Communications
in Computer and Information Science 1074

Commenced Publication in 2007
Founding and Former Series Editors:
Phoebe Chen, Alfredo Cuzzocrea, Xiaoyong Du, Orhun Kara, Ting Liu,
Krishna M. Sivalingam, Dominik Ślęzak, Takashi Washio, and Xiaokang Yang

More information about this series at http://www.springer.com/series/7899

César Benavente-Peces · Nancy Cam-Winget ·
Eric Fleury · Andreas Ahrens (Eds.)

Sensor Networks

6th International Conference, SENSORNETS 2017
Porto, Portugal, February 19–21, 2017
and 7th International Conference, SENSORNETS 2018
Funchal, Madeira, Portugal, January 22–24, 2018
Revised Selected Papers

 Springer

Editors
César Benavente-Peces
ETS Ingenieía y Sistemas de Teleco
Universidad Politécnica de Madrid
Madrid, Spain

Eric Fleury
École Normale Supérieure Lettres
et Sciences Humaines
Lyon, France

Nancy Cam-Winget
Cisco Systems
San Jose, CA, USA

Andreas Ahrens
Fakultät für Ingenieurwissenschaften
Hochschule Wismar
Wismar, Mecklenburg-Vorpommern
Germany

ISSN 1865-0929   ISSN 1865-0937   (electronic)
Communications in Computer and Information Science
ISBN 978-3-030-30109-5   ISBN 978-3-030-30110-1   (eBook)
https://doi.org/10.1007/978-3-030-30110-1

This Springer imprint is published by the registered company Springer Nature Switzerland AG
The registered company address is: Gewerbestrasse 11, 6330 Cham, Switzerland

Preface

The present book includes extended and revised versions of a set of selected papers from the 6th and 7th International Conference on Sensor Networks (SENSORNETS 2017 and SENSORNETS 2018). The 6th edition of SENSORNETS was held in Porto, Portugal, during February 19–21, 2017, and the 7th edition was held in Madeira, Portugal, during January 22–24, 2018.

SENSORNETS 2017 received 37 paper submissions from 24 countries and SENSORNETS 2018, received 30 paper submissions from 18 countries. In total, 15% of the papers submitted were included in this joint book. The papers were selected by the event chairs and their selection was based on a number of criteria that included the reviews and suggested comments provided by the Program Committee members, the session chairs' assessments, and also the program chairs' global view of all papers included in the technical program. The authors of selected papers were then invited to submit a revised and extended version of their papers having at least 30% new material.

Both editions of the International Conference on Sensor Networks (SENSORNETS) intended to be the meeting point of researchers and practitioners to share experiences and ideas on innovative developments in any aspect of sensor networks, including hardware of sensor networks, wireless communication protocols, sensor networks software and architectures, wireless information networks, data manipulation, signal processing, localization, and object tracking through sensor networks, obstacles, applications, and uses.

The papers selected to be included in this book contribute to the understanding and development of relevant trends of current research on sensor networks, including:

- Media access protocols which improve the throughput and reliability of wireless sensor networks (WSN) specially in harsh environment, such as industrial ones, where the contribution on channel modeling is fundamental for the successful development of WSN, and the use of appropriate operating systems aimed at low capabilities and low power consumption devices
- Contribution to design and development of WSN in critical services as those concerning transportation where engineers face specific problems and constraints, such as the railway, and specifically in high-speed trains
- Remote sensor applications for various purposes such as those using satellites for earth monitoring, for risk detection and disaster prevention, or climate phenomenon observation, where novel tools combining hardware and software solutions are required
- Development of new applications and services aimed at improving the quality of life for people with disabilities, such as promoting healthy-life through exercise with the support of wireless sensing and computing in mobile applications
- The development of novel techniques to provide localization and location-based services where the GPS does not provide coverage, i.e., in indoor environments and using ultra-low-power devices

We would like to thank all the authors for their contributions and also to the reviewers who have helped ensure the quality of this publication.

January 2018

César Benavente-Peces
Nancy Cam-Winget
Eric Fleury
Andreas Ahrens

Organization

Conference Co-chairs

César Benavente-Peces   Universidad Politécnica de Madrid, Spain
Nancy Cam-Winget   Cisco Systems, USA

Program Co-chairs

Eric Fleury   Inria Grenoble Rhône-Alpes, France
Andreas Ahrens   Hochschule Wismar, University of Technology
                            Business and Design, Germany

Program Committee

Served in 2017

Ahmad Lotfi   Nottingham Trent University, UK
Alberto Ferrante   Università della Svizzera Italiana, Switzerland
Ali Emrouznejad   Aston University, UK
Andri Riid   Tallinn University of Technology, Estonia
Athanasios Gkelias   Imperial College, UK
Bernardete Ribeiro   University of Coimbra, Portugal
Boris Kovalerchuk   Central Washington University, USA
Chiara Buratti   Università di Bologna, Italy
Cyril Onwubiko   Research Series Ltd., UK
Erik Buchmann   Hochschule für Telekommunikation Leipzig, Germany
Erwin Pesch   University Siegen, Germany
Francisco Martins   University of Azores, Portugal
Ioanis Nikolaidis   University of Alberta, Canada
Mateusz Tykierko   Wroclaw University of Technology, Poland
Michael Zink   University of Massachusetts Amherst, USA
Ozlem Incel   Galatasaray University, Turkey
Pangun Park   Chungnam National University, South Korea
Sergey Y. Yurish   IFSA Publishing, S.L., Spain
Shelley Minteer   University of Utah, USA
Yu Zhang   University of Lincoln, UK

Served in 2018

Amitava Chatterjee   Jadavpur University, India
Amy Murphy   Bruno Kessler Foundation, Italy
Antonio Lopez-Martin   Universidad Püblica de Navarra, Spain
Chia Chong   Sunway University, Malaysia

Klaus Volbert   Technical University of Applied Sciences Regensburg,
                             Germany
Marco da Silva   Universidade Tecnologica Federal do Parana, Brazil
Mario Alves   Politécnico do Porto, Portugal
Mattia Monga   Università degli Studi di Milano, Italy
Meng-Shiuan Pan   Tamkang University, Taiwan
Monika Maciejewska   Wroclaw University of Science and Technology,
                             Poland
Niina Halonen   University of Oulu, Finland
Nuno Pereira   Instituto Superior de Engenharia do Porto, Portugal
Sevil Sen   Hacettepe University, Turkey
Stefan Fischer   University of Luebeck, Germany
Susan Rea   Cork Institute of Technology, Ireland
Tarikul Islam   Jamia Millia Islamia (Central University), India
Victor Cionca   NIMBUS Centre for Embedded Systems Research,
                             Ireland
Xuemin Chen   Texas Southern University, USA

Additional Reviewers

Served in 2017

Florian Büther   University of Lübeck, Germany
Florian Lau   Universität zu Lübeck, Germany

Served in 2018

Pavel Novoa   Universidad Técnica Estatal de Quevedo, Ecuador

Invited Speakers

2017

Nancy Cam-Winget   Cisco Systems, USA
Nirwan Ansari   New Jersey Institute of Technology, USA
Thomas Gilbert   Alexandra Institute, Denmark

2018

Kort Bremer   Leibniz Universität Hannover, Germany
Leonhard Reindl   University of Freiburg, Germany
Luca Mottola   Politecnico di Milano, Italy, and SICS Swedish ICT,
                             Sweden

Contents

TinyOS-Based WSN Performance: Default Active Message Layer vs. TKN15.4

Diego V. Queiroz[1], Cesar Benavente-Peces[1(✉)] [iD], and Ruan D. Gomes[1,2,3]

[1] Signal Theory and Communications Department,
Universidad Politecnica de Madrid, Madrid, Spain
diego@sti.ufpb.br, cesar.benavente@upm.es, ruan.gomes@ifpb.edu.br
[2] Informatics Coordination, Federal Institute of Paraiba, Guarabira, Brazil
[3] Post-Graduate Program in Electrical Engineering,
Federal University of Campina Grande, Campina Grande, Brazil
http://www.upm.es

Abstract. The applications aimed at monitoring and controlling smart homes and buildings, health, industrial environments, traffic, energy consumption, resources, and so on, are being increasingly deployed due to the advantages they provide, increasing efficiency and decreasing costs. In this context Wireless Sensor Networks (WSN) have become a leading solution providing the appropriate mean to get and collect data and deliver it for their processing. Sensor nodes in a WSN have resource constraints, presenting low processing power and, in some cases, restrictions in power consumption. Resources availability constraints force researchers and engineers to develop proper Operating Systems (OS) aimed at low-power wireless devices, and one of the most important and in active use is the TinyOS. This paper describes an experimental analysis and evaluation which investigates relevant features and evaluates the performance (throughput, network delay, success rate, and energy consumption) of WSN under the constraint of using the low-power-consumption-aimed chosen operating system in an harsh outdoor industrial environment for with two different protocols: Active Message (AM) layer protocol and the fully 802.15.4 compliant protocol stack TKN15.4. Based on the results we conclude that TKN15.4 is better in energy consumption and success rate. On the other hand, AM protocol allows running multiple services using the same radio, but at the cost of an excessive energy consumption.

Keywords: Wireless Sensor Networks · TinyOS · TKN15.4 ·
Active message · IEEE 802.15.4 · Network throughput

1 Introduction

Wireless Sensor Networks (WSN) are preferred in the deployment of monitoring and control systems in industrial environments due to a number of

© Springer Nature Switzerland AG 2019
C. Benavente-Peces et al. (Eds.): SENSORNETS 2017/2018, CCIS 1074, pp. 1–22, 2019.
https://doi.org/10.1007/978-3-030-30110-1_1

advantages and a better performance they show compared to wired networks features, constraints and performance. The most remarkable advantages are low cost, high flexibility, reconfigurability, easy installation/maintenance, self-organization capabilities and local processing. In consequence, WSN are becoming promising platforms to implement online systems aimed at remote monitoring and controlling in distinct environments. Despite these advantages, WSN work in an inherently unreliable, and harsh communication medium. Hence, WSN performance is affected by typical disturbances in wireless channels such as attenuation, multipath, shadowing, fading, noise and interferences in the frequency band used for establishing the communication link (the free ISM bands), which is typically shared by a number of services and users, e.g. in the 2.4 GHz band [22].

There are many environments where the wireless nodes can be deployed. Among home, office, and industry, the industrial environment is harsher due to the unpredictable variations of temperature, pressure, humidity, and so on. The use of Industrial Wireless Sensor Networks (IWSN) to implement monitoring and control systems has some advantages, such as low cost and high flexibility to reconfigure the network. However, it is necessary to deal with typical problems of wireless networks, such as noise, electromagnetic interference, fading and high attenuation, due to the presence of many objects and obstructions. Many industrial environments also present characteristics that make the wireless channel non-stationary for long time periods [1].

In addition, the wireless channel in many industries is non-stationary for a long term, which can cause abrupt changes in the characteristics of the channel over time [2]. In industry, the coherence bandwidth is low due to the high level of multipath fading, which causes differences in the characteristics of the different channels, since they are uncorrelated in frequency, and the impact of multipath is different for different channels. In addition, changes in the topology of the environment, such as the movement of a large metal structure, people and reflections, may cause changes in the characteristics of the channel over time [12].

Another problem is the link asymmetry. Some protocols use acknowledgement per packet and, in this case, it is necessary to guarantee a good quality of communication in the two directions of the link. Spatial variations in the channel quality can also occur in IWSN. In [29], a coherence length of 5.5 cm was found for IEEE 802.15.4 radios operating in the 2.4 GHz band. Hence, two nodes positioned at a distance more than 5.5 cm apart from each other, and using the same channel, can be considered uncorrelated, and thus the channel can present a high quality for one node, and a low quality for the other. Some protocols use beacon packets to synchronize the nodes, and these packets are sent using a single channel. However, sometimes it may be difficult to pick a channel that is good enough for all links in the network.

The lack of reliability in the communication medium makes it difficult to establish Quality of Service (QoS) guarantees with reduced CAPital EXpenditure (CAPEX) and OPerational EXpenditure (OPEX). Therefore, the sensors, including their softwares, need to be low-cost, resulting in a set of restrictions, such as low data rate and low processing capabilities. For this reason, Operating Systems (OS) such as TinyOS, Contiki, OpenWSN, RIOT and FreeRTOS were developed, and designed to run on devices that are severely constrained in memory, power consumption, processing power, and communication bandwidth.

According to [3], TinyOS is the most suitable OS to operate in a resource-starved network, such as WSN. It is an OS designed for low-power wireless embedded systems. Basically, it can be considered a tasks scheduler and a collection of drivers for microcontrollers commonly used in wireless embedded platforms. TinyOS programs are composed of event handlers and tasks with run-to-completion semantics. When an external event occurs, such as an incoming data packet or a sensor reading, TinyOS calls the appropriate event handler to deal with the event [28]. Both the TinyOS system and programs developed for this OS are written in nesC, which is an extension of the C programming language. Figure 1 depicts the architecture of TinyOS.

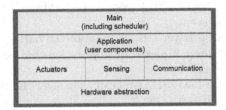

Fig. 1. TinyOS architecture.

As alternatives to TinyOS, stand out: Contiki, which is an open-source OS for the IoT, and connects tiny low-cost, low-power microcontrollers to the Internet; Berkeley OpenWSN, which is an open-source stack intending to implement low-power wireless standards such as IEEE 802.15.4e, 6LoWPAN, RPL and CoAP, and is rooted in the new IEEE802.15.4e TSCH; FreeRTOS, which is a popular Real Time Operating System (RTOS) that has been ported to many microcontrollers, and its preemptive micro-kernel has support for multi-threading with statically instantiated tasks; and RIOT, which is also a real time OS and was developed with focus on the requirements of IoT.

The latest version of TinyOS was released in 2012 (2.1.2), providing support for updated msp430-gcc (4.6.3) and avr-gcc (4.1.2), and a complete 6lowpan/RPL IPv6 stack. Currently, TinyOS development has been migrated to GitHub[1], where researchers and engineers can contribute to its development. The OS includes TOSSIM, a high-fidelity mote simulator that compiles directly from nesC code, scaling to thousands of simulated nodes. TOSSIM gives the programmer an omniscient view of the network and greater debugging capabilities. Server-side applications can connect to a TOSSIM proxy just as if it were a real sensor network, easing the transition between the simulation environment and actual deployments [17].

---

[1] https://github.com/tinyos - Access in 09/12/2016.

Fig. 2. Testbed set-up implemented for performance evaluation, XM1000 (Advantic-sys), and one coordinator connected to USB port [22].

Different types of hardware platforms support TinyOS in the WSN domain. These different platforms introduce their own interrupts relating to their hardware designs [16]. To port from one hardware platform to another, TinyOS developers have introduced a hardware abstraction architecture, and it can be classified into three layers [3,14], as follows:

1. Hardware Interface Layer (HIL): comprises hardware-independent components, interfaces and events;
2. Hardware Presentation Layer (HPL): close to the hardware layer. The components of this layer are not picked by applications but are used by hardware in some particular tasks;
3. Hardware Adaptation Layer (HAL): layer that favors hardware functionality, and is closer to the HPL.

Among the main platforms supported by TinyOS, are TelosB, Tmote Sky, MicaZ, Mica2, Zolertia Z1, GINA, IRIS, and XM1000, which is based on TelosB. In this paper, XM1000 platform is used to perform the experiments. In the experiments, seven motes were used, and five of them are depicted in Fig. 2.

The XM1000 is the new generation of mote modules, based on TelosB technical specifications, with upgraded 116Kb-EEPROM and 8Kb-RAM and integrated Temperature, Humidity and Light sensors. Besides TinyOS 2.1.2, it is also compatible with Contiki 2.7 (latest version of Contiki is 3.0^2). Its processor belongs to Texas Instruments MSP430 family, the RF Chip is CC2420 and has range of around 120 m (outdoor), and 20–30 m (indoor), in which longer ranges are possible with optional SMA antenna attached. Its current consumption is of 18.8 mA for RX, 17.4 mA for TX, and 1 μA when the device is in sleep mode.

The experimental analysis described in this research evaluates the performance of the default Active Message (AM) protocol of TinyOS and TKN15.4 protocol, and compares the main features of the protocols in order to choose the most appropriate for wide general-purpose applications, including industrial implementations. In this scenario, two exemplary applications designed for TinyOS and TKN15.4 were used for comparison purposes, in which one sends and receives packets using timers (to time-stamp), and the other uses the beacon-enabled mode of IEEE 802.15.4 standard, respectively. Actually, in this work both applications were adapted to perform the same tasks. The only difference between them is that in TKN15.4, beacons were used to synchronize

---

^{2} Released in 26 Ago 2015.

with its coordinator. The motivation for these tests is to see the feasibility of using those protocols for WSN in industrial environments/applications without stringent requirements on reliability and predictable real-time performance, as defined by [8]. Among the variety of application where they can be applied, remarkable applications with stringent timing requirements are those aimed at Military/Defence and Healthcare purposes, and in some hazardous and harsh industrial environments, such as chemical/biotechnology.

It is worthy to note that the IEEE 802.15.4 MAC frame format is different from the frame format used in default AM TinyOS protocol. Therefore, there is an optional implementation called *TKN154ActiveMessageP.nc* that abstracts AM over the nonbeacon-enabled variant of IEEE 802.15.4 MAC. In this optional implementation, the upper layer in TinyOS will see the actual AM payload, and before passing frames down to the 15.4 MAC, the implementation makes sure that the AM type (and network byte) are moved to the MAC payload portion. This workaround involves extra *memmove* functions (C library function that copies n characters from *str2* to *str1*, which is a safer approach than *memcpy* function for overlapping memory blocks). Since it requires more memory and processing than the protocols analysed in this paper, it was not considered.

DA	LSA	ML	GID	AM_TYPE	SM_ID	SC
FF FF	00 00	4	22	6	00 02	00 0B

Fig. 3. Message format used in AM Protocol [22].

The remainder of this paper is structured as follows. In Sect. 2, AM and TKN15.4 protocols are introduced highlighting the main features. Section 3 discusses the related investigations, remarking those which implement testbeds based on TinyOS. Section 5 describes the measurement techniques, implementation details of the protocols, and the experimental methodology. The analysis of the results and the concluding remarks are given in Sects. 6 and 7, respectively.

2   TinyOS Protocols

Sensor nodes are network-centric devices. A large part of their software complexity is produced by the network protocols and their interactions. TinyOS provides a number of interfaces to abstract the underlying communications services and a number of components which provide those interfaces. This set of interfaces and components uses a common message buffer abstraction, called "*message_t*", which is implemented as a *nesC struct* (similar to a C struct) in the following way:

```
typedef nx_struct message_t {
  nx_uint8_t header [ sizeof ( message_header_t )];
  nx_uint8_t data [TOSH_DATA_LENGTH];
```

```
nx_uint8_t  footer [ sizeof ( message_footer_t )];
nx_uint8_t  metadata [ sizeof ( message_metadata_t )];
} message_t;
```

Some of the basic interfaces of TinyOS are briefly described as follows [10]:

- *Packet*: Provides the basic accessors for the *message_t* abstract data type;
- *Send*: Provides the basic address-free message delivering interface;
- *Receive*: Provides the basic message receive interface;
- *PacketAcknowledgements*: Provides mechanism for requesting acknowledgements (ACK) on a per-packet basis;
- *RadioTimeStamping*: Provides time stamping information for radio transmission and reception.

Both protocols under analysis (AM and TKN15.4) use some of these interfaces to transmit and receive packets. To clarify this operation a brief introduction is developed in the following subsections to evaluate the two protocols in TinyOS.

2.1 The Active Message Protocol

As having multiple services sharing the same radio link to data exchange is very common, the TinyOS defines the AM layer to multiplex the access to the radio.

AM packets have a field named *AM_TYPE* (8 bits) which describes what the rest of the packet looks like. This term refers to the field used for multiplexing, and its functionality is similar to the Ethernet frame type field, IP protocol field, and UDP port field. All of them are used to multiplex the access to a communication service [10]. Figure 3 depicts an example of the overall message structure (ignoring the first 00 byte), where the meaning and length of each field is as follows:

- DA: Destination Address (2 bytes);
- LSA: Link Source Address (2 bytes);
- ML: Message length (1 byte);
- GID: Group ID (1 byte);
- AM_TYPE: Active Message handler type (1 byte);
- PA: Payload (up to 28 bytes), in which:
  - SM_ID: Source Mote ID (2 bytes);
  - SC: Sample Counter (2 bytes).

As AM services, TinyOS implements *AMPacket* and *AMSend*. The first one is similar to *Packet*, defined in Sect. 2, and provides the basic AM accessors for the *message_t* abstract data type. This interface provides commands for getting a node's AM address, and packet's destination/type. The second one is *AMSend*, which is similar to *Send*, and provides the basic AM sending interface. The key difference between *AMSend* and *Send* is that *AMSend* takes a destination AM address in its send command.

The AM accessors provide the functionality for querying packets. AM is a single-hop communication protocol, therefore, fields such as source and destination represent the single-hop source and destination. Multihop sources and destinations are defined by the corresponding multihop protocol (if any). Variants of the basic AM stack exist that incorporate lightweight, link-level security [17].

Several components implement the communications and active message interfaces, as follows[3]:

- *AMReceiverC* - Provides the Receive, Packet, and AMPacket interfaces;
- *AMSenderC* - Provides AMSend, Packet, AMPacket, and PacketAcknowledgements as ACK;
- *AMSnooperC* - Provides Receive, Packet, and AMPacket;
- *AMSnoopingReceiverC* - Provides Receive, Packet, and AMPacket;
- *ActiveMessageAddressC* - Provides commands to get and set the node's active message address.

The basic components of programming a mote with AM are exemplified as follows, with methods to get the payload of a packet, to send and receive the messages:

```
uses interface Packet;
uses interface AMSend;
uses interface Receive;
...
BlinkToRadioMsg* btrpkt =
    (BlinkToRadioMsg*)(call Packet.getPayload(&pkt,
        sizeof(BlinkToRadioMsg)))
...
call AMSend.send(AM_BROADCAST_ADDR,
        &pkt, sizeof(BlinkToRadioMsg)) == SUCCESS
...
event message_t* Receive.receive(message_t* msg,
        void* payload, uint8_t len){...}
...
```

The data payload of a data link frame is always at a fixed offset of a message. The position in which a component can put its header or data depends on what the underlying components of headers introduce. Therefore, in order to be able each component to find out where to put its data, it must arrange the components in a query below it. The *Packet interface* defines this mechanism:

---

[3] http://tinyos.stanford.edu/tinyos-wiki/ - Access 12/12/2016.

```
interface Packet {
    command void clear(message_t* msg);
    command uint8_t payloadLength(message_t* msg);
    command void setPayLoadLength(message_t* msg, uint8_t len);
    command uint8_t maxPayloadLength();
    command void* getPayload(message_t* msg, uint8_t len);
}
```

A component can obtain a pointer to its data region within a packet by calling *getPayload()*.

2.2   The TKN15.4 Protocol

While the first steps in protocol design can often be made with the help of analytical models and simulation, the last steps require the use of real hardware, in realistic environmental conditions and experimental setups. TKN15.4 provides a stable, open-source 802.15.4 MAC platform independent implementation for the 2.1 and later releases of TinyOS [15]. It was developed by the Telecommunication Networks (TKN) Group from Technical University Berlin on March 2009.

TKN15.4 Architecture. The TKN15.4 protocol architecture is depicted in Fig. 4. At the lowest level, the *RadioControlP* component manages the access to the radio. Thanks to an extended TinyOS 2 arbiter component, it controls which of the components at the level above is granted to access the radio at what point in time. Most components on the second level represent different parts of a superframe: the *BeaconTransmitP/BeaconSynchronizeP* components deals with beacons, *DispatchSlottedCsmaP* manages frame communication during the CAP (Contention Access Period), and *NoCoordCfpP/NoDeviceCfpP* components are responsible for the CFP (Period). *ScanP* and *PromiscuousModeP*

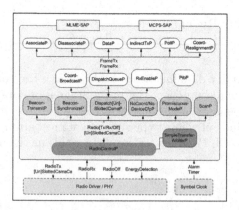

Fig. 4. TKN15.4 protocol architecture where components are represented by rounded boxes, interfaces by connection lines. Radio driver and symbol clock components are external to TKN15.4 [22].

components provide services for channel scanning and promiscuous mode, respectively. Finally, the components on the top level implement the remaining MAC data and management services, for example, PAN association or requesting (polling) data from a coordinator. Components at this level typically provide a certain MAC MLME/MCPS primitive to the next upper layer, e.g., *DataP* component provides the MCPS-DATA primitive to the next upper layer to transmit a frame to a peer device.

An example of how a mote is programmed with the TKN15.4 configured in a beacon-enabled mode implementation is as follows:

```
uses  interface  MCPS_DATA;
uses  interface  MLME_RESET;
uses  interface  MLME_GET;
uses  interface  MLME_SCAN;
uses  interface  MLME_SYNC;
uses  interface  MLME_BEACON_NOTIFY;
uses  interface  IEEE154Frame as Frame;
uses  interface  IEEE154BeaconFrame as BeaconFrame;
...
event void MLME_RESET.confirm(ieee154_status_t
   status){...}
...
event message_t* MLME_BEACON_NOTIFY.indication
   (message_t* frame){...}
...
event void MCPS_DATA.confirm{...}
```

TKN15.4 Applications. As default, in TKN15.4 implementation of TinyOS there are 11 examples of applications to help the developers to build their own applications; six applications for beacon-enabled mode networks (*TestAssociate, TestData, TestGTS, TestIndirect, TestMultihop and TestStartSync*), four for nonbeacon-enabled mode networks (*TestActiveScan, TestAssociate, TestIndirectData and TestPromiscuous*), and one application that works as packet sniffer.

In this work, the application *TestData* for beacon-enabled mode networks was adapted to fit the experiment, since it is a basic application example which implements data direct transmissions from a device to the PAN (Personal Area Network) coordinator, which is also known as *sink node*. In this application, the coordinator periodically transmits beacons and waits for incoming DATA frames. The remaining nodes act as devices, and scan the pre-assigned channel to detect the beacons transmitted by the coordinator. Once a beacon is found, they try to synchronize to and track all the following beacons. Then, the nodes can start to transmit DATA frames to the coordinator (direct transmission during the Contention Access Period - CAP).

The IEEE 802.15.4 standard defines the Beacon Interval (BI), also called Superframe, as the time interval between two beacon frames, which is divided into an active period and an optional inactive period. During inactive periods, nodes can be kept in sleep mode to conserve their energy. The length of the active period is Superframe Duration (SD) and contains 16 equal length time slots (from 0 to 15). The 16 time slots in the superframe are subdivided into smaller slots known as the Backoff Period (BP). The active period comprises CAP and Contention Free Period (CFP). During CAP, nodes use the slotted CSMA/CA algorithm to access the channel. During CFP, up to seven Guaranteed Time Slots (GTS) can be allocated by the coordinator for each superframe, which allow the node to operate on the channel that is dedicated exclusively to it. A node with an assigned GTS has full access to the channel during its GTS. Nodes activity during it should be completed before the start of the next GTS or the end of the CFP, as depicted in Fig. 5.

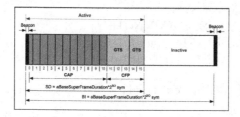

Fig. 5. Superframe structure with BO and SO parameters [22].

In the case of mesh networks, when using CSMA/CA transmissions and duty-cycles (the fraction of time in which the node is awake) lower than 100%, the delay in the communication will mainly depends on the network load (application data traffic) and the number of hops to the sink node as well [27].

The duty-cycle (DC) is the ratio of the length of an active period SD to the length of a BI, and it is determined by $(\frac{1}{2})^{BO-SO}$. The default values defined by the standard for both parameters are $0 \leq SO \leq BO \leq 14$. The constant *aBaseSlotDuration* represents the number of symbols, and it has 60 symbols. Considering each symbol is $16\,\mu s$ in length for the 2.4-GHz band, it is possible to calculate the DC of the combination BO × SO. If BO = 5 and SO = 5 (TKN15.4 default values), the DC is calculated as follows:

- *aBaseSlotDuration* = 60 symbols;
- *aBaseSuperframeDuration* = 60 symbols × 16 µs = 960 µs;
- $BI = 960 \times 2^5$ symbols = 491520 µs (≈491 ms);
- $SD = 960 \times 2^5$ symbols = 491520 µs (≈491 ms);
- $DC = \frac{SD}{BI} = 1$;

This implementation has a DC of 100% with active and inactive periods (SD) of 0.491 s and BI of 0.491 s. In this example, the PAN coordinator will generate around 2 beacons/second (1000/491BI ≈2). During each BI, the devices work for about 491 ms (SD) and would keep quit for the rest of time, if there was any in this case. If SO was defined as 0, for example, it would minimize the ON time for the device during the CAP. If it were increased, it would allow more packets to be transferred during the CAP at the expense of higher power consumption.

Due to non-deterministic nature of CSMA/CA transmissions, an exact calculation of delay cannot be provided nor can specific delay limitations be guaranteed [6]. To guarantee specific delay requirements, the network parameters cannot be selected randomly. Therefore, before comparing AM (does not use IEEE 802.15.4 MAC) and TKN15.4 protocols, this paper provides a delay analysis with regard to different MAC layer parameters so the best configuration of those can be selected.

The results of several works studying the behaviour of the protocol when considering the DC configuration have been described in the literature, and how the setting of configuration influences the performance of the network as well. Usually, the experiment analysis is evaluated by using appropriate simulation tools. Some of the works implemented experiments using real devices providing valuable results, as in [9]. Since the parameters are dependent on the packet rate and the environment, in order to increase the number of packets received and to improve the energy-efficiency (lowering the consumption) at the same time, it is important performing this analysis before its implementation.

3 Related Works

The related works presented in this Section are classified based on experiments performed with one of the two protocols related in this paper.

In [23], the authors carried out various experiments sing TinyOS using a MicaZ platform. They proposed a localized algorithm to enable detection, localization and extent determination of damage sites using the resource constrained environment of a WSN. The data collection stage starts at a given time, as requested by the sink node. A message is sent from the sink to the cluster managers, and those are responsible for sending messages to schedule the next sensing task on their subordinated sensors. For their paper, the default implementations of 802.15.4 protocol for lower level communication handling, and AM protocol for higher-level communication handling in TinyOS 2.1 were used. The reason for this choice was that they wanted a lean implementation of the whole system in their prototype.

In [20], the authors present a low cost and energy efficient wireless sensor mote platform for low data rate monitoring applications, called DZ50. This platform is based on ATmega328P micro-controller and RFM12b transceiver, and is compared with MicaZ and TelosB platforms. They ported all device drivers of DZ50 to TinyOS 2.x, which eases the programming of the platform and allows using many protocols already developed for TinyOS platform. As well as the previous paper, this one used AM to transmit and receive packets via an abstract interface.

In [30], the authors study passive discovery of IEEE 802.15.4 networks operating in beacon-enabled mode. To validate their analytical model, they performed experimental evaluations with an implementation on Tmote Sky using TKN15.4 protocol.

The work in [6] presents the InRout route selection algorithm, where local information is shared among neighbouring nodes to enable efficient, distributed route selection while satisfying industrial application requirements and considering sensor node resource limitations. They used data frames size of 127 bytes, which is the maximum possible size in IEEE 802.15.4 networks. Given the sensor nodes have a reduced memory space, the buffer size at MAC layer for all nodes is limited to 10 packets. A buffer size choice of 10 packets is selected based on the default buffer size defined in the IEEE 802.15.4 MAC standard implementation for TinyOS-2.x with the TKN15.4 protocol.

In [19], the authors analysis and evaluate the performance of a Listen-and-Suppress Carrier Sense Multiple Access (LAS-CSMA) scheme in order to reduce power consumption, network bandwidth usage and delays by suppressing node unnecessary packet transmissions. The scheme is evaluated with IRIS and MicaZ platforms, and AM protocol. The authors argue that AM allows for the overlap and integration of communication and computation, which is critical in sensor networks to improve the efficiency in-network data aggregation. In addition, it also allows multiple applications to simultaneously use communication resources.

In [21], it is introduced the concept, design, and implementation of the proxy mote, a Linux-based TinyOS platform able to execute a TinyOS applications, called ProxyMotes. The main use case for the proxy mote is to expose a non-TinyOS ("legacy") sensor/actuator device to TinyOS applications. To evaluate the proxy network, the authors used an oscilloscope application – a TinyOS demo, which delivers AM packets to generate the traffic and controlling the channel congestion.

In [7] the authors presented a visualization toolkit for TinyOS 2.0 to give support in the program comprehension. To make the concepts more concrete, they considered a variant of the Blink application included as part of TinyOS distribution, which uses AM protocol.

In [24], it is presented the PowerTOSSIM, a scalable simulation environment for WSN that provides an accurate, per-node estimate of power consumption. For the experiments, the authors used Mica2 sensor node and oscilloscope, and used AM protocol.

4   Industrial Environments Wireless Channel Features

Industrial environments usually contain RF signals absorbing/reflecting elements and materials as metal, and mobile objects, such as robots, cars and people. Every one influences both the large-scale and small-scale fading. The power of the signals received at the front-end depends on the transmitted power, the antennas gains, the distance between transmitter and receiver (which produces signal attenuation) and the effects caused by the particular environment.

Even with the same values for the aforementioned parameters, there is a variation in the mean received power, depending on the place where the measurement is performed, which is known as log-normal shadowing. The log-normal shadowing model has been used to model the large-scale path loss and shadowing in industrial environments [25].

Besides path loss and shadowing, it is also necessary to analyse the small-scale channel fading due to fast changes in the multipath conditions of the environment, which is mainly provoked by the movement of the various elements around the receiver and transmitter. Distinct experiments demonstrated that, in industrial environments, the attenuation variation with time follows a Rice distribution. In industrial environments the K factor of the Rice distribution has a high value. For the experiments described in [25], in industrial environments, K took values between 4 dB and 19 dB, while in indoor office environments, values between −12 dB and −6 dB were found, as discussed in [25]. This behaviour can be explained by the open nature of industrial buildings and facilities, and the large amount of elements which produce reflections. In consequence, the model is characterized by many time invariant rays and only a small part of the multipath profile is affected by moving objects.

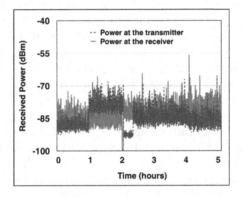

Fig. 6. Asymmetric and time variant behaviour of the wireless channel in industrial environments.

The IEEE 802.15.4 standard defines sixteen channels in the 2.4 GHz band, with 2 MHz of bandwidth, and channel spacing of 5 MHz. Thus, the channels are highly uncorrelated. Experiments described in [4] have found that changing the communication channel can lead up to 30 dB difference in the received power, in an office environment. Varga *et al.* [26] performed experiments for a short range, in an environment without multipath, and with line-of-sight. In that experiment, differences up to 10 dB were observed for some channels. Thus, besides the variation in shadowing observed depending on the place that the nodes are positioned, there is also a variation in shadowing regarding the different channels. In the experiments described in [11], differences of up to 15 dB were found for different channels in an indoor industrial environment, but only one link was analysed.

Figure 6 shows the received power in both directions of two nodes link showing the asymmetric and time variant behaviour of the channel in industrial environments.

5   Experiments Methodology

In order to compare AM and TKN15.4 protocols scalability, quantitative metrics are used to measure and evaluate the performance of both protocols. For all metrics, the average over multiple experiments is determined. The set of performance metrics used for comparing the selected protocols of this work can be described briefly as follows [13]:

- *Packet generation rate*: it is the number of packets that the sensor node transmits in one period, which is usually one second.
- *Network throughput*: the end-to-end network throughput measures the number of packets per second received at the destination. It is considered here as an external measure of the effectiveness of a protocol;
- *Network delay*: it measures the average end-to-end delay of data packet transmission. This delay implies the average time taken between a packet initially sent by the source, and the time for successfully receiving the message at the destination. This measure takes into account the queuing and the propagation delay of the packets;
- *Success rate*: it is the total amount of packets received at the destinations verses the total number of packets sent from the source;
- *Energy consumption*: it is the energy consumed by a node in the network in which the periods of transmission, reception, and idling are taken into account. Assuming each transmission consumes an energy unit, the total consumption is equivalent to the total number of packets sent in the network. Note that there are many factors influencing the overall energy consumption, and the results presented in this paper should only be regarded as indicative for what is possible to achieve in systems with similar hardware.

In this work, seven nodes were used in a star topology, working on channel 26 (2.480 GHz) and with -20 dBm of transmission power. In TKN15.4, one node plays the coordinator role, and the others play the device role. In both protocols, the devices send two packets per second, and all the end nodes send packets at the same time in order to analysed the *Network throughput*, *Success rate*, and the *Network delay* metrics.

The sink node is connected to a USB port of the computer to forward the packet information (payload) to it, and the devices are set to send 2000 packets to their coordinators without ACK. It is important to notice that interference occurs in the laboratory, since the nodes are working on 2.4 GHz frequency, and the laboratory receives the signal of seven Wi-Fi networks.

In some cases, the channel in which the nodes are working is full of interference caused by other networks, and multipath problems, produced by the movements of people and the presence of metallic objects, which decreases its quality. Therefore, after seven experiments with this structure, both networks had their channels exchanged for the results to become fairer.

For both protocols, the application tasks were the same, just changing the parameters of sending the packets. The TKN15.4 application in this work was developed with beacons enabled, so before sending the packets, the nodes need to synchronize with their coordinator. The beacon packets were not considered in the *Network throughput*, *Success rate*, and *Network delay* metrics, since AM does not use beacons to communicate with its sink node. However, the beacon packets were evaluated in the *Energy consumption* metric.

In order to measure the power consumed by the devices, a power supply and an oscilloscope were used, as depicted in Fig. 7, where a loop is used to measure the current and shows its shape in the oscilloscope.

The environment where the experiments were performed is as depicted in Fig. 8. It is a laboratory with around $43\,m^2$ with some metal objects and people moving around. The nodes were put in random location, some of them with line of sight (LOS), and some without LOS. In Fig. 8, one sender and the receiver (coordinator) nodes are in the extremes right and left of the picture as an example without LOS. There were performed eight replications for each protocol.

As stated before, in order to define the best parameters to achieve low power consumption for ZigBee devices, there were stablished varying values for BO and SO, and the values adopted were used to compare TKN15.4 and AM protocols. For each value, four replications were performed, and the results are in Table 1.

In this table, it is shown the percentage of packets received in different values of BO and SO. For each one, four replications were performed. The values of

Fig. 7. Measurement set-up: power supply and oscilloscope connected to the transmitter [22].

Fig. 8. Environment where the experiments were performed [22].

X were not used in the experiments because of the limitation in IEEE 802.15.4 standard, as discussed in Sect. 2.2 ($SO \leq BO$). Since the duty-cycle in N values of the table leads to a decrease in the number of packets received, as can be seen in $BO = 4/SO = 2$, $BO = 5/SO = 2$, and $BO = 5/SO = 3$, they were not analyzed in this work. Such values of packet reception are not acceptable. In this table, the best values of packet reception are using $BO = 5/SO = 5$ and $BO = 6/SO = 6$, and had almost the same results. Since in $BO = 6/SO = 6$, BI lasts more than in $BO = 5/SO = 5$, it spends more energy, so $BO = 5/SO = 5$ parameters were used to compare TKM15.4 and AM protocols.

Table 1. Percentage of packets received by changing BO and SO parameters [22].

SO	BO			
	4	5	6	7
2	58	41	N	N
3	70	48	N	N
4	82	61	N	N
5	X	92	61	N
6	X	X	91	59
7	X	X	X	83

6   Results

Regarding the first metric to evaluate the performance of both protocols, *Packet generation rate*, this value was set to two packets per second. It takes 1000 s (nearly 17 min) to send 2000 packets. In TKN15.4, the beacon time synchronization was not considered, which lasts around 491 ms for $BI = 5$, and around 983 ms for $BI = 6$.

Each node is set to send 2 packets/s, i.e., the network sends 12 packets to the sink node. The sink node could not process correctly all packets that were received when the transmission rate was more than two packets per second for each of the six nodes, so this rate was adequate for the amount of packets to be processed and forwarded to the computer. With this configuration, the metric *Network Throughput* results in an average of 11 packets per second received/processed by the sink in the AM protocol. This result can be explained because AM is a very simple protocol, and it cannot deal with so much packets at the same time. Only TRUE or FALSE attribute is used as congestion control method to determine if the sink is busy with processing of other packet. If so, the next packet will be discarded. Concerning TKN15.4, a device must sense an idle channel twice before it may transmit, as explained in Sect. 2.2, so the control is more organized and therefore the sink node will process more packets.

Table 2. Performance evaluation with metrics [22].

Metrics/ Protocols	Packets sent	Packet rate (pkts/s)	Network throughput (pkts/s)	Network delay (ms)	Success rate (%)	Energy consumption (Joules)
AM	2000	2	11	488.25	90.7	486
TKN15.4	2000	2	12	488.2	94.8	100

Regarding the *Network delay* metric, for each replication, each node was analyzed considering the time when it sends one packet, and the time when the packet is received by the sink. For all the packets received by the sink, for each sender, it was calculated the average time from sending to receiving tasks, and for AM protocol, the average value was 488.25 ms. That is, the first packet from "Sender 1" was sent at 0 ms; after 488.25 ms, this packet was received by the sink; 11.75 ms after that, the second packet was sent by "Sender 1", and then this packet was received by the sink at 988.25 ms, and so on. Almost the same results were obtained by TKN15.4 protocol that lasted 488.2 ms to send a packet, and this one to be received by the sink node.

Concerning the energy of TKN15.4, besides data packet transmitted, it must be considered the beacons received from the coordinator. Figure 10 depicts one

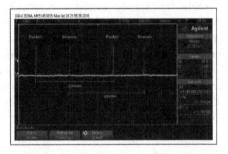

Fig. 9. Beacon and packet traces [22].

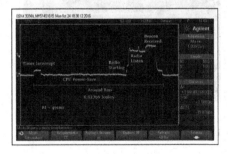

Fig. 10. Characteristic of Beacon Packets [22].

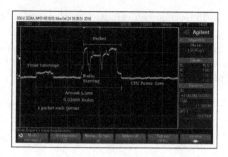

Fig. 11. Characteristic of TKN15.4 packets [22].

beacon received by the node. After receiving it, the node waits 491 ms (BI) to receive the next one. The process of sending all packets lasts 10^6 ms, and each packet is sent every 500 ms, as depicted in Fig. 9. Without considering the first milliseconds of beacon packets for synchronizing, which is performed once, when the button is pushed to start, the node begins to send packets, and the time is started. After the first packet sent, the first beacon is received from the coordinator.

Depicted in Fig. 10, the energy consumption of one single beacon is shown, which results in about 0.023 Joules. Figure 11 depicts the amount of energy of a single data packet, which consumes around 0.026 Joules. Depending on the platform, these results might be slightly different, even if the same application is used. In other periods than the packet interval, the node enters in a CPU Power-Save mode, therefore this time interval was not considered in the consumption, as it can be neglected compared to the main consumption. In 10^6 ms, the node received around 2036 beacons, resulting in a total of 48 Joules of energy consumption for the beacon packets. The amount of data packets during all the experiment results in a consumption of 52 Joules. The result for TKN15.4 packets is around 100 Joules, as illustrated in Table 2.

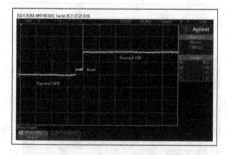

Fig. 12. Restart of AM protocol [22].

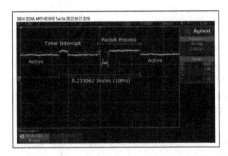

Fig. 13. Characteristic of AM packet [22].

Regarding AM protocol, as seen in Figs. 12 and 13, it does not implement CPU Power-Save mode, i.e., the node remains active all the time, with around 18 mA (54 mW), even without receiving or transmitting any packet. Figure 12 depicts the moment when the node is restarted, and Fig. 13 shows the packet transmission. The time from processing and sending the packet in AM protocol lasts around 10 ms and consumes 0.233 Joules for each packet (466 Joules for 2000 packets, 20000 ms). Considering that the node sends packet almost immediately after restarting, and the processing of packet lasts around 10 ms, the period that the node does nothing in the interval between two packets is 490 ms, resulting in 500 ms for each packet sent. During the 2000 packets sent, the interval when the nodes does nothing (but remains in active) is 980000 ms, which corresponds to around 20 Joules. Adding the consumption of active period, and packet processing, the total consumption is around 486 Joules, almost five times more than TKN15.4 during 16.7 min. Figure 14 shows the energy consumption for individual data and beacon packets for both AM and TKN15.4 protocols.

TKN15.4				AM	
Beacon	Joules	Packet	Joules	Packet	Joules
Timer Interrupt	0.000716316	Timer Interrupt	0.001792393	Timer Interrupt	0.026630544
Beacon Packet	0.022948176	CPU Power-save	0.0	Active Packet	0.081082163
		Data Packet	0.024297984	Data Packet	0.125348845
Total	0.023664492	Total	0.026090377	Total AM	0.233061552
Total TKN15.4		0.049754869			

Fig. 14. Energy consumption for individual data and beacon packets for both AM and TKN15.4 protocols in Joules [22].

The most important differences of the measurement set-up regard the *Success rate* and *Energy consumption*. It is worthy to note that TKN15.4 protocol shows a higher success rate than AM protocol, and has much less energy consumption than AM Protocol. Therefore, AM protocol is not appropriate to monitor environments with restriction of energy and large amount of data.

7 Conclusions

Wireless Sensor Networks (WSN) deployment to develop monitoring and control systems in industrial environments, show some advantages compared to wired networks, such as low cost and high flexibility. However, it is necessary to deal with typical problems of wireless systems, such as electromagnetic interference [18], and industrial environment high attenuation, due to the presence of many objects and obstructions [25].

In this context, this investigation as aimed at analysing and evaluating the performance of two protocols developed for TinyOS for communication in WSNs. The AM protocol is simpler to implement than TKN15.4. Additionally it allows running multiple services using the same radio (channel) to establish the link. The TKN15.4 protocol is based on the IEEE 802.15.4 standard and uses CSMA/CA to reduce packets collisions and retransmissions. It can be used for a variety of applications, and in the case of this paper, the application with beacon-enabled mode, was implemented and compared to the case of using the AM protocol regarding network throughput, network delay, success packet rate, and energy consumption.

Although simpler and allowing multiple services, the AM protocol shows several drawbacks. The only congestion control method used is a variable (flag) which indicates whether the sink node is busy or not. The AM baaed set-up also noticeably consumes more power, although in this investigation the duty-cycle used in TKN15.4 was 100% (maximal power consuming mode). The TKN15.4 is superior in energy consumption and success rate, since it uses CSMA/CA to access control. These are two decisive parameters for choosing TKN15.4. Maybe with more nodes and during a longer observation period, the results would become even more different, remarking the aspects with best performance. The positive feature of using the AM protocol is that it allows setting multiple services sharing the same radio, but it shows an excessive power consumption limiting wireless node operating time.

However, when considering stringent requirements such as reliability and predictable real-time performance, the TKN15.4 (IEEE 802.15.4) is not considered a good choice because of its several limitations, already highlighted by many studies, such as in [5]. The main limitations of the IEEE 802.15.4 [8], are inefficiency of slotted CSMA/CA in beacon-enabled mode, and in non-beacon-enabled mode for a network with a large number of nodes transmitting at the same time, and without protection against interference/fading.

Ongoing and future works will extend the experiments and results shown in this paper to face the development of the IEEE 802.15.4e standard in TinyOS based nodes, specifically the DSME (Deterministic and Synchronous Multi-Channel Extension) behaviour mode. The implementation of DSME in TinyOS will improve the old standard of TKN15.4 introducing appropriate mechanisms, such as time slotted access, multichannel communications and channel hopping. In a different way than the other behaviour modes, DSME keeps using the CAP and CFP channel access methods derived from IEEE 802.15.4, which smooths its implementation.

Acknowledgements. The authors would like to thank the support of the Institute for Advanced Studies in Communications (Iecom), the Brazilian Council for Research and Development (CNPq), the Coordination for the Improvement of Higher Education Personnel (CAPES), and the SMART 2 Project of the Erasmus Mundus Programme.

References

1. Agrawal, P., Ahlén, A., Olofsson, T., Gidlund, M.: Long term channel characterization for energy efficient transmission in industrial environments. IEEE Trans. Commun. **62**(8), 3004–3014 (2014). https://doi.org/10.1109/TCOMM.2014.2332876

2. Agrawal, P., Ahlen, A., Olofsson, T., Gidlund, M.: Characterization of long term channel variations in industrial wireless sensor networks. In: IEEE International Conference on Communications, pp. 1–6 (2014)

3. Amjad, M., Sharif, M., Afzal, M.K., Kim, S.W.: TinyOS - new trends, comparative views, and supported sensing applications: a review. IEEE Sens. J. **16**(9), 2865–2889 (2016)

4. Amzucu, D.M., Li, H., Fledderus, E.: Indoor radio propagation and interference in 2.4 GHZ wireless sensor networks: measurements and analysis. Wirel. Personal Commun. **76**, 245–269 (2014)

5. Anastasi, G., Conti, M., Di Francesco, M.: A comprehensive analysis of the MAC unreliability problem in IEEE 802.15.4 wireless sensor networks. IEEE Trans. Ind. Inform. **7**(1), 52–65 (2011)

6. Carballido Villaverde, B., Rea, S., Pesch, D.: InRout - a QoS aware route selection algorithm for industrial wireless sensor networks. Ad Hoc Netw. **10**(3), 458–478 (2012)

7. Dalton, A.R., Wahba, S.K., Dandamudi, S., Hallstrom, J.O.: Visualizing the runtime behavior of embedded network systems: a toolkit for TinyOS. Sci. Comput. Program. **74**(7), 446–469 (2009)

8. De Guglielmo, D., Brienza, S., Anastasi, G.: IEEE 802.15.4e: a survey. Comput. Commun. **88**, 1–24 (2016)

9. Despaux, F., Song, Y.Q., Lahmadi, A.: Measurement-based analysis of the effect of duty cycle in IEEE 802.15.4 MAC performance. In: 2013 IEEE 10th International Conference on Mobile Ad-Hoc and Sensor Systems, pp. 620–626. IEEE October 2013

10. Developers, T.: Official tinyos documentation wiki (2013). http://tinyos.stanford.edu/tinyos-wiki

11. Gomes, R.D., Queiroz, D.V., Filho, A.C.L., Fonseca, I.E., Alencar, M.S.: Realtime link quality estimation for industrial wireless sensor networks using dedicated nodes. Ad Hoc Netw. **59**, 116–133 (2017). https://doi.org/10.1016/j.adhoc.2017.02.007. http://www.sciencedirect.com/science/article/pii/S1570870517300434

12. Gomes, R.D., et al.: Evaluation of link quality estimators for industrial wireless sensor networks. In: XXXIV Simposio Brasileiro de Telecomunicacoes e Processamento de Sinais, pp. 1–5 (2016)

13. Hac, A.: Wireless Sensor Network Designs (2003)

14. Handziski, V., Polastre, J., Hauer, J., Sharp, C., Wolisz, A., Culler, D.: Flexible hardware abstraction for wireless sensor networks. In: Proceeedings of the Second European Workshop on Wireless Sensor Networks, pp. 145–157. IEEE (2005)

15. Hauer, J.H.: Tkn15.4: An IEEE 802.15.4 MAC. implementation for tinyos 2. Technical report, Technical University Berlin (2009)

16. Hill, J., Culler, D.: A wireless embedded sensor architecture for system-level optimization. Technical report, UC Berkeley (2002)
17. Levis, P., et al.: Tinyos: an operating system for sensor networks. In: Ambient Intelligence. In: Weber, W., Rabaey, J., Aarts, E. (Eds.) Springer-Verlag (2009). https://people.eecs.berkeley.edu/~culler/papers.html
18. Lima-Filho, A., Gomes, R., Adissi, M., Borges da Silva, T., Belo, F., Spohn, M.: Embedded system integrated into a wireless sensor network for online dynamic torque and efficiency monitoring in induction motors. IEEE/ASME Trans. Mech. **17**(3), 404–414 (2012). https://doi.org/10.1109/TMECH.2012.2187354
19. Macbeth, J., Sarrafzadeh, M.: Press the cancel button! a performance evaluation of scalable in-network data aggregation. In: 2009 International Conference on Information and Multimedia Technology, pp. 449–457. IEEE (2009)
20. Ouadjaout, A., Lasla, N., Bagaa, M., Doudou, M., Zizoua, C., Kafi, M.A., Derhab, A., Djenouri, D., Badache, N.: DZ50: energy-efficient wireless sensor mote platform for low data rate applications. Procedia Comput. Sci. **37**, 189–195 (2014)
21. Paczesny, T., Tajmajer, T., Domaszewicz, J., Pruszkowski, A.: ProxyMotes: Linux-based TinyOS platform for non-TinyOS sensors and actuators. In: 2012 IEEE 10th International Symposium on Parallel and Distributed Processing with Applications, pp. 255–261. IEEE (2012)
22. Queiroz, D.V., Gomes, R.D., Benavente-Peces, C.: Performance evaluation of default active message layer (AM) and TKN15.4 protocol stack in tinyos 2.1.2. In: Proceedings of the 6th International Conference on Sensor Networks (SENSOR-NETS 2017), Porto, Portugal, 19–21 February 2017, pp. 69–79 (2017). https://doi.org/10.5220/0006204200690079
23. dos Santos, I.L., et al.: A localized algorithm for structural health monitoring using wireless sensor networks. Inf. Fus. **15**, 114–129 (2014)
24. Shnayder, V., Hempstead, M., Chen, B.r., Allen, G.W., Welsh, M.: Simulating the power consumption of large-scale sensor network applications. In: Proceedings of the 2nd International Conference on Embedded Networked Sensor Systems - SenSys 2004, p. 188. ACM Press (2004)
25. Tanghe, E., et al.: The industrial indoor channel: large-scale and temporal fading at 900, 2400, and 5200 mhz. IEEE Trans. Wireless Commun. **7**, 2740–2751 (2008)
26. Varga, L.O., Heusse, M., Guizzetti, R., Duda, A.: Why is frequency channel diversity so beneficial in wireless sensor networks? In: IFIP Wireless Days. IFIP, Toulouse, France (2016). https://hal.archives-ouvertes.fr/hal-01287518
27. Villaverde, B.C., Alberola, R.D.P., Rea, S., Pesch, D.: Experimental evaluation of beacon scheduling mechanisms for multihop IEEE 802.15.4 wireless sensor networks. In: 2010 Fourth International Conference on Sensor Technologies and Applications, pp. 226–231. IEEE July 2010
28. Wang, Q., Balasingham, I.: Wireless sensor networks - an introduction. In: Wireless Sensor Networks: Application-Centric Design. InTech December 2010
29. Watteyne, T., Lanzisera, S., Mehta, A., Pister, K.S.J.: Mitigating multipath fading through channel hopping in wireless sensor networks. In: 2010 IEEE International Conference on Communications, pp. 1–5 (2010). https://doi.org/10.1109/ICC.2010.5502548
30. Willig, A., Karowski, N., Hauer, J.H.: Passive discovery of IEEE 802.15.4-based body sensor networks. Ad Hoc Netw. **8**(7), 742–754 (2010)

Sensor Networks: Enlarging the Attack Surface

Nancy Cam-Winget[(✉)]

Cisco Systems Inc., San Jose, CA 95134, USA
ncamwing@cisco.com

Abstract. Sensor Networks are becoming ubiquitous as they are deployed in many applications, from the consumer electronics, home appliances, and modern vehicles to critical infrastructures and industrial control systems. With the promise of improved user experience, maintainability and automation, these sensor networks interconnect and communicate over the Internet by employing Internet-aware embedded systems: IoT devices. With such capabilities, not only can management and control systems better manage the sensor network's efficiency and capabilities, so too can the attackers gain insight and leverage these networks and devices for malicious intent. This paper provides an overview of the evolving threats and technology trends to help address them.

Keywords: Cyber physical systems · Cyber security · Attack surface · Attack vector · IoT

1 Introduction

Sensor networks are becoming commonplace not just in the workplace but in our everyday lives. With current innovations in sensor technology, Gartner, Inc. forecasts that 8.4 billion IoT devices are connected to the Internet today, with a projected increase to 20.4 billion devices by 2020 [1]. These IoT devices are increasingly used in the home, the workplace and in critical applications such as utilities, transport systems, manufacturing and critical infrastructures. Devices such conventional thermometers, motion sensors and programmable logic controllers are being updated with the ability to communicate through a sensor network so as to facilitate its control and monitoring, in essence, creating a cyber-physical systems (CPS) [2]. As these CPS deployments include these innovative IoT devices, many communicate over unsecured protocols [14, 15].

New technology trends such big data analytics is also emerging as cyber-physical systems increase in adoption. Big data algorithms are evolving to improve and provide services such as predictive maintenance [3, 4], energy efficiency and management [5] and higher order services such as improved experiences for cities and communities [6]. In these CPS deployments, the IoT devices generate vasts amounts of data through the Internet as they are continuously being controlled and monitored. As data is mined for many purposes, as is being demonstrated through the evolution of the various analytic algorithms, so do the challenges in security and privacy grow.

Highlighting the security challenges are the growing number of breaches and attacks in various cyber physical systems deployed across different disciplines. As

© Springer Nature Switzerland AG 2019
C. Benavente-Peces et al. (Eds.): SENSORNETS 2017/2018, CCIS 1074, pp. 23–30, 2019.
https://doi.org/10.1007/978-3-030-30110-1_2

these sensor networks are now connected through the Internet, the very communications used for command and control of our operating environments are now lucrative targets for attacks [7–11].

Section 2 provides an overview of the evolving attack surface by describing the security challenges arising from these sensor networks and how these IoT systems become both victims as well as attack vectors. Discussion of the recent industry trends towards addressing some of the challenges follows in Sect. 3.

2 Evolving the Attack Surface

In brief, an attack surface is the sum of all means by which an attack can occur, e.g. the sum of all possible attack vectors. Wherein, an attack vector is the means by which an uncontrolled access with exploit or malicious purpose is made. Metrics to determine a how the security of a deployment, or system design can be based on measuring its attack surface [12, 13].

Some common attack vectors include viruses, malware, phishing and malicious e-mail attachments. The success of these attacks have now been facilitated by sensor networks as these include the new embedded devices, e.g. IoT devices, that provide easier means for exploit:

- Constrained devices: while these embedded devices are now able to connect to the Internet, they are typically constrained in CPU power, memory and power consumption. These limitations can provide challenges in providing the appropriate level of security within the device. Such challenges include the inability to secure their boot process, verify the integrity of their software and often lack the ability to encrypt their communications.
- Open exposure: as these sensor networks are deployed, literally everywhere, the embedded device's ability to connect to the Internet can now be easily accessible both physically or through wireless networks easing the attacker's entry.
- Physical security: with the devices being deployed in the open, they often lack the appropriate physical security and appropriate monitoring techniques to detect tampering.
- Unsecured protocols: many of the communication and control protocols used in operational networks, designed well before ubiquitous Internet connectivity, did not account for the need to protect their data transport mechanisms.

This section will describe two types of attacks to demonstrate both, how these IoT devices are now being leveraged for malicious intent and how the attacks themselves are continuing to evolve as countermeasures improve over time.

2.1 DDoS Attacks: From Mirai to a New Potential, Reaper

The Mirai attack was a well-publicized attack launched on September 20, 2016 that demonstrated how these IoT devices were leveraged and infected with malware that could self-propagate to mount a large scale Distributed Denial of Service (DDoS) attack [16]. It is reported that over 380,000 IoT devices were infected and thus enslaved by the Mirai malware to attack Krebs' website [17]. Once a device is infected, the Mirai malware continuously scans the Internet for other vulnerable IoT devices to further infect and enslave. Figure 1 summarizes the process flow by which the Mirai attack works.

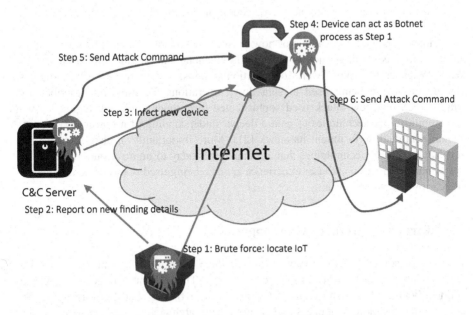

Fig. 1. Mirai attack: flow for affecting DDoS attack.

The Mirai Attack succeeds as it spreads using existing infected IoT devices to scan for additional IoT devices. Those that lack appropriate configurations, such as using the default (out-of-box) credentials and lacking in appropriate access or firewall protection. By scanning and thru trial and error, such devices can be discovered thru the Internet and infected as is shown in Steps 1 thru 3 in Fig. 1. With many of these infected devices, now under the control of the attacker's Command and Control center, a DDoS attack can succeed. As of the end of 2016, it was reported that over 2.5 million devices are infected with the Mirai malware [18].

These techniques and the Mirai process flow have been observed to continue to persist and evolve into what has recently termed as the Reaper or IoTroop [18, 19]. These new variants further exploit existing other software and hardware weaknesses in these IoT devices. The extent of its DDoS power is still unknown as the attack is yet to emerge. What is important to note however, is the efficacy in which the threats can evolve to attempt to skirt detection and to cause more serious harm.

2.2 Ransomware to Shutdowns: From Wannacry to CrashOverride

The latest attack type (e.g. ransomware), Wannacry, targeted and affected businesses across multiple disciplines from financial, government, educational to pharmaceutical across the world. The attack is based on two software modules; with the first module acting as a worm, exploiting a vulnerability in Microsoft Windows SMB Server Remote Code Execution to infiltrate a server and register itself as a legitimate service. With the worm and illicit service in place, the second module can then be launched (as a service dropped by the worm module) to perform its extortion activities. With the wide impact, an alert to facilitate the detection of this attack was posted by the U.S. Cert [20].

Wannacry is the first example of how ransomware attacks can also be leveraged to affect operations facilities such as those in the financial and pharmaceutical industries. While Wannacry's exploits were for extortionist gains, new malware exploits such as CrashOverride are being used to shut down operations facilities. As described by Dragos Inc., this new attack used sophisticated techniques while leveraging known vulnerabilities and techniques to gain a deeper understanding of a power grid's operational control flow to mount its attack [21]. More importantly, it also describes the very nature of how technologies that are innovated today to improve our connectivity, operational production and user experience are also being used to mount attacks and as such, grow the attack surface.

3 Addressing Security Challenges

Technology solutions exist today to aid in the detection and monitoring of CPS deployments though security challenges still exist. There is much ongoing work and effort in both academia and industry towards these evolving challenges using a combination of education, awareness and secure design architectures and practices.

Some of the technologies and efforts to address the security challenges, especially when using these IoT devices are discussed in this section and drawn from the following perspectives (shown in Fig. 2):

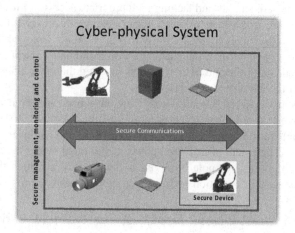

Fig. 2. Cyberphysical secure system.

- Hardening IoT devices: as these devices can be exposed to both physical and compute tampering, techniques to enable the devices to protect themselves from such attacks must be considered.
- Securing communications: with IoT devices transitioning from a physically siloed environment to communicating through the Internet, communications protocols across the networking e.g. Open Systems Intercommunication (OSI) stack.
- Management and monitoring: to ensure devices are configured with secure credentials, communications and software they must be continuously monitored and managed securely.

3.1 Securing IoT Devices

With these devices now being exposed with the potential for both physical tampering and infiltrations through the Internet, they must carry the means to protect themselves. Existing technologies such as hardware secure modules (HSMs) are being used and adapted to provide the first step in security, the means by which these devices can boot their software securely and provide a strong immutable identity [22].

Given the broad range of IoT devices available, several security architectures exist to suit the various device types [23, 24]. From suppliers of general componentsboth ARM and Intel provide architecture which are now widely used in mobile environments. These same technologies are showing increased use in sensor networks. The use of their security capabilities now allow for those IoT devices to identify themselves with a strong identity stored in their HSM modules, affording secure boot and where feasible, provide software verification through their attestation mechanisms. With these improvements, and coupled with technology trends facilitating virtual environments and containers, implementors are developing Trusted Execution Environments (TEE) and tools to aid applications their use. A TEE is a hardware secured module that includes both memory and storage along with the software and interfaces to provide an integrity-protected processing environment [25].

3.2 Securing Communications

Many of the technologies used to secure network communications protocols are being leveraged today to enable the IoT devices to communicate through the Internet. However, these protocols were often developed in environments where the devices are unconstrained from code size, computational power and battery utilization. To address the limitations imposed by IoT devices, several forums are adapting and creating new protocols to address these constraints.

One Internet focused standards group, IETF, has formed several working groups to address these constraints and requirements needed to provide secure connectivity in CPS. Some examples include:

– Constrained RESTful Environments (CORE): focuses defining protocols suitable for applications running in a constrained network such as Low-Power Wireless Personal Area Networks (LoWPANs).

- Authentication and Authorization for Constrained Environments (ACE): focuses on defining solutions to facilitate the authorized access in RESTful-like environments through the use of authentication and authorization protocols.
- Routing Over Low power and Lossy networks (ROLL): with many sensor networks utilizing low power and lossy networks (LLNs) such as IEEE 802.15.4 are interconnecting today to create these CPS deployments, this working group focuses on addressing routing issues for LLNs and define routing protocols to facilitate these interconnections.
- IPv6 over Networks of Resource-constrained Nodes (6lo): focuses on defining IPv6 based protocols to enable connectivity over these constrained sensor networks
- IP Wireless Access in Vehicular Environments (IPWAVE): focuses on defining IPv6 based protocols to enable secure communications between vehicles and other vehicles or stationary systems.

Full information of these groups and all IETF working groups, their charters, published specifications and current specifications under development can be found in [31].

Industries such as those in the Industrial Controls Sector have also recently published guidelines and recommendations for addressing security [27] and further evolving their protocols to be secured. One such example is the Common Industrial Protocol (CIP) updates to enable CIP Security [28].

An important protocol that is widely adopted and continues to be adapted for IoT devices is TLS [16]. In its current version 1.2, TLS is widely used in CPS deployments to secure the application layer protocols and in some cases, network layer protocols. This is implemented with the adaptation of using elliptic-curve or pre-shared keys as the credentials to facilitate the TLS authentication exchange. The use of pre-shared keys is provided to lower the computational cost affecting the authentication (or tunnel) establishment. The challenge presented now is in the management of the credentials, whether using x.509 certificates or pre-shared keys.

3.3   Awareness, Management and Monitoring

As the Mirai attack has demonstrated, even with the best protections in place, misconfigurations and lack of awareness for the need to practice good security measures, such as using strong credentials can still cause breaches. With these recent attacks demonstrating the mass and global span has heightened the need for raised awareness. As such, forums such as the National Institute of Standards and Technology (NIST) has created a public CPS working group to raise awareness. Thru this working group, a cybersecurity framework [29] has also been defined to describe core functions needed to secure CPS deployments with its core requirements including the need to facilitate continuous education and awareness and continuous monitoring (shown in Fig. 3).

With the heightened awareness, industry is also making their findings more public and providing timely reports and recommendations as potential breaches are observed [19, 21].

Identify	Protect	Detect	Respond	Recover
Risk Assessment	Access Control	Anomalies & Events	Response Planning	Recovery Planning
Risk Management Strategy	Data Security	Security Continuous Monitoring	Analysis	Communications
Asset Management	Information Protection	Detection Process	Mitigation	Improvements
	Awareness & Training		Improvements	
	Protective Technologies			

Fig. 3. NIST cybersecurity framework.

4 Conclusion

A study of the history of malicious software and attacks to the network indicate early techniques such as worms and viruses that presented themselves in the 1990's mounted attacks such as Blaster [30], forcing firewalls to be defined. These attack vectors have evolved enabling these worms to lay the ground work to more sophisticated attacks. Not only can they better propagate, but they often lay dormant and thus less detectable, all the while under the attacker's control. The attacks of yesterday were thwarted by the ability to create secure communication tunnels, access controls through network or application authentication and authorization to firewalls. These attacks have become more sophisticated to the point where no single technique is sufficient. This paper described a small representative set of challenges presented by the use of IoT devices and sensor networks as well as a small sampling of industry and standards trends that will continue to evolve as the attack surface evolves.

References

1. Gartner: https://www.gartner.com/newsroom/id/3598917
2. Khaitan, S.K., McCalley, J.D.: Design techniques and applications of cyberphysical systems: a survey. IEEE Syst. J. **9**(2), 350–365
3. Daily, J., Peterson, J.: Predictive maintenance: how big data analysis can improve maintenance. In: Richter, K., Walther, J. (eds.) Supply Chain Integration Challenges in Commercial Aerospace. Springer, Cham (2017). https://doi.org/10.1007/978-3-319-46155-7_18
4. Munirathinam, S., Ramadoss, B.: Big data predictive analtyics for proactive semiconductor equipment maintenance. IEEE International Conference on Big Data 2014
5. Karagiannidis, K.: Big data analytics for dynamic energy management in smart grids. Big Data Res. **2**(3), 94–101 (2015)
6. Sun, Y., Song, H., Jara, A., Bie, R.: Internet of things and big data analytics for smart and connected communities. IEEE Access **4**, 766–773 (2016)
7. Wired. https://www.wired.com/story/crash-override-malware

8. Theguardian. https://www.theguardian.com/technology/2017/jun/28/notpetya-ransomware-attack-ukraine-russia

9. Computerworld. https://www.computerworld.com/article/2519574/security0/stuxnet-renews-power-grid-security-concerns.html

10. Hernandez, G., Arias, O., Buentello, D., Jin, Y.: Smart nest thermostat: a smart spay in your home. In: Black Hat USA (2014)

11. Illera, A.G., Vidal, J.V.: Lights off! The darkness of the smart meters. In: Black Hat Europe (2014)

12. Manadhata, P., Wing, J.: An attack surface metric. IEEE Trans. Software Eng. Arch. **37**(3), 371–386 (2011)

13. Struckman, J., Purtilo, J.: Comparing and applying attack surface metrics. In: MetriSec 2012 Proceedings of the 4th international workshop on Security, pp. 3–6 (2012)

14. Modbus. http://www.modbus.org

15. 1815-2010: IEEE Standard for Electric Power Systems Communications – Distributed network Protocol (DNP3). 2010. ISBN 978-0-7381-6312-3

16. KrebsonSecurity. https://krebsonsecurity.com/2016/09/krebsonsecurity-hit-with-record-ddos

17. PCWorld. https://www.pcworld.com/article/3126362/security/iot-malware-behind-record-ddos-attack-is-now-available-to-all-hackers.html

18. Wired. https://www.wired.com/story/reaper-iot-botnet-infected-million-networks

19. KrebsonSecurity. https://krebsonsecurity.com/2017/10/reaper-calm-before-the-iot-security-storm/

20. US-CERT. https://www.us-cert.gov/ncas/alerts/TA17-132A

21. Dragos Inc. https://dragos.com/blog/crashoverride/CrashOverride-01.pdf

22. Trusted Computing Group (TCG), https://trustedcomputinggroup.org/

23. Costin, A., Zaddach, J., Francillon, A., Balzarotti, D.: A large-scale analysis of the security of embedded firmwares. In: USENIX Conference on Security Symposium. USENIX Association (2014)

24. Cui, A., Stolfo, S.J.: A quantitative analysis of the insecurity of embedded network devices: results of a wide-area scan. In: Annual Computer Security Applications Conference (ACSAC). ACM (2010)

25. Sabt, M., Achemial, M., Bouabdallah, A.: Trusted Execution Environment: What It is, and What It is Not. IEEE Trustcom/BigDataSE/ISPA (2015)

26. Dierks, T., Rescorla, E.: The Transport Layer Security (TLS) Protocol Version 1.2. https://tools.ietf.org/html/rfc5246

27. International Electrotechnical Commision: IEC 62443 International Standard

28. ODVA CIP Security Standard. https://www.odva.org/Technology-Standards/Common-Industrial-Protocol-CIP/CIP-Security

29. NIST Cybersecurity Framework. https://www.nist.gov/cyberframework

30. Computerworld. https://www.computerworld.com/article/2571072/malware-vulnerabilities/blaster-worm-spreading–experts-warn-of-attack.html

31. The Internet Engineering Task Force (IETF). https://ietf.org/

On the Performance of Industrial Wireless Sensor Networks: Channel Hopping vs. Channel Adaptive Protocols

Ruan D. Gomes[1,2,3], Cesar Benavente-Peces[3(✉)], Marcelo S. Alencar[1], Diego V. Queiroz[3], and Iguatemi E. Fonseca[4]

[1] Post-Graduate Program in Electrical Engineering,
Federal University of Campina Grande, Campina Grande, Brazil
`ruan.gomes@ifpb.edu.br, malencar@dee.ufcg.edu.br`
[2] Informatics Coordination, Federal Institute of Paraiba, Guarabira, Brazil
[3] Signal Theory and Communications Department,
Universidad Politecnica de Madrid, Madrid, Spain
`cesar.benavente@upm.es, diego@sti.ufpb.br`
[4] Informatics Center, Federal University of Paraiba, Joao Pessoa, Brazil
`iguatemi@ci.ufpb.br`

Abstract. The standard IEEE 802.15.4e shows several improvements which makes it outperforming the predecessor IEEE 802.15.4 standard. A remarkable improvement is the use of multiple channels and the capability to choose the most convenient depending on the network links state. Hence, different techniques can be provisioned to dynamically select the most appropriate channel for establishing the link through an adaptive mechanism. During the contention-free periods, the Time-Slotted Channel Hopping (TSCH) mode is based on channel hopping while the Deterministic and Synchronous Multi-channel Extension (DSME) mode uses either channel hopping or channel adaptation. In scenarios where channel diversity techniques are used for channel adaptation nodes links are established using the same channel as long as the channel quality (SNR) is high enough. In consequence to guarantee link best performance, its quality must be measured periodically to decide whether continue in the same channel of switch to a better performance one. Our investigation focuses on the analysis of the performance of three different approaches which pretend to take advantage of the multichannel capabilities of the new standard, based on the DSME protocol: CH-DSME which is based on a simple channel hopping mechanism, CA-DSME which employs channel adaptation, and a novel hybrid approach (H-DSME) which combines channel hopping and channel adaptation. This investigation shows that, in an industrial environment, the H-DSME outperforms both CH-DSME and CA-DSME approaches. In this work, the Castalia simulator was used to perform the simulations, using a reliable simulation model, which captures the characteristics of the wireless channel in industrial environments in long range basis. The analysis demonstrates that channel adaptation is better than channel hopping for unicast packets transmission, when links quality are continuously measured. Nevertheless, the

C. Benavente-Peces et al. (Eds.): SENSORNETS 2017/2018, CCIS 1074, pp. 31–57, 2019.
https://doi.org/10.1007/978-3-030-30110-1_3

coordinator transmit packets in broadcast mode, it is demonstrated that using channel hopping is a good alternative to deal with the quality spatial variation of the network channels.

Keywords: Industrial wireless sensor networks · Channel modelling · Channel performance · Channel diversity · Adaptive-dynamic channel allocation

1 Introduction

Traditional industrial monitoring systems operate in an off-line mode or use wired networks to transmit the data to a central host. In the case of monitoring systems based on wired networks, the operations to deploy cables and sensors usually has higher cost than the sensors themselves [26]. Furthermore, that approach has limited flexibility, which makes the network installation and maintenance processes more cumbersome and expensive.

A lower cost alternative to implement such systems is the use of wireless networks, which have significant advantages, including high flexibility, reconfigurability, easier deployment and maintenance [19]. More specifically, Wireless Sensor Networks (WSN) have additional advantages, such as the ability of self-organization and local processing, and can ne considered as a promising platform for the implementation of monitoring and controlling systems in industrial environments.

The use of WSN, to implement monitoring and control systems in industrial environments, has some advantages when compared with the use of wired networks, such as low cost and high flexibility. However, it is necessary to deal with typical problems of wireless systems, such as electromagnetic interference [25], and industrial environment high attenuation, due to the presence of many objects and obstructions [32]. Many industrial environments also present characteristics that make the wireless channel non-stationary, for long time periods, which can cause abrupt changes in the characteristics of the channel over time [3].

Link asymmetry is another remarkable problem in WSN. To cope with this issue some protocols use acknowledgement per packet, and hence guaranteeing a good bi-directional link quality is required. Spatial variations in the channel performance happen often in IWSN. Spatial correlation arises because the high density in the network topology, here nodes are spatially close and in consequence the observations are highly correlated here correlation degree increases with inter-node distance decrease [4]. In [34], a coherence length of 5.5 cm was found for IEEE 802.15.4 radios operating in the 2.4 GHz band. Hence, two nodes positioned at a distance more than 5.5 cm apart from each other, and using the same channel, can be considered uncorrelated, and thus the channel can show a high quality for one node, and a low quality for the other. Some protocols use beacon packets to synchronize the nodes, and these packets are transmitted using a single channel. However, sometimes it may be difficult to pick a channel whose performance is good enough for all links composing the network.

To overcome these limitations, appropriate mechanisms allowing the network to self-adapt to the variations that occur in the link quality over time need to be implemented, such as adaptive routing [11] or dynamic channel allocation [15]. Other important aspect is the energy consumption and management, which is a key issue in industrial WSN, given network motes are usually powered by batteries. Some appropriate strategies, as energy aware geographic routing in lossy WSN, can be developed [7].

The deployment of Industrial Wireless Sensor Networks (IWSNs) presents advantages in comparison to the use of wired networks, such as greater flexibility and low cost. However, it is necessary to deal with typical problems of wireless networks such as interference and the high level of small and large scale attenuation due to the existence of many moving objects and obstacles in the environment. One way to circumvent the variations in channel quality in an industrial WSN is the use of multichannel protocols and dynamic channel allocation strategies. This is justified by the fact that the channels are frequency uncorrected in environments that have a large effective delay spread, as is the case in several industrial environments. Through the use of multichannel protocols, associated with the use of dynamic channel allocation strategies, it is possible to deal with the variation in the quality of the channels in different places of the network and also with the non-stationary characteristics of the channels in long periods of time. In this article, some characteristics of industrial WSNs are discussed and the use of multichannel protocols and dynamic channel allocation is presented as a possible solution to improve the quality of service (QoS) of these networks.

Some standards have been proposed in the last years with a focus on industrial applications, such as the WirelessHART and the ISA100.11a. Both WirelessHART and ISA100.11a are based on the physical layer of IEEE 802.15.4, but defines its own MAC layer. Instead of using CSMA/CA, as defined by the IEEE 802.15.4 standard, they use a MAC layer with Time Division Multiple Access (TDMA). By using TDMA, collisions are avoided and the power consumption can be optimized. They also use frequency hopping and blacklisting, to mitigate the problems related to interference and fading. However, without an adequate management of the blacklist, the communication performance may be lower for these standards [31].

More recently, the IEEE 802.15.4e standard was released. The goal of this standard is to propose solutions for applications that require high reliability, such as industrial applications [18]. Five modes of operation are defined, that is: Time-Slotted Channel Hopping (TSCH), Deterministic and Synchronous Multi-Channel Extension (DSME), Low Latency Deterministic Network (LLDN), Asynchronous Multi-Channel Adaptation (AMCA), and Radio Frequency Identification Blink (BLINK). However, only the modes TSCH, DSME, and LLDN have been explored in the literature until recently. In general, the modes of the IEEE 802.15.4e are based on TDMA or frequency hopping to reduce collisions and mitigate the effects of interference and fading, and to satisfy the requirements of industrial applications in terms of reliability and determinism.

One of the main differences between the new standard IEEE 802.15.4e in comparison to the previous IEEE 802.15.4 standard is the use of multiple channels. The TSCH mode employs channel hopping. When using this mechanism, the nodes usually switch to a new channel before each transmission, which makes the network more robust against problems that affect only a subset of the channels. However, if a proper management of the blacklist is not made, the network performance can be significantly degraded [17]. In the DSME mode, channel hopping can also be used in the contention free periods. It is also possible to use a channel adaptation mechanism instead of channel hopping. When using channel adaptation, a pair of nodes communicate using only one channel during a large time period. A channel switch only occurs when the channel in use starts to present low quality. Thus, a procedure is necessary to evaluate the quality of the links continuously, in order to use the channel adaptation mechanism properly. The implementation of this procedure is not defined by the standard.

In this paper, the performance of three different approaches for channel diversity, based on the DSME mode of the IEEE 802.15.4e standard, were evaluated. The first one is based on a simple channel hopping mechanism, the second one employs channel adaptation, and the third one is a novel approach that uses both channel hopping and channel adaptation. The simulations were performed using the Castalia simulator, which is an event-driven simulator for WSN. A realistic channel model was used, which includes the effects of fading, shadowing, and the non-stationary characteristics of the channel in industrial environments. When using this model, which was first described in [14].

By using the Castalia simulator and the appropriate channel model, it is possible to observe and predict the performance of the protocols under investigation, while considering the non-stationary behaviour of the wireless channel in industrial environments. This simulation model was also used in [12] to evaluate link quality estimators for industrial WSN.

The remaining part of this paper is organized as follows Sect. 2 reviews the main characteristics of the IEEE 802.15.4e standard. In Sect. 3 the considered DSME-based protocols are introduced. In Sect. 4 the main properties of IWSN channel properties are shown. Section 5 describes the evaluation methodology used in the performance analysis. Section 6 shows and discusses the results obtained in this investigation. Finally, in Sect. 7 the most relevant conclusions and remarks are described.

2   Review of the IEEE 802.15.4e Standard

In networks that use the IEEE 802.15.4 standard, it is difficult to establish strict latency boundaries, due to the CSMA/CA protocol used in the MAC layer, since the access to the communication medium occurs in a distributed and random way. Hidden and exposed terminal problems can also affect the performance of the network, making it even more unpredictable. The MAC protocols defined by the IEEE 802.15.4 use a single channel for communication, which is a single point of failure, and increases the number of collisions in the network. Due to these limitations, the new standard IEEE 802.15.4e was proposed, for applications with more stringent requirements of reliability and determinism.

Five modes of operation are defined by the standard, but only modes TSCH, DSME, and LLDN have been more extensively studied until recently [18]. Modes TSCH, DSME and LLDN use TDMA as the channel access method, which allows to reduce the number of collisions, and increases the determinism of the network, since each node has specific time slots allocated to it, and the access can be done without contention. Besides, it is possible to reduce the energy consumption, since the nodes can sleep during time slots in which they are not transmitting or receiving packets. Modes TSCH, and DSME also employ multichannel communication and three types of topology (star, mesh or tree), while the LLDN define only star networks that use a single channel to communicate. However, some works have proposed the use of a tree topology and multiple channels in LLDN networks [29,30].

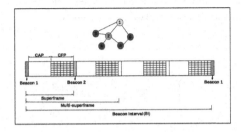

Fig. 1. Example of a superframe structure for a DSME network [16].

In the next sub-section more details about the DSME mode are provided, since the protocols proposed and evaluated in this paper are based on this mode.

2.1   The DSME Mode

The DSME (Deterministic and Synchronous Multi-Channel Extension) mode is the most complex and flexible mode of the IEEE 802.15.4e standard [18]. It extends the beacon-enabled mode of the IEEE 802.15.4, which is based on a superframe structure, that is managed by the network coordinator. The coordinator sends beacon frames to delimit two consecutive superframes. The main differences between the beacon-enabled mode of the IEEE 802.15.4 and the DMSE mode is that the DSME mode allows the use of a higher number of Guarantee Time Slots (GTS), and allows communication using multiple channels during the contention free period. Thus, multiple nodes can transmit simultaneously during the same GTS in different channels, increasing the overall WSN throughput.

Figure 1 shows an example of a superframe structure defined according to the DSME mode of the IEEE 802.15.4e standard [1]. Each superframe is composed by a Contention Access Period (CAP), and a Contention Free Period (CFP).

Different from the beacon-enabled mode of the IEEE 802.15.4, there is no inactive period. In the CAP, the nodes can access the communication medium using CSMA/CA or ALOHA [18]. The beacon frames, referred in the standard as Enhanced Beacons (EB), delimit the superframes. The EB frames are transmitted using the same channel, defined in the starting process of the network [1], which is also used in the CAP period.

Multiple superframes can be grouped inside a multi-superframe, and multiple multi-superframes can be grouped inside the same Beacon Interval (BI). This time structure is configured using some parameters, that is: *macSuperframeOrder* (SO), *macMultisuperframeOrder* (MO), and *macBeaconOrder* (BO), in which $0 \leq SO \leq MO \leq BO \leq 14$. The parameter SO defines the size of the superframes, MO defines the size of the multi-superframes, and BO defines the BI. In the example shown in Fig. 1 the parameters $MO = SO + 1$, and $BO = MO + 1$. Each superframe has 16 time slots. Thus, the value of SO defines the duration of each slot. Optionally, the number of CAP can be reduced in a multi-superframe, through a mechanism called *capReduction*. When the *capReduction* is enabled, only the first superframe in the multi-superframe has the CAP.

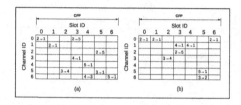

Fig. 2. Channel diversity mechanisms defined for DSME networks [16].

In the DSME networks there are three types of nodes: PAN coordinator, coordinator, and end node. The PAN coordinator sends a EB every BI. The coordinator is the sink node for some of the network nodes. A coordinator sends a beacon at least once per multi-superframe, in the beacon slot, in order to register its presence in the network [5]. In Fig. 1, Node 1 is the PAN coordinator, Node 2 is a coordinator, and the remaining are end nodes. The coordinators can forward packets from end nodes that do not reach the PAN coordinator directly. In the same network multiple coordinators nodes are allowed.

The DSME mode defines two types of channel diversity, that is: channel hopping, and channel adaptation. Figure 2 shows two examples of scheduling for the CFP period, using channel hopping in (a), and channel adaptation in (b). When using the channel hopping, the nodes receive packets in different channels depending on the channel offset of the node, the slot ID, the superframe ID, and the sequence number of the EB sent by the coordinator. For example, in the example illustrated in Fig. 2(a), Node 1 receives a packet using Channel 0 in the first time slot, using Channel 1 in the second time slot, and so on. The nodes that receive packets inside the same superframe need to have different channel offsets, in order to avoid collisions.

When using channel adaptation, a fixed channel is allocated for a given time slot inside the superframe, and a given pair of nodes. For example, in the example illustrated in Fig. 2(b), Channel 0 was allocated for the communication from node 2 to node 1, in all slots. The channel is only changed if the allocated channel starts to present bad quality. The standard does not define how to select the communication channels when using channel adaptation [18]. In this paper, an algorithm to estimate the link quality is proposed, and used to implement the channel adaptation mechanism.

Some nodes of the network, called coordinators, periodically transmit EBs, which contains all the information regarding the definition of the transient period *superframe*. The EBs are also used to ensure synchronization between the nodes of the network. DSME mode also defines two modes of channel diversity, one adaptive and the other based on frequency hopping. In the adaptive mode, communication between two nodes occurs on the same channel as long as it presents good quality. If a drop in channel quality is identified, another channel is allocated for communication between the two nodes. In frequency hopping mode, a channel sequence is defined equally for each node in the network. However, to avoid collisions, each node starts sequencing in a different time slot, based on an *offset* value. The channel allocation is based on the receiver, and the transmitter must use the receiver channel to send packets. In TSCH the channel allocation is based on the connection and not on the receiver.

Another interesting characteristic of the DMSE is the possibility of using group acknowledgement (GACK), in which two time slots of the multi-superframe are allocated for the GACK frames (G1 and G2). The coordinator uses G1 to acknowledge all packets received until the G1 time slot. The G2 is used to acknowledge all packets received after the G1 time slot and before the G2 time slot. If the GACK is not used, all packets transmitted to the coordinator are acknowledged individually [1]. With this mechanism, a node can retransmit a lost packet inside the same multi-superframe, if one slot before the G1 and other slot between G1 and G2 are allocated to the node.

Some nodes of the network, called coordinators, periodically transmit EBs, which contains all the information regarding the definition of the transient period (*superframe*). The EBs are also used to ensure synchronization between the nodes of the network. DSME mode also defines two modes of channel diversity, one adaptive and the other based on frequency hopping. In the adaptive mode, communication between two nodes occurs on the same channel as long as it presents good quality. If a drop in channel quality is identified, another channel is allocated for communication between the two nodes. In frequency hopping mode, a channel sequence is defined equally for each node in the network. However, to avoid collisions, each node starts sequencing in a different time slot, based on an *offset* value. The channel allocation is based on the receiver, and the transmitter must use the receiver channel to send packets. In TSCH channel allocation is based on the connection and not on the receiver.

2.2 Related Research

Some authors have proposed mechanisms to improve the performance of IEEE 802.15.4e networks, through the use of dynamic channel allocation or dynamic configuration of the blacklist for TSCH networks. In [17] an experiment was performed to analyze the performance of a TSCH network inside an aircraft cabin, with external interference caused by Wi-Fi networks. In the experiments described in [17] the Packet Error Rate (PER) was 35%, when using the 16 available channels, due to interference problems. In general, when fewer channels were used, the performance was better, as the interference is lower. For example, when using only one channel, the less affected by the interference sources, the PER was 5%. However, a mechanism is needed to estimate the quality of the channels and to dynamically configure the blacklist.

In [9,10] the use of adaptive frequency hopping for TSCH networks was proposed, in order to avoid using channels affected by interference sources. In this approach, two time slots in each cycle are used to perform readings of RSSI values, in order to identify interference sources. Based on these measurements, the blacklist is updated to avoid the channels with a high level of interference. In [9] experiments were conducted considering different sizes for the blacklist. It was observed that the higher the size of the blacklist, the better the communication performance. This result corroborate the results presented in [17]. However, this type of behaviour only occurs if an adequate monitoring of the quality of the channels is performed, in order to properly configure the blacklist in real time. One limitation of the approach presented in [9,10] is that only interference problems are considered. Other aspects that can affect the quality of the links are not considered, such as shadowing and fading. Besides, the channel quality monitoring is performed by all nodes and using time slots that could be used for communication, which incurs in a high overhead, and in an increase of latency.

Some authors have proposed the use of techniques for channel diversity and multi-channel communication based on the IEEE 802.15.4e standard for LLDN networks, which use originally only one channel. In [29] a multi-level and multi-channel protocol based on the LLDN mode, called the MC-LLDN, was proposed. The goal is to increase the scalability of the network through the use of a multi-level topology, data aggregation, and multi-channel communication. The drawback is that the channels are allocated to the sub-networks in a static way. Thus, it is not capable of dealing with the variations that occur in the channel quality over time. The protocol described in [30] is an evolution of the MC-LLDN, called PriMuLa, which incorporates adaptive channel selection. One limitation of the proposed protocol, which is due to the characteristics of the LLDN, is that a same channel is allocated to all nodes in the sub-network. However, spatial variations in the channel quality can occur, as well as asymmetry problems. In the approaches developed for the present paper, the channel quality is assessed in a per-link basis, as well as the channel allocation.

The experiments described in [21] and [24] evaluated the performance of the DSME mode in comparison to the beacon-enabled mode of the IEEE 802.15.4. The experiments verified that, in some scenarios, the throughput of the IEEE

802.15.4e DSME network can be 12 times higher than the IEEE 802.15.4 beacon-enabled network, and with a lower energy consumption, due to the use of a TDMA-based medium access. In the experiments frequency hopping was used, and no dynamic management of the blacklist was employed. In [24] the influence of interference caused by Wi-Fi networks was evaluated, but other problems that can affect the channel quality in industrial environments, such as shadowing and fading, were not considered.

In [8] simulation studies to verify the performance of DSME networks are described, and some enhancements to optimize the energy consumption are proposed. However, the paper focuses mainly on energy consumption, and did not consider in the experiments the problems that can affect the channel quality, such as interference and fading. Besides, although in the simulations described in [8] the channel adaptation mechanism was considered, the details about the implementation of this mechanism are not provided.

In [5] a comparison between DSME and TSCH in process automation scenarios is described. Simulations were performed to verify the delay, reliability, and scalability of each mode. The TSCH presented better results for small networks, with up to 30 nodes. For larger networks, with more than 30 nodes, the DSME presented better results. The simulations described in [5] used realistic parameters for the log-normal shadowing, but the effect of fading and the non-stationary characteristics of the wireless channel were not considered. In addition, only the channel hopping mechanism of the DSME were analyzed. The simulation model used for the present paper considers more aspects that can affect the channel quality, that is: shadowing, fading, asymmetry, and the non-stationary characteristics of the channel in long time periods. Besides, a comparison between channel hopping and channel adaptation is performed.

In [23] a comparison between TSCH and DSME is described, in terms of energy consumption and performance. In the scenarios under consideration, the energy consumption of DSME was slight better than TSCH, as well as the performance. For applications that send less data, the TSCH under-utilize the bandwidth, due to the fixed size of the time slots. In the experiments described in [23] only channel hopping was considered, and without group ACK. In the present paper, channel adaptation are also considered, as well as group ACK.

3 Considered DSME-Based Protocols

The design and deployment of WSN-based for smart-grid applications must take into account the performance of WSN communication protocols in harsh environments given the disturbances affecting the links quality. In [35] the performance of the state-of-the-art WSN medium access control (MAC) protocols, such as IEEE 802.15.4, IEEE 802.11, CSMA, TDMA, and Z-MAC, are analysed and investigated to better identity which are the main advantages and drawbacks of the MAC protocols under analysis in this work, with the constraints imposed by a harsh smart-grid environments affected by noise, interferences, shadowing, and fading.

A sensor node shares the environment and spectrum with other nodes composing the WSN. Furthermore, network nodes are in general sharing the spectrum band (in particular free ISM bands) with a number of wireless devices, as nodes belonging to different wireless networks and, other RF devices (among others WiFi, Bluetooth, Zigbee, LoRa, etc.). Under this situation, in order to guarantee the appropriate WSN performance, it is necessary to design proper network MAC layer to structure the WSN links to provide quality communications. In the WSN literature, a number of MAC layer techniques and technologies have been analysed and developed. In a general way, they can be included in one of the next three groups: *Contention-based MAC Layers, Reservation-based MAC Layers* and *Hybrid MAC Layers* [36].

The IEEE 802.15.4e standard describes the requirements for the slotted MAC scheme for the development of short-range communication devices aimed at low data-rate transmission, i.e., low capabilities wireless devices. The IEEE 802.15.4e standard describes a number of MAC schemes for different applications such as *Time Slotted Channel Hopping* (TSCH), *Low Latency Deterministic Networks* (LLDN), *Deterministic and Synchronous Multi channel Extension* (DSME), *Radio Frequency Identification blink* (RFID), and *Asynchronous Multi-Channel Adaptation* (AMCA). A different one is the DSME mode which is proposed in the IEEE 802.15.4e standard. It is mainly designed for applications requiring low energy consumption, short range transmission and narrow bandwidth (low data rate), as the living monitoring, process automation, industry monitoring, smart-grid, smart-home, smart-building, leisure, smart-health and many other applications [22].

In this paper, three approaches for the DSME mode are implemented and evaluated, called CH-DSME, CA-DSME, and H-DSME. The CH-DSME is based on the channel hopping mechanism, and without blacklist. Most papers, described in Sect. 2.2, evaluated the DSME with this type of channel diversity. In [8] the channel adaptation mechanism was considered, but the details about the implementation of this mechanism were not provided. The CA-DSME is based on the channel adaptation mechanism for the CFP periods of

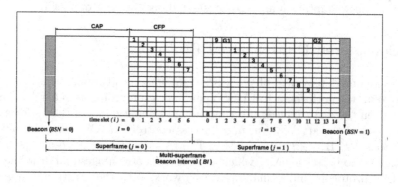

Fig. 3. The time structure used in the simulations [16].

the superframes. An algorithm to estimate the quality of the links is used to decide when a channel switch is needed. The H-DSME is a hybrid approach that uses channel adaptation in the CFP periods, and channel hopping for the beacons, and GACK frames.

This paper focuses in channel diversity techniques. Thus, to simplify the analysis at this point, a star topology was considered. In future works, the extension of the proposed approaches for tree and mesh networks, and considering a larger number of nodes, will be studied.

3.1 CH-DSME

Figure 3 shows the frame structure implemented for the CH-DSME. A network with 10 nodes, and star topology was considered, in which nine end nodes (Node 1 to Node 9) are connected, and transmit packets directly to the PAN coordinator (Node 0), and only one transmission occurs in each time slot. In Fig. 3 the numbers in the time slots indicate the ID of the end node that performs a transmission in each time slot. The *capReduction* was enabled, and thus only the first superframe has the CAP.

Each node has two time slots to transmit packets. The first one is before the first GACK (G1), and the second one is placed between G1 and the second GACK (G2). Thus, if the transmission in the first attempt fails, the end node can try again, using other channel, inside the same multi-superframe. The second time slot of each node is used only for retransmission. If the first transmission occurs successfully, the second time slot is not used. The beacons, and GACK frames are always transmitted using the same channel (Channel 0 in Fig. 3). For transmission of data packets, the channel to be used in a given time slot i is determined using

$$c(i) = (i + j \times l + macChannelOffset + BSN)\%16,$$

where j is the superframe index, $macChannelOffset$ is the channel offset of a receiver node, BSN is a sequence number of the beacon sent by the PAN coordinator. The value of l is equal to 15 if CAP reduction is enabled and j is not equal to zero, or 7 otherwise. In the implementation built for this paper, the $macChannelOffset$ is equal to the ID of the receiver node. All the 16 channels were considered, thus the value of $c(i)$ is an integer between 0 and 15, which represents the channel identification.

3.2 CA-DSME

The CA-DSME also uses the frame structure shown in Fig. 3, but with a different channel diversity mechanism. In CA-DSME all nodes transmit to the coordinator using only one channel, without channel hopping. All the nodes use the same channel at the beginning. Since only one transmission occurs in each time slot, the end nodes can use the same channel in the transmissions. In scenarios with more than one transmission at the same time, the channels need to be allocated in order to avoid collisions. A channel switch only occurs when the channel of a given link starts to present bad quality, and only the channel of the affected link is changed.

When using channel adaptation in the CFP periods, it is possible to pick good channels for all links, if the link quality estimator is able to quickly and accurately estimate the link quality. The experiments described in [9,17] showed that by using only one channel, the network performance is higher than using a channel hopping mechanism with a larger set of channels. However, the channels to be used need to be properly chosen.

Since the nodes try to retransmit a lost packet only once, and inside the same multi-superframe, it is possible to calculate the Packet Reception Rate (PRR), using the information obtained from a set of received packets. The Algorithm 1 was used to calculate the Packet Reception Rate of each link, in which each packet has an ID (a sequence number that identifies the packet) and the information about in which slot it was received, that is, before G1 (slot 1) or after G1 (slot 2). If the same packet is received twice due to a fail in the reception of G1, only the first received packet is put on the packet list to be analyzed by the algorithm. This algorithm also considers that the second time slot is used only for retransmission.

Algorithm 1. Algorithm to calculate the Packet Reception Rate.

Input: a list of packets $packet\_list$ with N packets, and the expected id for the first
    packet in the list fp_{id}
Output: the Packet Reception Rate (PRR)
1: $fail\_cont := 0$
2: **for** each $packet$ in $packet\_list$ **do**
3:    **if** $packet.slot = 1$ **then**
4:       $fail\_cont := fail\_cont + 2 \cdot (packet.id - fp_{id})$
5:    **else**
6:       $fail\_cont := fail\_cont + 2 \cdot (packet.id - fp_{id}) + 1$
7:    **end if**
8:    $fp_{id} := packet.id + 1$
9: **end for**
10: PRR $:= \frac{N}{N+fail\_cont}$
11: **return** PRR

Using the Algorithm 1 the coordinator calculates the PRR for each link using a window of N packets. A threshold can be defined for each link, in order to trigger the channel switch procedure. In the implementation built for this paper, $N = 10$, and a threshold equal to 0.9, for all nodes, were used. Each new PRR value obtained using the Algorithm 1 is combined with the last calculated value using an Exponentially Weighted Moving Average (EWMA) filter with history control factor $\alpha = 0.3$, to make the calculated PRR more stable over time. Higher values for α can make the estimator more stable, but the reactivity becomes smaller.

In the beacon frame, there is a bitmap to indicate to each node if it needs to perform a channel switch. When the PRR calculated for a given link is below its threshold, the coordinator sets the corresponding bit on the bitmap to 1. When the node receives a beacon indicating the need of a channel switch, it switches to the next channel, in a round-robin fashion. While the coordinator does not receive a packet in the new channel, it continues to send the beacon with the bit equal to 1 in the bitmap. After receiving the first packet in the new channel, the coordinator clears the bit. Since the beacon frames are always sent using the same channel, if the transmission of a beacon fails, the nodes can wait for the next beacon to re-synchronize.

A mechanism to identify deep fading problems was also implemented. As the coordinator needs to receive data packets to calculate the PRR using the Algorithm 1, when the link between a given end node and the coordinator enters in a deep fading state, no packets can be received while the channel remains in that state. Thus, when the coordinator does not receive packets from a given end node during a long period, it starts the channel switch procedure for that node. In the implementation built for this paper, the coordinator starts a channel switch procedure when no packet is received from a given end node during 10 consecutive BI.

In both CH-DSME and CA-DSME the channel used to transmit the beacons and the GACK frames is a single point of failure. In these protocols, it is possible to deal with problems that affect the quality of a subset of channels through channel hopping or channel adaptation, but they are not capable of dealing with problems that affect the channel used to transmit the beacons and the GACK frames. Thus, in this paper a new hybrid approach is proposed (the H-DSME), which is better explained in Sect. 3.3.

3.3   H-DSME

The beacon and GACK frames are transmitted in broadcast mode to all the end nodes connected to the coordinator. Therefore, the channel used to transmit these frames needs to present good quality for all links between the coordinator and the end nodes. However, spatial variations in the channel quality can occur. The coherence length is used to quantify the maximum change in distance that will result in the channel being highly correlated. In experiments described in [34], it was verified a coherence length of 5.5 cm for IEEE 802.15.4 radios operating in the 2.4 GHz band. Thus, two nodes positioned more than 5.5 cm apart from each other, and using the same channel, can be considered uncorrelated, and thus the channel can present high quality for one node, and low quality for the other.

Although the use of only one channel during a large time period can be advantageous for the CFP periods, as explained in Sect. 3.2, it may be difficult to guarantee a good qualify of service for all end nodes when using only one channel for the transmission of beacons and GACK frames. Thus, the H-DSME uses channel adaptation for the CFP periods (in the same way of CA-DSME), and channel hopping for the transmission of beacons and GACK frames.

The channels are used in a round-robin fashion to transmit the beacons and GACK frames. Using this mechanism, the end nodes do not remain disconnected for a large time period, when one channel begins to decrease its quality regarding the coordinator link.

The IEEE 802.15.4e standard defines that the channel used in the set-up of the network needs to be used to transmit the beacons and for the transmissions in the CAP period [1]. However, the modification to use multiple channels can be done with no interference with the other parts of the protocol.

When dynamic addition of nodes is considered, the nodes that want to join the network need to listen in some channel during up to 16 BI. If no beacon is received, the node can start to listen in another channel during other 16 BI. When only one channel is used to transmit the beacon frames, as defined originally by the standard, the node listens in one channel during only one BI. However, if the end node doesn't know the channel used to transmit the beacons a priori, in some cases it will be necessary to wait for multiple BI (16 in the worst case) until a beacon is received. In addition, if the channel in use to transmit the beacons presents a very low quality for the link between the coordinator and the new node, the delay to join the network can be very high. This aspect will be better evaluated in future works.

To accommodate the use of channel hopping in the transmission of the beacons, it is necessary to have a mechanism to maintain the network synchronized in case of failures during the reception of a beacon. To do this, a timer is used in the end nodes to identify that a beacon has been lost. The coordinator sends a new beacon for each BI, thus the timer is configured to expire after a time equal to $BI + \frac{SD}{16}$ ms, where $\frac{SD}{16}$ is the duration of a time slot. The values of BI and SD depend on the values of the parameters BO and SO, respectively. If a node receives a new beacon before the timer expires, the timer is reseted. Otherwise, the node switches the channel, and waits for the next beacon, which maintains the synchronization.

4   Channel Properties

Industrial environment is harsh and many effects affect the channel quality decreasing link reliability. In [20], despite the movement of people and equipment in the environment, over a short interval of time the channel can be regarded as wide-sense stationary or quasi stationary.

In [27], the authors analyse and formulate in detail two models for generating phase of individual multipath components in an indoor environment: deterministic phase increment model (model I) and random phase increment model (model II). These models were previously introduced in [20]. Intensive computer simulation were carried out in order to validate the models. In the first model, the phase of each multipath component is updated in a deterministic way by using a number of independent random scatterers. In the model II, the phase of each multipath component is updated by adding independent random phase increments. The number of scatterers and statistical properties of phase increments are studied, and simulated to analyse, and compared the effect on

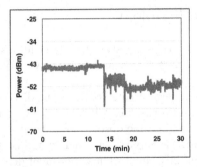

Fig. 4. RSS measurements (in dBm) for 30 min with Link 1.

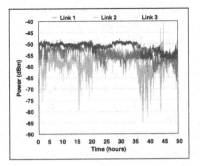

Fig. 5. Experiment with three links during 50 h.

both models. A major conclusion is that both models show a satisfactory performance when choosing an appropriate set of parameters.

In a measurement campaign in [14] performed by the authors of this investigation it was observed that the link properties could change dramatically over long periods of time due to the motion of the various elements in the environment. Figure 4 shows the appearance of abrupt changes in the link quality during 30 min where just on link was used. Figure 5 extends the same experiment up-to 50 h of observation with three different links. In the experiments, a star topology network was settled connecting three nodes, which are monitoring three motors simultaneously, and the three nodes communicate with the same sink node, using the same channel. Some of the observed changes are due to movements of different objects around the nodes in the measurement site.

Due to variations in channel characteristics that occur over long periods of time, in order for the network to continue operating with a certain level of quality of service over long periods of time, it may be necessary to employ strategies for dynamic channel allocation for clusters. To achieve the best performance, the channel allocation mechanism must take into account the network topology in order to avoid neighbouring clusters using the same or adjacent channels. There should also be some mechanism to estimate the quality of the channels in each cluster, since it is very likely that spatial variations in the channel quality is experienced.

5 Evaluation Methodology

The wireless channel can be considered as stationary for a short term, despite the moving parts around the transmitter and the receiver. However, the properties of the channel can change significantly over time due to changes in the topology of the environment, which are not considered in the distributions used to model the fading. This may require the recalculation of the distribution parameters, since these parameters may become obsolete over time [3].

A characterization of the wireless channel in industrial environments was performed for a long term (20 h) in [2]. The experiment demonstrated that abrupt changes in the channel characteristics can occur when the channel is analyzed for a long time, and differences on the mean value of the received power are observed, although the transmitter and receiver remain static. For example, in the experiment described in [2], the received power varied about −55 dBm during seven hours, and after this period the mean value of the received power changed abruptly to −46 dBm. An experiment described in [28] also presented similar behavior, showing the special nature of these environments.

To allow the simulation of protocols for industrial WSN, it is necessary to use a model that takes into account the channel characteristics for a long period of time. In a previous article [14], a simulation model was developed, which includes the effects of fading, log-normal shadowing, and the non-stationary characteristics of the channel. In this model, different channels can present different characteristics, since the channels defined by the physical layer of the IEEE 802.15.4e are uncorrelated in frequency. Experiments described in [6] have demonstrated that changing the communication channel can lead to a difference of up to 30 dB in the received power, in an office environment. In [33] it is shown the result of the experiments performed for a short range, in an environment without multipath, and with line-of-sight. In that experiment, differences up to 10 dB were observed for some channels. Experiments developed in an office environment are described in [34] showing that for distances greater than 6.5 m between transmitter and receiver, even the adjacent channels are uncorrelated.

In the current implementation, two instances of the model are used to model the wireless channel in the two directions of a link, to capture the asymmetry. In the model, abrupt changes in the channels characteristics can occur. A mean time of change is defined for the model, which is used to define the value of a parameter p, the probability that a change in the characteristics of the channels occur. Thus, it is possible to simulate environments that remain unchanged for a long period of time and environments that present frequent changes in the topology. The simulation result obtained using the model is compatible with results from experiments performed in industrial environments [3,13,28].

Figure 6 shows the reception power at a receiver (obtained from received packets) and a transmitter (obtained from received ACKs) during five hours of simulation to test the model. It is possible to notice the abrupt changes that occur in the channel characteristics over time, and the asymmetry between the two directions of the link.

To evaluate the performance of the three approaches, five replications of the experiment were made. Table 1 shows the parameters considered in the simulations for each replication. For the *lognormal* shadowing model the values of $n = 1.69$, $d_0 = 15\,\text{m}$, $L(d_0) = 80.48\,\text{dB}$, and $X_\sigma = 6.62\,\text{dB}$ were used.

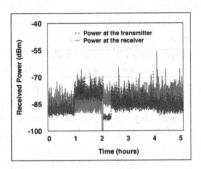

Fig. 6. Asymmetry and temporal variations in the received power [16].

Table 1. Parameters used in the simulation [16].

Area	$60 \times 60\,\text{m}$
Physical layer	IEEE 802.15.4
Bit rate	250 kbit/s
Simulation time	7200 s (2 h)
Transmission power	0 dBm
Packet transmission rate	1 packet/s
Mean time of change	40 min

Table 2. Position of the nodes in the simulations [16].

Node ID	Coordinates (X, Y, Z)	Distance to the coordinator (node 0)
0	$(-8.13, 7.66, 2)$	-
1	$(-14.53, 2.66, 2)$	8.12 m
2	$(-22.83, 8.91, 2)$	14.75 m
3	$(-12.25, -19.79, 2)$	27.76 m
4	$(16.66, -11.84, 2)$	31.54 m
5	$(-12.46, -15.26, 2)$	23.33 m
6	$(-1.93, 1.65, 2)$	8.63 m
7	$(-13.60, -20.99, 2)$	29.17 m
8	$(22.60, -5.45, 2)$	33.41 m
9	$(-15.30, 9.73, 2)$	7.46 m

These values were obtained from experiments in an industrial environment described in [32]. The mean time of change defines the average time between two changes in the characteristics of the channel.

To perform a fair comparison, for each replication the same seed was used to evaluate each approach, and different seeds were used for different replications. Thus, the three approaches were evaluated considering the nodes positioned at the same position and with the same channel characteristics during the replications. The positions of the nodes are shown in Table 2.

Figure 7 shows, in a polar plane, the nodes distribution regarding the coordinator which is located at the coordinates origin. In this example the nodes are randomly distributed except for the height which was fixed at 2 m. Nodes distances from the coordinator ranges from few centimetres up to a it more than 20 m. Nodes which are at a larder distance from the coordinator are the ones suffering more free-space attenuation. On the other hand, all of them can be affected by shadowing, fading, noise, and interferences. Distances between nodes are related to their random locations and different paths can be established from a given node to reach the coordinator by routing along the various nodes.

Table 3. Parameters of the frame structure [16].

macBeaconOrder (BO)	4
macMultisuperframeOrder (MO)	4
macSuperframeOrder (SO)	3
Time slot duration	7.68 ms
capReduction	Enabled
Group Ack	Enabled

The frame structure used in the simulations is shown in Fig. 3. Table 3 shows the values of the parameters that were used to configure the frame structure. In this configuration, the SO is equal to the BO, thus each BI has only one multi-superframe. Each multi-superframe has two superframes, in which only the first one has the CAP. With this configuration, the beacon interval has approximately 0.246 s, which is enough to accommodate the application implemented for the simulations, that transmits one packet per second.

6   Results

Four metrics were used to evaluate the approaches, that is: the Packet Reception Rate (PRR) at the application layer, the PRR at the MAC layer, the delay, and the maximum time between the reception of two consecutive packets. The PRR at the application layer considers the relation between the packets received and transmitted without considering the number of retransmissions at the MAC layer, while the PRR at the MAC layer considers the retransmissions. The delay is the time between the transmission of a packet and the reception of the packet at the application layer. The maximum time between the reception of two packets was analysed to investigate the time in which the nodes remain disconnected due to low channel quality.

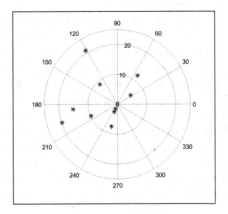

Fig. 7. Nodes locations. Coordinator is located at the origin [16].

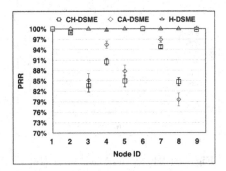

Fig. 8. PRR at the application layer [16].

Figure 8 shows the PRR at the application layer for the nine end nodes. The averages and confidence intervals were calculated considering the data obtained from all replications. For the nodes positioned further apart from the sink node, the PRR was smaller when using CH-DSME and CA-DSME. When using the H-DSME the PRR at the application layer was almost 100% for all nodes. When using CH-DSME and CA-DSME, most errors occurred due to failures in the transmission of the beacons.

In general, the performance of the CA-DSME was better than the CH-DSME, except for the End Node 8. This shows that in most cases the use of only one channel during a larger time period provides a better quality than the use of all available channels with channel hopping. However, in scenarios in which the quality of the link between the coordinator and the end node for beacon transmissions is very low, the channel adaptation mechanism implemented for this research can delay a long time to perform the channel switch. This was the case of the End Node 8. When using H-DSME the channel adaptation mechanism was more reactive, since multiple channels are used to transmit the beacons, which eliminates the single point of failure.

Figure 9 shows the PRR at the MAC layer. A transmission of a data packet in the MAC layer only occurs when a beacon is received at the end node. Thus, the failures in the beacon transmissions do not influence the PRR calculated at this layer, since only the transmissions of data packets from the end nodes to the coordinator are considered. It is worthy to note that when using CH-DSME the PRR at the MAC layer is significantly lower.

Since in the evaluated protocols two attempts are possible per packet, and in the CH-DSME different channels are used in each attempt, in most cases the packet is delivered at the application layer. However, when more retransmissions are needed the energy consumption of the end nodes can increase significantly. Again, the End Node 8 was the only exception, and the PRR was lower for the CA-DSME than for the CH-DSME for this end node. Even both CA-DSME and

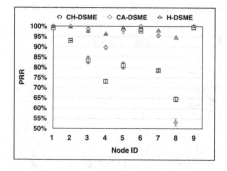

Fig. 9. PRR at the MAC layer [16].

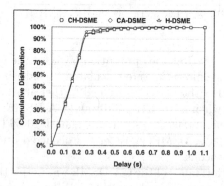

Fig. 10. Delay at the application layer [16].

H-DSME use channel adaptation, the PRR at the MAC layer for the H-DSME was higher, since the channel adaptation mechanism was more reactive when using channel hopping for the beacons, as observed also in Fig. 8.

Figure 10 shows the cumulative distribution function of the delay. Since the beacon period is approximately 0.25 s, most of the packets (about 93%) were transmitted with a delay lower than 0.25 s, and 99% of the packets were transmitted with delay lower than 0.5 s, which is equivalent to two beacon intervals. Since the three evaluated approaches use the same superframe structure, the resulting delay distribution was very similar. However, the delay is only computed for the delivered packets, and for the computation of this parameter it does not matter whether the packets reached the destination or were lost packets.

Figure 11 shows the maximum time lapse between the reception of two packets, which represents the maximum time interval in which a node remains disconnected. Since CA-DSME, and CH-DSME use only one channel for beacon transmissions, sometimes this channel can present low quality, for some nodes, during a long time period, due to a deep fading. This is a critical situation given shadowing is randomly produced ans it last a random period of time which could collapse the network at all. Hence, this situation must be avoided when critical processes depends on the links availability. The same channel can present good quality for other nodes, due to the spatial variation in the channel quality.

When using CH-DSME and CA-DSME, End Nodes 3, 4, and 5 presented long disconnection times (88, 29, and 72 min) due to problems in the channel used to transmit the beacon frames. Since the H-DSME uses channel hopping to transmit the beacons, this protocol is more robust against deep fading problems that affects only some channels. Besides, it is possible to deal with the spatial variation in the quality of the channels. For the H-DSME the maximum time of disconnection was 1.6 min, for the End Node 4.

As an example of the implemented channel adaptation mechanism, Fig. 12 shows the reception power for End Node 8 in the first hour of simulation of the first replication, when using the H-DSME. In the charts, some moments in which the channel switch procedure is triggered are highlighted. It is possible to notice the difference in the characteristics of the different channels when the channel switch occurs.

Sometimes, the channel switch procedure is triggered several times in a short time interval, until the node picks a good channel. For example, between 1.38 and 3.13 min, the End Node 8 switched its channel five times. However, when the End Node picks a good channel, it can remain for a long time using the same channel. In some cases, as demonstrated in the experiments described in [2], the channels can maintain the same characteristics during several hours before an abrupt change in its characteristics occurs. In the simulations a threshold of 0.9 was defined. If the application supports lower thresholds, the channel switch procedure is triggered less often.

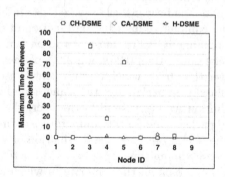

Fig. 11. Maximum time between the reception of two consecutive packets [16].

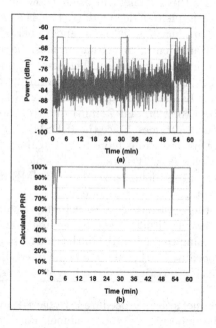

Fig. 12. Received power at the End Node 8 in (a) and the calculated PRR using the Algorithm 1 (b), using H-DSME [16].

Table 4. Summary of the performance of the different approaches.

Feature	CH-DSME	CA-DSME	H-DSME
PRR (app. layer)	Avg.	Avg.	Good
PRR (MAC layer)	Avg.	Avg.	Good
Delay (app. layer)	Good	Good	Good
Maximum time btw. 2 received pck.	Avg.	Avg.	Good

7   Conclusions

Industrial environment communications suffer from a number of disturbances which require proper techniques increasing the robustness to achieve an appropriate performance. This paper describes the outcomes of the developed research aimed at comparing the performance of industrial wireless sensor networks (IWSN) when using two different kinds of protocols: channel hopping and channel adaptation. In the analysis, three protocols, based on the DSME mode of the IEEE 802.15.4e standard, were implemented and evaluated using a realistic simulation model based on the industrial environment channel characteristics. The used model allowed measuring the performance of the protocols, considering the non-stationary and hazardous behaviour of wireless channels in industrial environments.

In order to improve the IWSN performance, a novel approach named hybrid-DSME (H-DSME) is proposed, whose operation is based on the use of channel hopping to transmit the beacons and ACK frames, and channel adaptation to data packets transmission. The results drawn by the simulation show that the use of channel adaptation outperforms the channel hopping performance in the industrial environment, where a network coordinator is continuously monitoring the links quality seeking for the most reliable.

Given beacon and ACK frames are transmitted in broadcast mode to a number of nodes, it is difficult guaranteeing that using a single channel provides the minimum required quality for all possible links between network nodes. Hence, transmitting frames using channel hopping seems to be a good option to face the channel quality spatial variation found in industrial environments.

Along this paper it is demonstrated that the proposed H-DSME approach outperforms the other two reference (existing) approaches. The results obtained through the simulations demonstrate that even for nodes which were located far away from the coordinator, and even considering the channel quality fluctuations over time, the packet-reception-rate achieved at the application layer is nearly 100% when using the H-DSME, and the number of packet retransmissions is lower. Besides, 99% of the packets were delivered with a delay lower than 0.5 s, which corresponds to two beacon intervals, and the resulting nodes maximum disconnection time is only 1.6 min. Anyway, from the point of view of the delay at the application layer the considered approaches perform in a similar way. From the perspective of the PRR at the application layer, the approach based on the H-DSME clearly outperforms the other one achieving a high value. This is remarkable for nodes 3, 4, 5 and 8 as depicted in Fig. 8. Furthermore, as shown in Fig. 9 H-DSME also performs much better than the other approaches under study, specially in our simulation for nodes 3, 4, 5, 7 y 8.

In this paper the results of analysing the use of channel adaptation to implement industrial WSN based on the DSME mode are shown. Nevertheless, to estimate the link quality it is used an algorithm assuming that all the operation of the transmitter is predictable, that is, just one retransmission is permitted in this case, and different slots are used to transmissions and retransmissions.

Table 4 Summarizes the comparative performance of the approaches regarding the various features considered in this investigation. It is worthy to note the superior performance of the H-DSME approach which outperforms the both CH-DSME and CA-DSME.

In non-industrial open environment, where no objects interrupts the line-of-sight between each couple of nodes and no object moves between nodes (free of shadowing and fading), in which all the wireless sensor nodes con be considered are being disturbed by the same noise and interference levels, routing protocols can be much more simple and are mainly driven by the shortest cumulated distance along nodes up to the coordinator as the attenuation is the main issue affecting the signal-to-noise ratio, determining the link quality. In the case of industrial wireless sensor networks node-to-node communication links are affected by a number of additional disturbances which impact paths with different level and changing along the time and at distinct frequencies. Hence, routing protocols are much more complex and smart to mitigate the impact, as the distance (attenuation) becomes one more among the various disturbances. In this paper three approaches have been analysed and compared to solve the problem. Particular characteristics of the environment should be taken into consideration as they can affect in different ways.

In order to improve network throughput and performance, time slots are managed more flexibly, e.g., transmitting two different packets in the same multi-superframe, and using a variable number of retransmission attempts. This approach can lead the algorithm to show lower accuracy, unless further links state information is collected at the end nodes are delivered to the coordinator, such as the average number of transmission attempts per packet.

Another issue which is worthy to be considered in further steps is the overhead produced by the algorithm operation. Some experimental analysis will be conducted to determine whether continuous monitoring of links quality is affordable using low-cost sensor nodes. The use of dedicated nodes to monitor channel quality, as proposed in previous investigations in [15], as well as the use of estimators based on physical layer metrics will be also studied. Experiments considering different network topologies will also be performed.

Acknowledgements. The authors would like to thank the support of the COPELE-UFCG, the Institute for Advanced Studies in Communications (Iecom), the Brazilian Council for Research and Development (CNPq), the Coordination for the Improvement of Higher Education Personnel (Capes), and the SMART 2 Project of the Erasmus Mundus Programme.

References

1. IEEE standard for local and metropolitan area networks-part 15.4: low-rate wireless personal area networks (LR-WPANs) amendment 1: MAC sublayer. IEEE Std 802.15.4e-2012 (Amendment to IEEE Std 802.15.4-2011), pp. 1–225, April 2012. https://doi.org/10.1109/IEEESTD.2012.6185525

2. Agrawal, P., Ahlen, A., Olofsson, T., Gidlund, M.: Characterization of long term channel variations in industrial wireless sensor networks. In: IEEE International Conference on Communications, pp. 1–6 (2014). https://doi.org/10.1109/ICC.2014.6883285

3. Agrawal, P., Ahlén, A., Olofsson, T., Gidlund, M.: Long term channel characterization for energy efficient transmission in industrial environments. IEEE Trans. Commun. **62**(8), 3004–3014 (2014). https://doi.org/10.1109/TCOMM.2014.2332876

4. Al-Murad, T., Alouini, M.: Outage probability analysis of wireless sensor networks in the presence of channel fading and spatial correlation. In: 2011 7th International Wireless Communications and Mobile Computing Conference, pp. 1636–1641, July 2011. https://doi.org/10.1109/IWCMC.2011.5982780

5. Alderisi, G., Patti, G., Mirabella, O., Bello, L.L.: Simulative assessments of the IEEE 802.15.4e DSME and TSCH in realistic process automation scenarios. In: 2015 IEEE 13th International Conference on Industrial Informatics (INDIN), pp. 948–955, July 2015. https://doi.org/10.1109/INDIN.2015.7281863

6. Amzucu, D.M., Li, H., Fledderus, E.: Indoor radio propagation and interference in 2.4 GHz wireless sensor networks: measurements and analysis. Wirel. Pers. Commun. **76**, 245–269 (2014)

7. Anastasi, G., Conti, M., Francesco, M.D., Passarella, A.: Energy conservation in wireless sensor networks: a survey. Ad Hoc Netw. **7**(3), 537–568 (2009). https://doi.org/10.1016/j.adhoc.2008.06.003. http://www.sciencedirect.com/science/article/pii/S1570870508000954

8. Capone, S., Brama, R., Ricciato, F., Boggia, G., Malvasi, A.: Modeling and simulation of energy efficient enhancements for IEEE 802.15.4e DSME. In: 2014 Wireless Telecommunications Symposium, pp. 1–6, April 2014. https://doi.org/10.1109/WTS.2014.6835017

9. Du, P., Roussos, G.: Spectrum-aware wireless sensor networks. In: 2013 IEEE 24th Annual International Symposium on Personal, Indoor, and Mobile Radio Communications (PIMRC), pp. 2321–2325, September 2013. https://doi.org/10.1109/PIMRC.2013.6666532

10. Du, P., Roussos, G.: Adaptive channel hopping for wireless sensor networks. In: 2011 International Conference on Selected Topics in Mobile and Wireless Networking (iCOST), pp. 19–23, October 2011. https://doi.org/10.1109/iCOST.2011.6085828

11. Gnawali, O., Fonseca, R., Jamieson, K., Moss, D., Levis, P.: Collection tree protocol. In: Proceedings of the 7th ACM Conference on Embedded Networked Sensor Systems, pp. 1–14, SenSys 2009. ACM, New York (2009). https://doi.org/10.1145/1644038.1644040. http://doi.acm.org/10.1145/1644038.1644040

12. Gomes, R.D., Alencar, M.S., Queiroz, D.V., Fonseca, I.E.: Evaluation of link quality estimators for industrial wireless sensor networks. In: XXXIV Simpósio Brasileiro de Telecomunicações e Processamento de Sinais, pp. 1–5 (2016)

13. Gomes, R.D., Fonseca, I.E., Alencar, M.S.: Protocolos multicanais para redes de sensores sem fio industriais (in Portuguese). Revista de Tecnologia da Informação e Comunicação **5**(2), 25–32 (2015)

14. Gomes, R.D., Queiroz, D.V., Fonseca, I.E., Alencar, M.S.: Modelo para simulação realista de redes de sensores sem fio industriais (in Portuguese). In: XXXIII Simpósio Brasileiro de Telecomunicações, pp. 1–5 (2015)

15. Gomes, R.D., Rocha, G.B., Filho, A.C., Fonseca, I.E., Alencar, M.S.: Distributed approach for channel quality estimation using dedicated nodes in industrial WSN. In: 2014 IEEE 25th Annual International Symposium on Personal, Indoor, and Mobile Radio Communication (PIMRC), pp. 1943–1948, September 2014. https://doi.org/10.1109/PIMRC.2014.7136489

16. Gomes, R.D., Alencar, M.S., Queiroz, D.V., Fonseca, I.E., Benavente-Peces, C.: Comparison between channel hopping and channel adaptation for industrial wireless sensor networks. In: Proceedings of the 6th International Conference on Sensor Networks (SENSORNETS 2017), Porto, Portugal, 19–21 February 2017, pp. 87–98 (2017). https://doi.org/10.5220/0006206800870098

17. Gürsu, M., Vilgelm, M., Zoppi, S., Kellerer, W.: Reliable co-existence of 802.15.4e TSCH-based WSN and Wi-Fi in an aircraft cabin. In: 2016 IEEE International Conference on Communications Workshops (ICC), pp. 663–668, May 2016. https://doi.org/10.1109/ICCW.2016.7503863

18. Guglielmo, D.D., Brienza, S., Anastasi, G.: IEEE 802.15.4e: a survey. Comput. Commun. **88**, 1–24 (2016). https://doi.org/10.1016/j.comcom.2016.05.004. http://www.sciencedirect.com/science/article/pii/S0140366416301980

19. Gungor, V.C., Hancke, G.P.: Industrial wireless sensor networks: challenges, design principles, and technical approaches. IEEE Trans. Ind. Electr. **56**, 4258–4265 (2009)

20. Hashemi, H.: The indoor radio propagation channel. Proc. IEEE **81**(7), 943–968 (1993). https://doi.org/10.1109/5.231342

21. Jeong, W.C., Lee, J.: Performance evaluation of IEEE 802.15.4e DSME MAC protocol for wireless sensor networks. In: 2012 First IEEE Workshop on Enabling Technologies for Smartphone and Internet of Things (ETSIoT), pp. 7–12, June 2012. https://doi.org/10.1109/ETSIoT.2012.6311258

22. Jeong, W.C., Lee, J.: Performance evaluation of IEEE 802.15.4e DSME MAC protocol for wireless sensor networks. In: 2012 The First IEEE Workshop on Enabling Technologies for Smartphone and Internet of Things (ETSIoT), pp. 7–12, June 2012. https://doi.org/10.1109/ETSIoT.2012.6311258

23. Juc, I., Alphand, O., Guizzetti, R., Favre, M., Duda, A.: Energy consumption and performance of IEEE 802.15.4e TSCH and DSME. In: 2016 IEEE Wireless Communications and Networking Conference, pp. 1–7, April 2016. https://doi.org/10.1109/WCNC.2016.7565006

24. Lee, J., Jeong, W.C.: Performance analysis of IEEE 802.15.4e DSME MAC protocol under WLAN interference. In: 2012 International Conference on ICT Convergence (ICTC), pp. 741–746, October 2012. https://doi.org/10.1109/ICTC.2012.6387133

25. Lima-Filho, A., Gomes, R., Adissi, M., Borges da Silva, T., Belo, F., Spohn, M.: Embedded system integrated into a wireless sensor network for online dynamic torque and efficiency monitoring in induction motors. IEEE/ASME Trans. Mechatron. **17**(3), 404–414 (2012). https://doi.org/10.1109/TMECH.2012.2187354

26. Lu, B., Gungor, V.C.: Online and remote motor energy monitoring and fault diagnostics using wireless sensor networks. IEEE Trans. Ind. Electron. **56**, 4651–4659 (2009)

27. Nikookar, H., Hashemi, H.: Phase modeling of indoor radio propagation channels. IEEE Trans. Veh. Technol. **49**(2), 594–606 (2000). https://doi.org/10.1109/25.832991

28. Olofsson, T., Ahlén, A., Gidlund, M.: Modeling of the fading statistics of wireless sensor network channels in industrial environments. IEEE Trans. Signal Process. **64**(12), 3021–3034 (2016). https://doi.org/10.1109/TSP.2016.2539142

29. Patti, G., Alderisi, G., Bello, L.L.: Introducing multi-level communication in the IEEE 802.15.4e protocol: the multichannel-LLDN. In: Proceedings of the 2014 IEEE Emerging Technology and Factory Automation (ETFA), pp. 1–8, September 2014. https://doi.org/10.1109/ETFA.2014.7005204

30. Patti, G., Bello, L.L.: A priority-aware multichannel adaptive framework for the IEEE 802.15.4e-LLDN. IEEE Trans. Ind. Electron. **PP**(99), 1 (2016). https://doi.org/10.1109/TIE.2016.2573754

31. Petersen, S., Carlsen, S.: Performance evaluation of wirelessHART for factory automation. In: IEEE Conference on Emerging Technologies & Factory Automation, pp. 1–9 (2009)

32. Tanghe, E., Joseph, W., Verloock, L., Martens, L., Capoen, H., Herwegen, K.V., Vantomme, W.: The industrial indoor channel: large-scale and temporal fading at 900, 2400, and 5200 mhz. IEEE Trans. Wirel. Commun. **7**, 2740–2751 (2008)

33. Varga, L.O., Heusse, M., Guizzetti, R., Duda, A.: Why is frequency channel diversity so beneficial in wireless sensor networks? In: IFIP Wireless Days. IFIP, Toulouse, France (2016). https://hal.archives-ouvertes.fr/hal-01287518

34. Watteyne, T., Lanzisera, S., Mehta, A., Pister, K.S.J.: Mitigating multipath fading through channel hopping in wireless sensor networks. In: 2010 IEEE International Conference on Communications, pp. 1–5 (2010). https://doi.org/10.1109/ICC.2010.5502548

35. Yigit, M., Yoney, E.A., Gungor, V.C.: Performance of MAC protocols for wireless sensor networks in harsh smart grid environment. In: 2013 First International Black Sea Conference on Communications and Networking (BlackSeaCom), pp. 50–53, July 2013. https://doi.org/10.1109/BlackSeaCom.2013.6623380

36. Yildirim, G., Tatar, Y.: On WSN heterogeneity in IoT and CPSS. In: 2017 International Conference on Computer Science and Engineering (UBMK), pp. 1020–1024, October 2017. https://doi.org/10.1109/UBMK.2017.8093421

Advanced Infrastructure for Environmental Monitoring and Early-Warning System Integration

Stefania Nanni[1(✉)] and Gianluca Mazzini[2(✉)]

[1] LepidaSpa, Viale della Liberazione 15, 40128 Bologna, Italy
stefania.nanni@lepida.it
[2] Engineering Department, University of Ferrara, Ferrara, Italy
g.mazzini@ieee.org

Abstract. In order to increase the resilience of the regional territory to extreme rainfall phenomena, LepidaSpA has enhanced an already existing IOT platform, Sensornet, created to manage heterogeneous sensor networks extended all over the entire territory of the Emilia-Romagna Region, introducing some new "virtual sensors" [1] not related to physical measures, such as rivers level or amount of rainfall, but to their estimation and forecast. The ability to manage both real and "virtual sensors" grants the possibility to integrate conventional monitoring systems, based on observed data, with innovative ones, based on estimated and forecast data, providing an advanced monitoring infrastructure not only capable to monitor the phenomena and their evolution, with greater accuracy and spatial distribution, but also to generate early warning in case of critical thresholds with a forecast up to 12/24 h, according to the simulation model used for forecast.

Keywords: Virtual sensors · Estimated data · Hydrological simulation model · Early-warning system · Extreme rainfall phenomena

1 Introduction

Sensornet is the Internet of Things Platform of the Emilia-Romagna Region, collecting data and information from thousands of objects distributed across the territory, building in time a digital map of the reality we live in (Fig. 1).

Whether they are generated by inclinometers for landslide monitoring, rain gauges or inductive coils for the traffic monitoring, data generated by the sensors define a snapshot of a reality made of continuously updating information, allowing a better knowledge of what is happening in cities and in territories [2].

Usual rain gauges, like the ones integrated on Sensornet platform, are not so effective during intense precipitation since their operating principle is based on mechanical tilting parts, which makes their measurements unreliable during this type of phenomena. Besides, their measurements provide limited spatial resolution, since they only represents the immediate proximity of the measurement spot, as well as limited temporal resolution.

© Springer Nature Switzerland AG 2019
C. Benavente-Peces et al. (Eds.): SENSORNETS 2017/2018, CCIS 1074, pp. 58–73, 2019.
https://doi.org/10.1007/978-3-030-30110-1_4

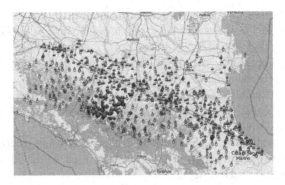

Fig. 1. Sensornet platform [1].

Lastly, given the rapidity of this type of phenomena evolution, traditional real-time monitoring systems are not sufficient for an anticipated recognition of critical scenarios.

For the purpose of dealing with heavy rain events and with the possible consequent flooding events, that are affecting not only Italy, but all regions in Europe in the recent years [3], it is therefore necessary to update and integrate the current hydropluviometric monitoring infrastructure both through the use of innovative technologies, able to exploit the pervasiveness of cellular networks, and through the use of hydrological simulation models, able to foresee in advance water rivers level status.

The first part of the article describes the purpose of the project starting from the analysis of the environmental problems from which it was born (hydrogeological risk due to extreme rainfall) (Fig. 2), and the description of the currently available methodologies for their mitigation.

The second part illustrates the innovative use of the beforementioned instruments within Sensornet platform, which derives both from their novel and unitary implementation and from their integrated and synergic use.

The last part summarizes the results, giving evidence of the achievement of the intended purpose.

2   The State of the Art

Fig. 2. Parma flash-flood October 2014 [1].

The microwave rainfall monitoring system is an innovative, but already tested technology [7], exploiting the microwave links used in commercial cellular communication networks.

Radio signals propagate across microwave links from the transmitting antenna of a base station to the receiving antenna of another base station.

Rain-induced attenuation and, subsequently, path-averaged rainfall intensity can be retrieved from the signal's attenuation between transmitter and receiver by applying, almost in real-time, a rainfall retrieval algorithm.

A distributed monitoring system can be developed by using received signal level data from the massive number of microwaves links used worldwide in commercial cellular communication networks.

Many studies are currently addressing, not only the problem of monitoring critical environmental phenomena in real-time, but also that of predicting them.

Some of them are not based on forecasting system, but rather on real-time monitoring systems [8] or on certain percutaneous parameters of the phenomena [10].

In other cases, the forecasting system is based on the integration of the predictive algorithm in physical sensor networks and is strictly bound to all the problems and limitations associated with this type of solution [9]. In other cases, the predictability aspect of the phenomenon is only mentioned as one among many others involving in the management of critical events [11].

The preparation and reaction to such disruptive phenomena can increase the resilience of the territory in short time as early warning of hazardous conditions and in medium term as territorial planning and preparation to emergency response.

The management of extreme rain events can not, therefore, solely rely on traditional real time monitoring systems, but must also include the use of new and distributed technologies, like microwaves one, and new forecasting systems based on hydrological simulation models and meteorological modeling.

3   RainBO Life

The analysis of climate variability over the municipality of Bologna, as resulted from the BlueAp LIFE project (Bologna Local Urban Environment Adaptation Plan for a Resilient City 2012–2015), reveals important changes observed in the main climatological variables.

During the last two decades, years with intense precipitation have been frequently registered in Bologna, having an important impact on the city and its citizens.

The quantity of precipitation shows a slightly negative trend during winter, spring, and summer and a positive trend during autumn, over the period 1951–2011.

With regards to seasonal extreme of precipitations, the dry days index presents a positive tendency over 1951–2011 period, more intense during summer.

Analysis performed on intense precipitation time series evidence a slightly positive trend of the frequency of days with intense precipitation (based on 90th percentile as a threshold) in all season, except on spring.

The flooding risk of small water courses is a major problem in several urban areas (especially in Italy): the constant growth of urbanization, with the consequent decrease of soil permeability and loss of space for river and stream beds, is leading to increased flood hazard and vulnerability; in such conditions, severe rainfall events over steep catchments of limited area can produce dramatic consequences; in addition, ongoing climate changes are likely to increase the occurrence of severe precipitation events, thus increasing flash flood hazard.

Historical and recent records report that the urban areas of Bologna located beneath the highland are prone to severe flood events caused by small water courses. The most severe event occurred in 1932, when rainfall of 134 mm within a few hours caused flooding of a large urban area, including a portion of the Ravone catchment area.

Another severe flood event occurred in the Bologna area in 1955, while in 2002 a further flood event affected several small municipalities nearby. In all of these cases, the recorded hourly peak intensity exceeded 50 mm/h.

Despite its relevance, the risk of flooding of small water courses in urban areas is often underestimated and few measures are taken for prevention and mitigation [4].

The high level objective of RainBO LIFE project (2016–2019), that is a follow-up of BlueApp one, is the improvement of knowledge, methods and tools for the characterisation and forecast of heavy rains potential impact due to the hydrological response, not only of medium and large basin, but also of the small ones and for the evaluation of the vulnerability of assets in the urban areas.

RainBO project aims to achieve its goal developing an advanced infrastructure based both on traditional monitoring systems and on innovative ones, such as cellular communication network monitoring, and implementing an early warning system based on hydrological models driven by fileds of precipitation for the forecasting of flash floods in small and large basins.

Since RainBO monitoring system is based on Sensornet platform, its goals have been achieved through the incremental integration, within the platform, of new "virtual" sensors associated to estimated data calculated from the attenuation of microwaves links and to forecast data from hydrological simulation models and meteorological modelling.

4   The Microwave Rainfall Monitoring Network

The microwave rainfall monitoring network exploits the Microwave links (MWL) used worldwide in commercial cellular communication networks. Along such links, radio signals propagate from a transmitting antenna at one base station to a receiving antenna at another base station. Rain-induced attenuation and, subsequently, path-averaged rainfall intensity can be retrieved from the signal's attenuation between transmitter and receiver by applying, almost in real-time, a rainfall retrieval algorithm.

The algorithm chosen for this purpose is the RAINLINK retrieval algorithm developed from Aart Overeem and Remko Uijlenhoet from Wageningen University (Wageningen, the Netherlands) and Hidde Leijnse from the Royal Netherlands Meteorological Institute (KNMI) in 2015. The code is an open source R package (https://www.r-project.org) available for free download on GitHub (https://github.com/overeem11/RAINLINK).

The implementation of the algorithm for the specific needs of the Italian test areas, as well as code debugging and improving, is done by MEEO, one of the partner of RainBO LIFE project [13], in close contact with the original authors.

The great advantage of this technology is related to the high resolution (15 min and 1 KM^2) of 2D rainfall maps to monitor and forecast rainfall events even on geographical area not covered by traditional gauges network but equipped with mobile telecommunication antennas.

RainBO adopted as rainfall estimation method the RAINLINK algorithm, which is already suited for a midlatitude flat land like the Netherlands and is easily portable to the Pianura Padana. The algorithm capabilities over the hilly areas of the Appennino have been investigated and results obtained are encouraging.

The limit of this technology is substantially related to the data availability from the telecommunication operators.

So far, microwave links data for RainBO project are provided from Lepida and Vodafone telecommunication operators. The data consists in near real time receiving power readings, collected at time intervals of one (Lepida) or fifteen (Vodafone) minutes. The algorithm works with 15-min maximum and minimum received powers, from which signal attenuation are calculated and, through the link's pathlength information, the instantaneous path-averaged rainfall depths are estimated.

Data are representative of the link between two points in space, as the first internal output of the algorithm is the rainfall estimation on the midpoint between the transmitter/receiver, derived from the power attenuation data measured on the antennas.

The ordinary kriging interpolation is applied on these middles points of the links on a 1 km by 1 km grid, taking into account the other values and obtaining more reliable map of rainfall data, on a 5 km by 5 km.

High density network coverage is needed for best performances. The interpolation grid adopted by RainBO project is the one already in use at Arpae for the meteorological interpolated maps and for the limited area models.

This choice was done to simplify the validation of microwaves links data through many comparisons with data, radar and ERG5 (interpolated rain gauges) ones, by carrying out qualitative and statistical analysis. The deliverable C2_5 of RainBO project describes this activity and its results in detail.

The Algorithm evaluates the signal attenuation along the link and assigns the related rainfall intensity to its average point that we call, in this project, "Microwaves Virtual Sensors". In particular "Microwaves Virtual Sensors" map published in RainBO are based on data provided by Lepida. Rain gauge data provided by Vodafone cannot be published as project output for data confidentiality, but they were fundamental for the comparison between the microwaves maps and those obtained from the traditional systems, radar and ERG5, for the purposes of the algorithm validation process.

5   Hydrological Models

5.1   Medium and Large Basins: Random Forest Method

Following the flooding of the Baganza river in Parma on October 2014 (Fig. 2), caused by heavy rains, which flooded several neighborhoods southwest of the city, the Civil Protection Agency of the Emilia-Romagna region required ArpaE the development of a hydrological simulation model to be able to recognize in advance the probability of overcoming the three alert thresholds fixed for the main rivers of Emilia-Romagna region: Warning (threshold 1), Pre-alarm (threshold 2), Alarm (threshold 3).

Hydrological modeling for medium and large basins is based on a statistical method, Random Forest, which uses decision trees.

The Random Forest model, applied to hydraulic modeling, provides the probability of overcoming the alert thresholds of some observation point of the medium and large basins, for the next 6–8 h, depending on the dynamics of the river.

In particular, the Random Forest hydrological model gives the following forecast data:

1. Probability of not exceeding threshold 1
2. Probability of exceeding threshold 1
3. Probability of exceeding threshold 2
4. Probability of exceeding threshold 3

5.2   Small Basins: Criteria 3D Model

Forecasting models of heavy rainfall initiating flash flood from small basins are different from other models (e.g. from large basins or waterways).

The size of the small basin results in very rapid response times to heavy rainfall.

In other words, the time interval between the start time of the precipitation and the span peak can be reached in less than two hours, which in reality would make the prediction of the event very difficult and therefore the alert system.

For this reason, it is considered essential to develop a hydraulic simulation model for small basins, and the installation of specific measuring points, allowing hydrometric observations to its validation.

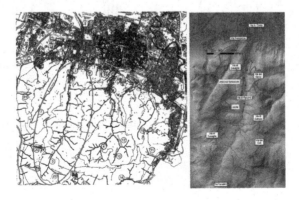

Fig. 3.   Ravone creek [1].

Criteria3D is a three-dimensional hydrological model, which also simulates water infiltration into the soil, developed by ArpaE-SIMC of Emilia-Romagna region.

The model was developed starting from the study of the river Ravone, which is one of the creek that from the hills south of Bologna goes down to the city (Fig. 3).

In this basin, all those critical and valuable factors that are present in the hilly waters, such as the effects of the strong anthropization that currently characterizes the end of the valley and the crossing of the city, are also present (Fig. 4).

Figure 5 shows the good result of the test of simulation of the water level at the stream gauge of Ravone in the event of 2015-02-05.

Fig. 4. Ravone's suture and measure point [1].

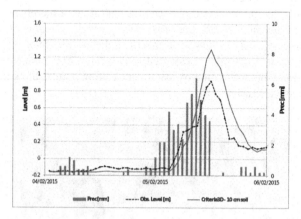

Fig. 5. Criteria3D simulation of the water level at the stream gauge of Ravone in the event of 2015-02-05 [1].

6   Meteorological Modeling Cosmo-Lami

The numerical meteorological model limited area Cosmo-Lami [5], called Lami for brevity, carried out in consortium between national civil protection department, USAM Air Force, Harp ArpaE Piemonte and ArpaE Emilia-Romagna, provides numerical forecasts with a spatial resolution at 7 km and 2.8 km and temporal validity respectively three and two days.

Predictions based on this model are carried out twice a day, at 00 and at 12 UTC, at the supercomputing Cineca center, in accordance to a contract with the IdroMeteo-Clima Service and the Department of National Civil Protection.

Data are provided in grid format, GRIB [6], and each file contains forecast data for various meteorological parameters, including precipitation, either at the surface or close to it, at an hourly or three-hourly in dependence on the parameter.

The data relating to the meteorological modeling can be used both at the level of maps to have, for example, an overview of the precipitation forecast, but also at the numerical level to have, for example, the detail on hourly precipitation provided on a given grid cell, as in the case of Ravone creek, which constitutes the basic information for the prediction of the hydrometric level corresponding starting from the product simulations scenarios resulted from the 3D hydrological model for small basins.

Data from meteorological modelling, limited to the Emilia-Romagna region, are distributed GRIB format on the open date platform of ArpaE of Emilia-Romagna.

7   Advanced Environmental Monitoring and Early-Warning System Integration

The implementation of an advanced infrastructure for environmental monitoring and of an early-warning system is based on incremental integration within Sensornet platform of new "virtual sensors", using the same data model initially defined for physical ones.

Unlike real sensors, virtual ones are not associated with observed measurements, but with estimated data starting from other measures observed related to them, as in the case of rain estimates through the attenuation of radio signals, or starting from simulation models hydrological systems, which provide a future estimate of the river level at the observation point.

The concept of "virtual sensor" allows, indeed, to integrate information from non-traditional systems, georeferencing them with respect to the same reference system and synchronizing them over time.

The integration of these new "virtual sensors" into the Sensornet platform has been accomplished in a simple and immediate way, using the same data model defined for the physical sensors, without the need for any extension or specialization and providing the platform with an enhanced monitoring infrastrucuture and a new feature crucial for recognition and generation of early-warning reports.

The integration of sensors data coming from different monitoring systems in Sensornet is realized through a federated approach whose main advantage is to preserve the investments made on already existing systems and to protect the technical, technological and organizational autonomy of the individual systems and of their owners.

The architecture implemented in Sensornet platform provides an interconnection middleware between the different data sources and the central system, acting as a data collector from different sources and a data normalizer towards the central system, as shown in Fig. 6.

It consists of a series of atomic modules for data retrieval from individual sources and of their manager, which oversees their activation and coordination.

Each module contains the access rules and the required commands for retrieving data from a specific source or database and for storing them in a standard format on the centralized database.

In order to acquire data from heterogeneous sources and use them in a contextual and correlated mode, a standardization process is necessary.

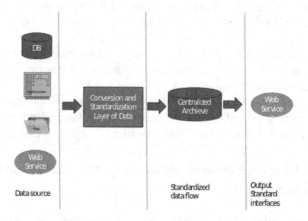

Fig. 6. Flow of collection, standardization, storage and access of the data [1].

The creation of a standardized data stream is one of the added values offered by Sensornet platform, which transforms the data from the different sources into a single standard format, regardless of the technologies, the interfaces, formats and data type of the sources [2].

The integration of data form cellulars communication networks and the hydrological simulation models and meteorological modelling data in Sensornet has been achieved through the definition of "virtual" sensors, which, unlike the real, are not associated with physically measured data, but to the forecasted ones provided by the models.

This type of solution allowed to completely integrate these new types of "virtual" sensors with the real ones, while maintaining the consistency of data and their modeling within the Sensornet platform.

7.1   Microwave Rainfall Monitoring Network Integration

In addition to the data coming from the conventional real-time monitoring system of ArpaE, mainly consisting of regional hydrometers stations to measure temperature, rain and hydrometric levels, Sensornet platform also integrates those belonging to Microwaves Rainfall Monitoring Network.

The new "virtual Microwaves sensor" has been defined in Sensornet platform to allow the integration of data related to microwaves links, as well as a new "Microwave" module data acquisition.

Microwave data supplied by Lepida, cover the Apennini region of the Emilia Romagna. At present time, data corresponding to the metropolitan areas of Bologna and Parma (i.e. the test site of RainBO project) have been integrated, for a total of 53 sensors.

The integration of all Lepida Wireless Network Links, corresponding to a hundred additional sensors, is expected by the end of this year.

Figure 7 shows the "virtual Microwaves sensors" currently integrated on Sensornet Platform.

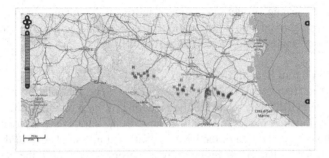

Fig. 7. Microwaves virtual sensors integrated in sensornet platform.

7.2 Water Hold Capacity Data Integration

The Water Hold Capacity index provides the maximum amount of water the soil can hold, given the current conditions of soil moisture.

It is one of the input parameters to identify the hydrological scenario for small basins. The WHC index for the Ravone creek test case is daily estimated through a mono-dimensional restriction of the Criteria3D water balance model and it is calculated on the first 35 cm of soil. It becomes zero when the soil is above the field capacity and is no longer able to retain water. To compute this index, the model uses as input soil, crop and weather data (temperature and precipitation) that Arpae collects for all the Emilia-Romagna region.

The use of an estimated value of soil moisture instead of a measured one has the advantage that it can be estimated on all the similar sites of the region and it is not affected by lack or failures of sensors nor by local peculiarity

As shown in the graph relating to Fig. 8 the soil drainage capacity is higher in summer than in autumn or winter (when rain is more frequent). The water status of the basin is updated every 24 h.

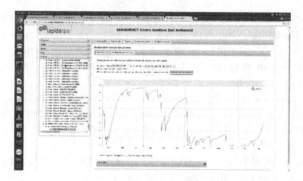

Fig. 8. WHC virtual sensor graphic.

7.3   Forecast Data Integration

Sensornet early-warning system integration is based on the integration of forecast data into the platform through the configuration of new virtual sensors based on hydrological simulation models and meteorological modelling.

7.3.1   Lami Virtual Sensor Integration

The new "virtual Lami sensor" has been defined in Sensornet platform to allow the integration of the GRIB data related to the modeling of the weather, needed for the 3D hydrological simulation model for small streams. In the case of the Ravone stream, as in most small streams, the size of the basin is contained in a single cell of the reference grid, whose data can then be represented by a sensor placed within the cell itself.

From the datum for cumulative rain, collected from GRIB data at the beginning of each run for each cell, it is possible to calculate the corresponding precipitation per hour. Once a precipitation threshold has been established, it is possible to determine when a precipitation starts and when it finishes, to infer the duration as well as the peak and the accumulated of the corresponding event.

The algorithm to calculate the significant parameters of a rainy event, starting from the data for the cumulative hourly precipitation, can be described as follows:

- starting from the GRIB data (the cumulative hourly precipitation from the beginning of the run), the hourly precipitation is extracted with simple subtractions;
- the hours in which rain is expected and when it is not (0–1) are calculated according to the established threshold (normally 0,2 mm);
- depending on the distribution of 0 and 1, it is estimated when a rainy event starts and when it ends;
- at this point it is possible to calculate the duration, the accumulated (constitutes from all the hourly precipitation included in the event) and the maximum intensity relative to the event (peak).

The storage of the main parameters of a rainfall event, calculated as it has been described, is made by defining four corresponding measures associated with each "virtual" Lami sensor:

- hourly precipitations
- event
- cumulative hourly precipitations
- peak

The integration of the new type of Lami virtual sensor inside the Sensornet platform, indeed, required the implementation of a new GRIB data acquisition and processing module, the definition of a new type of Lami sensor, to which the four measures previously described are associated, and the configuration of a new Lami type sensor at the Ravone stream, identified by the coordinates of the corresponding grid cell.

The integration of other sensors related to the meteorological forecasts at another stream, simply requires the configuration of another Lami type virtual sensor associated with the coordinates of the corresponding grid cell.

Currently, eight more virtual Lami sensors have been integrated in correspondence of the cells adjacent to those of the Ravone basin, to take into account rain forecasts around the basin.

Figure 9 shows an example of graphing data for the Lami sensor defined for the Ravone cell (lat 44.46 and lon 11.31) provided at 00:00 on 30/06/2017 and valid for 72 h later.

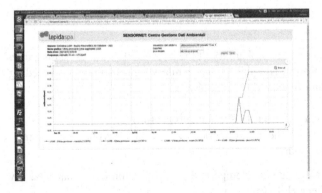

Fig. 9. Example of graphic data of Lami virtual sensor [1].

In the example shown, the expected rainfall is below the defined threshold (normally 0,2 mm) and is therefore not a source of rain for a rainfall event.

7.3.2 Random Forest Virtual Sensor Integration

The new "virtual" Random Forest sensor has been defined to allow the integration the data related to hydrological modeling for medium and large basins.

The integration of the new type of Random Forest virtual sensor inside the Sensornet platform required the implementation of a new data acquisition and processing module of the .csv files (provided by ArpaE every 10 min on a ftpServer, hosted by LepidaSpa), the definition of a new type of Random Forest sensor, to which the previously described four probabilities are associated, and the configuration of two new Random Forest type sensors in correspondence of Parma and Baganza rivers, identified by the station ID of the corresponding hydrometer.

The integration of other data related to hydrological modeling for medium and large basins, simply requires the configuration of others Random Forest type virtual sensor associated to corresponding .csv files.

Figure 10 shows a graphical representation data for the Random Forest sensor defined for the Baganza river provided at 14:40 of 18/07/2017 and valid for 6 h later.

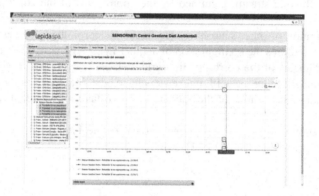

Fig. 10. Example of virtual sensor Random Forest data graphication [1].

In the example, the probability of the river level of not exceeding threshold 1 in the point of observation is equal to one, while the probability of exceeding threshold 1, threshold 2, and threshold 3 is equal to zero.

7.3.3   Criteria 3D Virtual Sensor Integration

The predictions of the hydrometric level of the Ravone stream, are based on the following three sources of information:

- observed weather data (temperatures and precipitation) that feed a water balance model (Water Hold Capacity)
- forecast rain in the next 72 h, from Lami meteorological modelling
- hydrometric level of Ravone in the observed point during calibration and validation

The forecasting process includes the following phases:

- The water status of the basin (WHC) is updated every 24 h
- Every 12 h, the platform receives the LAMI +72 predictions on the cell in which the basin falls (and the 8 neighbouring cells); precipitation events are identified and in particular the cumulative and maximum hourly intensity.
- The predicted precipitation values are updated based on the data observed by the Paderno rain gauge.
- To take account of any LAMI underestimation on the maximum intensity, maximum intensities increased by + 33% are also considered possible.

- These values are passed to the estimation equation of the maximum drainage waterway producing a statistical distribution of the forecast

The algorithm must be performed on the 9 cells (the one referring to the Ravone basin and the eight adjacent ones) and must be performed both for the peak value of the event estimated for each cell, from Lami Virtual Sensor, and for the same values increased by 30%, for take account of possible underestimation.

The output algorithm is a statistical distribution of the possible 18 water levels, associated with the peak time of the expected event. In particular, the algorithm outputs the 5 percentile values: 5°, 25°, 50°, 75° and 95°, in addition to the time when the peak is expected.

Figure 11 show an example of graphic output.

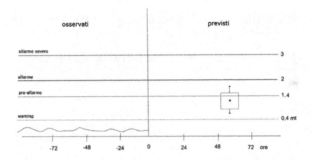

Fig. 11. Example of graphic data of Criteria 3D VirtualSensor.

8 Results

The use of "virtual sensors" and "microwave links" technology allowed the integration into Sensornet of dozens of measurement points, without the addition of any more infrastructure compared to those already existing in the territory.

The geographical and temporal integration of the "virtual sensors" with the real ones, allows their overlap and comparison.

Figure 12, for example, shows the correlation between rain gauges and microwaves estimates.

Figure 13 shows the correlation between soil moisture sensor and WHC index. In particular, it can be noted the ratio of inverse proportionality of the two parameters and the perfect correspondence between their derivatives.

With regards to hydraulic risk, the possibility of early detection of extreme pre-cipitation events and their effects on the river level allows to recognize in advance critical scenarios and to support their management or, vice versa, to give evidence of the absence of critical conditions.

Figure 9, for example, shows the rain forecast for the next 72 h on Ravone's cell.

The graph gives evidence of the expected rainfall and its cumulated level, whose duration and intensity are not sufficient to generate a significant event to report.

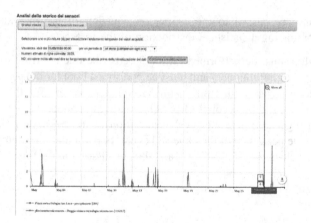

Fig. 12. Example of correlation between Raingauge and MW-Links estimates values.

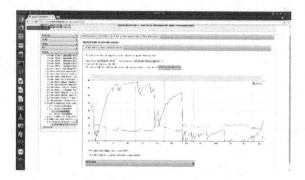

Fig. 13. Example of correlation between soil moisture sensor and WHC index.

Figure 10 shows that the probabilities of the level of Baganza River to not exceeding threshold 1 is one, while it is equal to zero the probability that it exceeds any of the three defined alert thresholds, for the next 6 h.

Integration of forecast model data is the right prerequisite for the creation of an early-warning system that allows recognition and signaling of critical thresholds over with an anticipation that depends on the simulation model used.

In particular, the integration of forecast data related to the hydrometric level for medium-sized basins and rainfall events for small ones allows to identify critical scenarios in advance with a margin of some hours in the case of medium-sized basins and up to a few days for those small ones.

The concept of "virtual sensor" made it possible to describe estimated and forecast data with the same model defined for those observed, creating an advanced and integrated monitoring and early-warning infrastructure.

9   Conclusions

The management of events of intense precipitation and the risk of flooding connected to them is an ever more current topic, which requires new actions.

The risk of these events can be mitigated through the upgrading and integration of monitoring infrastructures suitable for this type of phenomena, but also through the development of early-warning systems [12] that allow their forecast with a significant margin of advance.

In this sense, hydrological simulation models and metereological modelling play an extremely important role and their continuous development is fundamental in order to increase their level of reliability.

The availability of a platform, like Sensornet, able to integrate all the available, observed, estimated and forecast data, allows to realize an advanced and integrated monitoring and early-warning infrastructure for extreme precipitation measurements and water rivers level forecast, for the purposes of mitigating the hydraulic risks of the territory.

References

1. Nanni, S., Mazzini, G.: Proceedings of the 7th International Conference on Sensor Networks. Madeira, 22–24 January 2018
2. Nanni, S., Mazzini, G.: From the smart city to the smart community, model and architecture of a real project: SensorNet. JCOMSS **10**(3) (2017)
3. http://www.eea.europa.eu/media/publications/climate-impacts-and-vulnerability-2012
4. Grazzini, F., Dottori, F., Di Lorenzo, M., Spisni, A., Tomei, F.: Nubifragi e rischio idraulico nella collina bolognese: il caso studio del Ravone. Arpa-Simc, BOLOGNA, Ottobre 2013
5. https://www.arpae.it/dettaglio_generale.asp?id=2584&idlivello=32
6. http://apps.ecmwf.int/codes/grib/format/grib1/
7. http://www.pnas.org/content/110/8/2741.full.pdf+html
8. Baxter Jr, J.F.: Early warning detection and notification network for environmental conditions. U.S. Patent No. 6,023,223. 8 February 2000
9. Basha, E.A., Ravela, S., Rus, D.: Model-based monitoring for early warning flood detection. In: Proceedings of the 6th ACM Conference on Embedded Network Sensor Systems. ACM (2008)
10. Chaczko, Z., Ahmad, F.: Wireless sensor network based system for fire endangered areas. In: Third International Conference on Information Technology and Applications, ICITA 2005, July 2005
11. Basha, E., Rus, D.: Design of early warning flood detection systems for developing countries. In: International Conference on Information and Communication Technologies and Development, ICTD 2007, 2007 December
12. Zschau, J., Kuppers, A.N.: Early Warning Systems for Natural Disaster Reduction. Springer, Heidelberg (2003)
13. http://www.meeo.it/wp/?lang=it

On Update Protocols in Wireless Sensor Networks

Tobias Schwindl, Klaus Volbert, and Maximilian Schwab[⊠]

Ostbayerische Technische Hochschule Regensburg, Prüfeninger Straße 58,
93059 Regensburg, Germany
{tobias2.schwindl,klaus.volbert,maximilian1.schwab}@oth-regensburg.de

Abstract. There has been a lot of research been done in the domain
of Wireless Sensor Networks in recent years. Nowadays, Wireless Sensor
Networks are in operation in a wide range of different scenarios and applications, like energy management services, heat and water billing as well
as smoke detectors. However, research and development will be continued
in this domain. During the operation of such a network, software updates
need to be done seldom. In contrast to this, software updates need to
be done very frequently during development and testing for uploading
a new firmware on umpteen nodes. In this paper, we examine such a
software update for a particular, but popular and often used sensor network platform. There are already interesting research papers about the
process of updating sensor nodes. Our specific focus relies on the technical part of such an update process. We will argue why these already
existing update processes do not cover our defiances. The objective of
our software update protocol is to enable the developer to update many
nodes in a reliable and very fast fashion during the development and
testing process. For this reason, energy consumption is considered only
marginally. We do not need a multi-hop protocol, due to the fact that
all devices are in range, e.g. in a laboratory. In this paper we survey well
known update protocols and architectures for software updates in WSN,
discuss the solutions and compare them to our approach. As a conclusion of our extensive simulation follows to sum up that the developed
protocols do a fast and scalable as well as a reliable update.

Keywords: WSN · Software update · Low-power devices

1 Introduction

Wireless Sensor Networks are used in different environments. Some of the basics
of such wireless networks are described in [4,6,8,14,22]. Special constraints
regarding power and time management in these systems are shown in [7] and [2].
Many example applications and its areas are shown in [3,12,17,21]. Since most of
these sensor networks are energy constrained one of the main goal of each application in such an environment is to make sure that the lifetime of every node is
as long as possible and at the same time reach a satisfactory performance level.

© Springer Nature Switzerland AG 2019
C. Benavente-Peces et al. (Eds.): SENSORNETS 2017/2018, CCIS 1074, pp. 74–97, 2019.
https://doi.org/10.1007/978-3-030-30110-1_5

In specific circumstances, e.g., after production of devices, a initial firmware must be flashed to the nodes. This requires that every device gets the firmware and could be realized with a wireless update mechanism.

A company which produces a lot of radio hardware, e.g., smart devices like wireless smoke detectors or heat cost allocators does not want to flash and/or update all devices one after the other. They usually want to update all devices at once. In this laboratory-like use case, the update process must ensure that the firmware is flashed entirely and without any errors. All nodes should receive the firmware. It should not happen that a node does not receive the update. The whole update process should happen automatically, this means that no user is required to update the nodes. Due to the fact that many wireless sensor nodes are driven by battery most update processes have the aim to reduce power consumption as well as minimizing the update time. Most of the update protocols use different approaches to ensure these points. We show in Sect. 2 that most of the update mechanisms resolve more issues than needed, hence this results in additional effort to realize this update protocols on a real hardware.

This is one reason for us to develop a new update protocol optimized for a specific use case. This use case is the flashing of software on all used sensor nodes during the development process for a wireless sensor network. This means sensor nodes need an update for either to test new code or to extend the current code base to more than one device. This includes the possibility that the firmware update is needed for a small amount of nodes at the beginning of the development as well as a very large amount of nodes in later stages of the development that need to be updated. If the sensor nodes do not support a wireless update protocol they usually are programmed with a simple hardware tool like the so called Gang-Programmer [28]. This kind of programmer can update a small amount of nodes in parallel. Such a device is used, e.g., in Germany to flash nodes which are ready for production use. Since we had known the different scenarios for the update process itself, the scalability of such a design for the complete process was one important requirement. The next goal of our update model was the minimization of the programming time of each and every node. Every time a new software is flashed to the nodes in the sensor network there is a delay until new software can be tested, i.e. the programming time of the nodes. Furthermore, in a deployed wireless sensor network the amount of updates should be minimized because the update itself uses a lot of power and therefore battery lifetime is strongly reduced. This implies that power consumption of an update process is one of the most important things in a deployed network, but in our scenario not the main goal.

The protocol we designed tries to reduce the power consumption as much as possible, but there are possibly more sophisticated approaches to achieve this aim (done in other protocols). The flawless and complete transmission of the new code are naturally important factors because the update protocol would otherwise not be reliable. As a result of either manual intervention or many update runs would be needed to secure that all devices receive the new software. This said, such an update mechanism would not be very useful.

A preliminary version of this paper was presented at the 2018 SENSORNETS Conference [23].

2   Background and Related Work

The problem of programming nodes in wireless sensor networks is discussed in several articles. A survey is given by [20] and in [18], a brief overview of some update mechanism is also shown in [5]. There are many solutions for several hardware platforms and specific use cases. While some of these protocols are designed for a specific hardware to run on, or only allow partial updates efficiently, e.g, by incremental/compressed or differential updates shown in [13] and [16], try others to be a more generic solution for the process of software updates in WSNs.

Software updates in a WSN require data dissemination protocols. The main differences between protocols for gather sensor data and updates are described in [20]. In the following section we discuss some of the update protocols and compare them to our solution.

2.1   Trickle

Nodes in a wireless sensor network that implement the Trickle [15] protocol transmit code updates throughout the network. These code updates are sent by an node if it has not heard a few other nodes nearby transmitting the same updates using a maintenance algorithm ("polite gossip"). All messages sent by Trickle will be sent to the local broadcast address. The two possible options to a Trickle broadcast are: every node that receives the updates are up to date or the code version of a receiving node is out-of-date. The detection itself can be the result of an out-of-date node receiving new code updates by another node or an updated node hearing a node nearby has outdated code.

It does not matter which node transmits first as long as all the nodes in the WSN can be reached somehow. There is no master node that needs to be in range of all the other nodes although there must be one node injecting updates from outside the network. Due to the nature of Trickle the need for an update can be detected through a reception or transmission of a message. This allows the protocol to operate in sparse as well as dense networks.

In comparison to our update protocol, Trickle allows multi-hop updates throughout the network. Not every node needs to be in range of the node transmitting new code updates. These multi-hop updates have a negative effect on the power consumption because nodes must forward data to other nodes regardless of the need to send own data. During the development process we can arrange the nodes in range of a single transmitter to update all devices at once to save energy. Disseminating data via multi-hop in a large wireless sensor network can be very time consuming. To achieve a rapid propagation as well as a low maintenance overhead, the nodes adjust the length of their gossiping attention spans. This means the nodes in the network communicate more often when there is an update. One of the biggest drawbacks of Trickle is that it assumes the nodes are always on. Due to this fact, nodes can not be run on battery because of the high energy consumption resulting from continuous listening for code updates. The probability of missing code updates by a node which is not always on and wakes up occasionally for receiving code updates is given. Such a node needs to be either listening for update packages until it receives an package or needs to define times for code updates within the WSN. A WSN usually has very low duty cycles to save energy. Therefore nodes are most of the time in sleep mode and not often able to receive messages.

2.2 Deluge

Deluge [11, 20] is a reliable data dissemination protocol based on Trickle to distribute large amounts of data among a WSN. It allows to transfer code updates from one or more source nodes to multiple other nodes via multi-hop. Representing the data object as a set of fixed-sized pages provides a manageable unit of transfer which allows for spatial multiplexing and support for efficient incremental updates distinguished by incremental version numbers. The identical data object is distributed to all of the nodes. Therefore the data is split into fixed size pages which is the basic unit of transfer to provide the following advantages: it restricts the number of states a receiver has to maintain while receiving the data, it allows efficient incremental upgrades from prior versions and spatial multiplexing. The pages itself are split into fixed sized packets. The packets and pages include a 16-bit cyclic redundancy check (CRC). The nodes broadcast advertisement packets containing a version number as well as a bit vector for all new pages received. The broadcast is a variable interval based on the updating activity. For incremental updating its image to a more recent version, a node listens to supplementary advertisements. After that it requests the required page numbers from a distinct neighbouring node. When the node receives the last package to complete a page it sends an advertising broadcast prior requesting further pages to improve pipe lining within the network. Deluge does neither support ACKs or NACKs. The requesting node pulls data by inquiring packets for a new page or for a missing packet from a previous page.

In comparison to our approach Deluge is robust to asymmetric links, where a link in one direction can have a significantly different loss rate in the other direction. A three-phase handshake protocol helps to ensure a bidirectional link exists prior transmitting data. Furthermore, if a node has not completely received its update after making a certain amount of requests, it searches for a new neighbour to request data, rather than hanging to a bad link. This approach helps to send updates fast, because sticking to a bad link leads to packet loss and therefore to a longer transmission due to the fact that packages need to be requested more often. Because the packages arrive more reliable and faster, less energy is wasted through slow or repeated transmission of packages. Bad links are a common problem for field deployments and can be minimized through decreasing the distance to the transmitter during the development. Deluge dynamically adjusts the advertisement rate to enable quick propagation. The use of spacial multiplexing allows parallel transfers of data. A downside of the use of spacial multiplexing is that the entire network must remain powered on to achieve the full benefits of spatial multiplexing. This increases the power consumption of the nodes and makes it impossible to run them on battery. Another drawback is that Deluge is not supporting fault detection and recovery. As we said we assume for the development and testing each of the nodes to be in range of a transceiver for programming the nodes, a multi hop protocol is not needed. Furthermore, a multi-hop protocol is usually harder to implement than a single-hop protocol.

2.3   Deployment Support Network (DSN)

A Deployment Support Network [9] is basically an architecture instead a particular implementation of a protocol for software updates. It is a possible choice for accessing the sensor nodes independently by providing a parallel network for maintenance. Accessing each node individually for software updates or maintenance in general is usually unattainable because of the inaccessibility of the nodes and the huge amount of nodes. Accessing the nodes via the WSN has distinct downsides. It postulates on the network being working, it has an negative effect on the network performance due to increased load and increases the energy consumption of the nodes. A DSN can face some of those problems by temporarily attaching small and portable nodes the WSN. This allows a host, e.g. a PC to connect to the WSN and open a virtual connection to any of the nodes and communicate with both, the attached DSN-Node and WSN-Node.

A DSN is advantageous during the whole development cycle. It allows convenient distribution of new code to all of the devices. In a later production and field deployment it allows to monitor, validate and measure with minimal impairment of the WSN.

In contrast to our update protocol, a DSN allows large-scale deployment without losing the ability to observe and control all nodes without the burden of fixed, wired infrastructure or changes to the target system. Due to the fact that it is an architecture it does not specify a protocol for node updates. Another disadvantage is that a parallel DSN network has to be managed and deployed in parallel to the WSN.

2.4   Four Step Update Process

Many update protocols in wireless sensor networks, e.g., Deluge [11], MOAP [24] or Trickle [15] use the idea of a four step process [20] to ensure the demanded functionality. This process is shown in Fig. 1 and includes four steps.

The first step (advertising) ensures that all nodes know the current software version. If there is more than one source that could provide the needed software, a target must choose the best source, e.g., by checking the link quality of the radio channel to the different possible sources (selection). These two steps include the concept of multiple sources and therefore multiple senders. At the same time these protocols often use the idea of multi-hop. This approach allows nodes to reach other nodes in a wide sensor network outside their own transmission area.

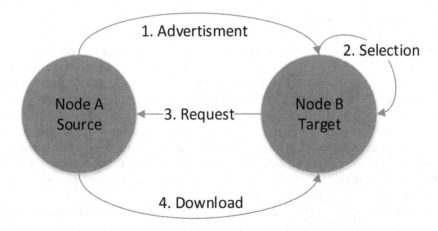

Fig. 1. Dissemination idea for update protocols [23].

So-called multi-hop protocols can distribute code to nodes which are not in direct reach of the source, but receive new software from in between nodes. This idea may be the best solution for some problems with appropriate hard- and software but does not fulfil our needs for the complete application programming of a large amount of wireless sensor nodes while developing software. All these programmable devices are within a small area, therefore reachable for one sender within this area. If the concept of multiple senders would be used, this could lead to interference with other sources in this network. Consequently, a mechanism would be needed to ensure that this kind of interference, i.e. colliding messages, does not occur.

Our update model does not include the idea of multiple senders. This allows us an easy mechanism to broadcast messages, due to the fact that there is only one sender and therefore this message can not collide with other messages. There are no other concurrent messages at all at the same time in the entire system. The third step (request) establishes a communication channel between source and target. The last step is the actual download of the inquired data for updating the target node. After the execution of all these steps, the new software is executable on each node that received the update.

Such sophisticated update models solve crucial problems to their specific use case(s). But the additional steps of advertising and necessary following selection would need more time and energy in our scenario. Because we have a very dense network these steps only bring their disadvantages, nonetheless they would work with such networks. Though the advantages of such an approach would be lost and therefore these kinds of methods add unnecessary overhead. Analysis of existing software update mechanisms is the reason for our different approach to the problem of updating sensor nodes. All these protocols are not satisfactorily for our challenges, admitting they cover their specific problems very well. The next chapter does introduce our protocol ideas to reach a fast and reliable update while developing new software for sensor networks.

3   Our Approach

In this chapter we describe the underlying ideas of the update protocol and give some reasons for their use. The process is designed to update an arbitrary amount of nodes in reasonable time. The update itself does only support full updates, i.e. it is not possible to update a part of the firmware while keeping other parts of the software. The complete flash memory is reprogrammed with the new program. Since we developed and implemented the update process for a specific hardware from Texas Instruments (TI) we used existing software and ideas where possible. However, these ideas can be easily adopted and used for other systems as well. The already available TI 1:1 update process was the cornerstone for the further development of our update process.

In the existing update mechanism a code distributor, described in the next chapter, communicates over USB with a pc application to collect the source code and send this new code to the update device, the sensor node. The TI update process needs a particular software on the sensor node, which will be updated, running. Due to this fact, the update process is only one-time executable. If the new loaded software does not support the specific sequence to launch and execute the update process, the complete process is not usable any longer, and must be manually flashed again. These limitations were another reason for designing a more practical update mechanism which fits better for our use case.

The TI software, after the wireless update is started and initialization process is complete, does use a simple stop and wait method. This means that after every single data packet an acknowledgement from the device is expected. If the validation is successful the next data packet is ready for transmission to the device. Otherwise, the current data packet will be sent again. This idea was extended and adapted to get it working with more than one device. The new approach does work similar, although at the moment not every packet is validated, but after a specific number of data packets the update device transmits an acknowledgement packet to advert the current position in the entire update process. This is also known as a go-back-N protocol. While the source code distributor receives good acknowledgement packets, i.e. no error occurred, it continues with the next valid data packet. A bad packet indicates an error and this data packet will be sent again as long as all update devices do not correctly receive it. The bad data packet is now the new position in the update and from this position all packets are transmitted. However, an error is not recognized immediately, but only with the next acknowledgement.

Since the process is designed to work with any amount of sensor nodes it must be guaranteed that all nodes know when to send their acknowledgement packet, otherwise some transmissions will collide because of interference with other possible transmissions. This is guaranteed by the used time division multiple access (TDMA) mechanism. Every node has a particular, fixed time slot when to send the acknowledgement. The initial easy idea and implementation uses the TDMA mechanism after a fixed amount of data packets regardless of the quality of the radio channel. A bad transmission channel could result then in slow error recognition. On the contrary when the radio channel is quite good the acknowledgement phase is kind a waste of time since an error is unlikely. An update protocol, which uses the information about the radio channel and its quality could save time as well as energy because it decides flexible when an acknowledgement phase is needed more often. The adaptation to the quality of the current radio channel is used in several environments. In some TCP/IP implementations there is a mechanism called AIMD (Additive Increase Multiplicative Decrease).

When the error rate is low the ack phase is used infrequently, but is increased by a multiplicative factor after an error appear, originally shown in [29]. A detailed analysis of the algorithms is presented in, e.g., [10] and [19]. A similar, simplified mechanism is used by our second developed update protocol. The idea was to get a better adaptation to the actual needed acknowledgement rate given by incorporating the physical quality of the radio channel. Mechanisms, messages and its sequences to initialize the update process are presented and analysed in Sect. 5.1. The complete update protocol, not only the acknowledgement phase of the process, is a time based, shared protocol, meaning all sensor nodes share the same system time. Data packets with new code come each fixed time step and all nodes are able to synchronize with the system time with every data packet which is received. This guarantees that every update device, which is correctly synchronized with the code distributor (master clock), can switch to receive mode very shortly before the packet is transmitted by the update distributor. This reduces energy consumption since update nodes are only in RX mode when it is absolutely necessary.

Because of the natural clock drift every update node must synchronize itself with the master clock, which in this case is the clock from the source code distributor. This guarantees that RX windows remain narrow. This basic idea is valid for many update scenarios. These concepts show that practical relevance of the update mechanism is of real interest here, as the theoretical background of our update model is not extremely difficult. In the next chapter we describe our particular hardware and software model on which we actually implemented and tested these update designs and protocols.

4   Software and Hardware Architecture

The software architecture and its distribution is based on the hardware devices used. Due to the fact that the update protocol has several tasks, we operate with different devices, which are suited for their specific function. The participants, which are involved in our update model are the sensor node (CC430), the distributor of the update code (access point) and the user interface represented as a desktop application.

The CC430 is a programmable watch delivered within the eZ430 Chronos development kit. This device (CC430F6137) is the sensor node in our environment and has an built-in sub-1 GHz wireless radio module based on the CC1101. It stores a bootloader (max. 2 KB) which handles the complete update process on watch side. Therefore, the code size of the complete update protocol software must be less than 2 KB, together with device drivers for the flash, ports and radio modules. This limitation allows only a small implementation as a more complex protocol could lead easily to a code size which will not suit the available bootloader ROM size. The eZ430 is equipped with 32 KB of internal flash memory and 4 KB of RAM [26]. The microcontroller supports different internal sensors and offers several power modes to save energy. While not in active mode (AM), but waiting for external/internal events, e.g., expired timers or incoming radio packets, it can switch to different low power modes (LPM0 – LPM4). In our scenario the most update time is spent in LPM3. The lowest power mode LPM4 disables all clocks, which are needed to provide a stable time base and hence, this mode cannot be used by our protocol.

The access point is a MSP430f5509 equipped with a CC1101 radio core [27] which is used for communication with the watch. The access point contains an USB interface for further communication with other USB devices like a pc. This device is responsible for dissemination of update messages, e.g., the new code, meaning it co-ordinates the complete sequence of the update. The last involved party is the user interface. This application handles the firmware file and partition into small update packages so the access point does not need to perform further actions with the packages, but only broadcasts them to the watches. The communication between the access point and GUI is handled via the USB interface. The complete structure of our update model is shown in Fig. 2. All watches

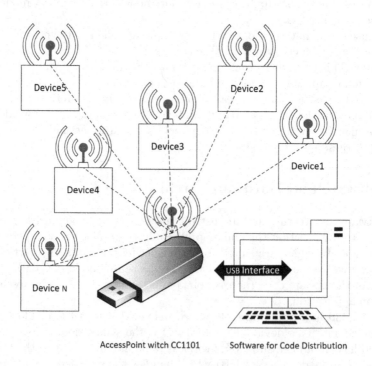

Fig. 2. Overview of update model [23].

are placed in a small area within radio reach of the access point. Besides that, no other additional requirements must be met. The update is initiated by the application. After starting the update process, no user intervention is required. The access point does now communicate with all watches within radio reach to update these nodes. In the design of the entire update protocol, communication among the different sensor nodes, i.e. the CC430 devices, is not planned. From the perspective of the update devices it is a 1:1 communication with the access point. On the other side the access point distributes code to all devices, hence this is a 1:n communication. The particular timings of messages and its sequences are presented in the next chapter.

5   Analysis

In this chapter we analyse the update protocol itself and its several states. We show how we calculated the power consumption as well as the computation of the execution time of the update process.

5.1   Protocol Overview

All sort of messages within the system are summarised in Fig. 3. As seen in the protocol messages, the hardware settings of the radio communication incorporate a 4 byte preamble as well as a 4 byte sync word. The preamble is an alternating series of ones and zeros, i.e. 0xAA is transmitted. The sync word consists of application specific data which is used for byte synchronization. Moreover, it allows a distinction among systems with the same hardware as the radio writes only data to the internal buffer if the correct synchronization word is received [25]. In our application it is used twice with the value of 0XD391 to get a 4 byte sync word. Because of the enabled 16 bit checksum calculation, there is no need to check for errors in software as erroneous packets are removed automatically. The data packets data field is adaptable, meaning during the update run the access point could decide to increase or decrease the length of the payload. This mechanism is currently not in use, but could be used in future versions of the update process. All other messages have a fixed length and can not change its size during protocol execution. The exact sequence of the complete update process is shown in Fig. 4. At the beginning of the firmware update mechanism all watches must execute its bootloader software. This can be done via reset of the device manually as well as by triggering a software reset if this is supported by the current firmware. Then the bootloader is executed where it is possible to start the update (automatically if in a specific time interval no user input was performed) or execute the application. After the device has initiated the execution of the bootloader, the update device transmits every specific time interval, e.g., 3 s, the RFU (ReadyForUpdate) message. When the access point receives such a message (this message comes from a watch which has not an update ID yet and therefore was not recognized yet) it replies with the RFU_ACK message and sets the update ID for this particular watch and update run. The frequency of

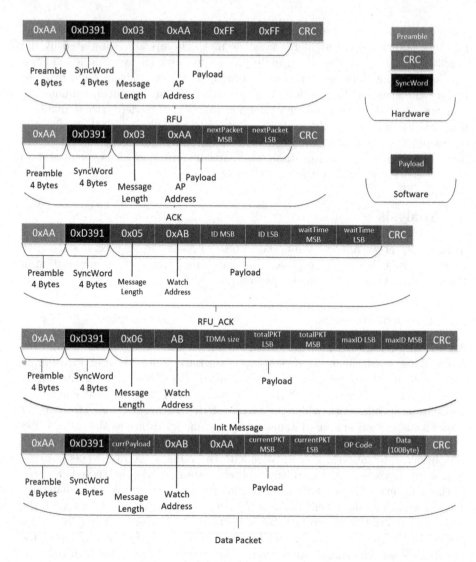

Fig. 3. Protocol messages in the update system [23].

the RFU message determines how often the watch can send its beacon in the context of the discovery phase of the update, e.g., if an error occurred or some other watch is sending simultaneously and another RFU message is needed.

There is a hardware mechanism used during the discovery phase to prevent most of the colliding messages. This stage is the only state where collision between different messages can occur. In all the other states is only one message at any time in the complete system. The watch switches to LPM3 after this short communication to save energy. After a particular and by the user configurable amount of time the discovery phase is done and the update goes into the next state, i.e. init state. At this stage all watches that need an update should be known by the access point. This is guaranteed by setting an appropriate amount of time for the watches to remain in the discovery update state. All watches wake up at the same time, very close before the first actual packet is send and now listen to the first update package, i.e. init packet. This is achieved by time information the devices gain from the previous communication with the access point, which is included in the RFU_ACK message.

The init packet does contain informations such as the update size, number of update devices and some information about the acknowledgement phase and its length. In the case a watch does not get an answer for the RFU message during this process or does not get the init message correctly this device does not participate in the following update process, rather resets itself. After the init mechanism for each node is successfully completed, the actual update starts. In this case an adjustable, but during the update process fixed amount of data packages is transmitted before the first acknowledgement phase is run. All packets come in specific time slots, so all watches can go into RX mode very close before the actual packet transmission starts. This guarantees that a very small amount of power is consumed, since RX time is not longer than absolutely necessary given by physical parameters and the calibration time. The time among data packets is 100 ms and 5 packets are sent one after the other before starting with the acknowledgement phase. This means the data packet duration is 500 ms. Afterwards, meaning 500 ms packet round with 5 sent packets is done, the update devices, whether they received packets successfully or not, trigger the next and final state, the TDMA phase. In the case of an error at the beginning of the data phase all further packets are lost as well. Because of the design of the protocol, an update device is only capable to save the current state in the complete update, but not single packets which are needed to complete the update. This behaviour could be changed in further versions to amend the update.

The entire TDMA windows is divided into small time slots for every single node. The length of this phase depends on the amount of sensor nodes, which participate in the update process. Each update node has the chance to send an acknowledgement packet which contains the packet number that is expected next, hence, this information covers the last successfully received packet number. The access point has all needed data, after this TDMA mechanism, to decide which packet should be transmitted next, i.e. the smallest packet number that was received by the access point. In the case an ack from a node is lost, for whatever reason, there will be no error handling performed. When the next ack phase starts there is a new chance for this node to send its ack successfully. The data phase is started again after every TDMA phase. This process is repeated as long as there are no more acks with a packet number below the highest possible packet number is received, therefore all nodes have the complete new code. Each node that has received all necessary packets successfully, resets itself automatically and starts the new application if there was user input, otherwise the bootloader waits for another update run, meaning the device starts with sending the RFU message. This process can be cancelled by particular input to easily start the application.

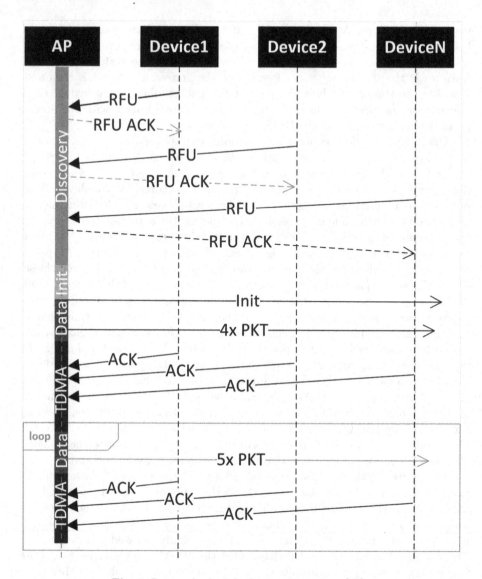

Fig. 4. Protocol schedule during the update [23].

The acknowledgement phase is the most complex phase of the complete update protocol. The more devices are participating in an update run, the longer this phase must be. The ack phase is always determined by a specific integer multiplicator of this 100 ms, dependent on how many devices need an update. This multiplicator does increase by 1 every 10 nodes. The decision to set these particular timing intervals were made after evaluating the USB communication between the access point and the pc application.

5.2   Calculations - Power Consumption

Because power consumption of an update protocol is an important requirement in the design of such a process the exact energy consumption of all messages are presented in this chapter. The power consumption of the update process is divided into four states of the watch: the active mode and LPM3 of the watch and its CPU, the receiving (RX) and the transmitting (TX) mode of the radio module. Table 1 shows several power levels of these states in mA. To guarantee a low power consumption, the completion time as well as radio transmissions should be minimized and update time should be remain in LPM3 whenever possible. The latter can be reached by an exact time based protocol as we have developed. The timings of each update state is known to every single device, hence the active time of any device is minimized to the actually needed active time. The rest of the update time is waiting for an event to get triggered or to let other devices finish their transmissions. The Power Consumption given in Ah, length of the messages in bytes and the timings (RX and TX) in ms of our messages are shown in Table 2 (from watches perspective, the access point power consumption is kind of negligible because its not battery driven and always on a secure power connection). The bytes added and removed automatically by hardware, i.e. the preamble, sync word and the checksum are already included, meaning the actual usable data is always 10 bytes less. This overhead is mandatory for all messages transmitted by the radio module. The shown power consumption is in 10^{-9} Ah. Timings and consequently power consumptions for these messages are valid for a transmission rate of 250,000 bits per second. Because the radio module needs calibration each time a communication is initilized a value of $721\,\mu s$ with a power consumption of 9.5 mA must be added to each receive or transmit operation [26]. This results in additional $1.9 \cdot 10^{-9}$ Ah per radio event. As we know all the necessary values to calculate the complete power consumption of the CPU and the radio module during one update run the following formula shows the power consumption for the radio module for all transmission:

Table 1. Power consumption @12 MHz [23, 26].

Voltage	IDLE + CPU active	TX	RX	LPM3
3.0 V	1.7 + 2.75	33	16	0.0022

Table 2. Power consumption of different messages [23].

Type	Length	TX time	RX time	Power
RFU	14	0.45	0.00	4.10
RFU_ACK	16	0.00	0.51	2.27
InitPacket	17	0.00	0.54	2.41
DataPacket	116	0.00	3.20	14.22
ACK	14	0.45	0.00	4.10

$$\text{radio\_power}_{\text{active}} = a \cdot \text{RFU} + a \cdot \text{RFU\_ACK} + \text{InitPacket} + b \cdot \text{DataPacket}$$
$$+ c \cdot \text{ACK} + (2a + 1 + b + c) \cdot 1.9 \cdot 10^{-9} \text{Ah}$$

where a stands for the number of RFU messages the watch transmits, b the number of data packets were received by the watch and c the number of acks the device is transmitting during the update run. Because the exact radio idle time is hard to determine we calculate the radio as always idle, knowing this is not correct but sound. This formula represents the radio power consumption for the idle state and must be added to the complete power consumption:

$$\text{radio\_power}_{\text{idle}} = 1.7 \, \text{mA} \cdot \text{updateTime}$$

The CPU is at least 90% of the update time in LPM3. The only CPU activity while updating the firmware, is before transmission and after or during receiving (when the FIFO hardware buffer is full) of a radio packet, since these events are interrupt-driven and wake up the CPU from all low power modes. Additional CPU active time is needed before the update starts as well as after a data packet was received, because this data must be written to internal flash memory. This is why we can calculate the worst case active CPU time and its power consumption with 10% of the update time, knowing the exact CPU active time is dependent on how many packets were received/transmitted. However the 10% calculated time is surely higher than in the actual implementation. Every 100 ms the radio waits for a data packet, which needs time for receiving (copy values, sync mechanism) and when successfully received the time for writing it to the flash memory. After some evaluation of these operations we can safely assume these operations do not need 10 ms and this would be the time amount to reach the 10% active CPU time. To get a wrong but safe bound we add, as the exact CPU active time is also hard to determine, for the complete run

$$\text{CPU\_power}_{\text{LPM}} = 0.90 \cdot \text{updateTime} \cdot 2.2 \, \mu\text{A}$$

and for the active state of the CPU

$$\text{CPU\_power}_{\text{active}} = 0.10 \cdot \text{updateTime} \cdot 2.75 \, \text{mA}.$$

The complete main flash memory of the device is erased and reprogrammed during an update run. These write operations also consume time and energy. Timings and power consumptions of all flash operations are shown in [26]. We calculate the power consumption during erase with the given typical value of 2 mA and during programming with 3 mA. While full erasing does need maximal 32 ms, the complete programming duration of the CC430 flash memory takes about 800 ms of active write operation. All flash instructions summarized result in $6.9 \cdot 10^{-7}$ Ah, which must be added to the power consumption of one update run.

The sum of $radio_{active}$, $radio_{idle}$, CPU_{LPM}, CPU_{active} and write/erase operations on the flash memory give now the complete power consumption necessary by one sensor device during one firmware update. The best case (one device, minimum amount of packets are sent) of an update with a size of 27 KB, a data packet payload length of 100 bytes and a TDMA window after each 5 data packets, can now be calculated. The minimum amount of packets necessary are 1 RFU message and its 1 ACK, the 1 init package which is followed by 270 data packets and in between of the data packets there are 54 acknowledgement packets needed. This results in 327 radio transitions. The minimum update time is 27 s, i.e. the 270 packets with one packet in 100 ms, plus discovery phase length which is calculated with 7 s – this is the value we used for our later shown experiments. This results in $6.01 \cdot 10^{-6}$ Ah for the active radio, $1.27 \cdot 10^{-8}$ Ah for the idle radio, $1.87 \cdot 10^{-8}$ Ah for the LPM of the CPU and $2.60 \cdot 10^{-6}$ Ah for the active CPU time. If exactly one device is involved in the update run, a total amount of $9.33 \cdot 10^{-6}$ Ah is used. The more devices are used the more the power consumption increases, but only because the time in LPM3 increases. With 1000 devices the additional power consumption for LMP3 is about $2.94 \cdot 10^{-7}$ Ah. This is much less than $1/10$ of the complete update process of one device, therefore does not significantly decrease the number of possible update runs for these devices. The number of radio transmissions and the CPU active times do not increase, but stay the same.

The eZ430 chronos watch contains a standard CR2032 lithium battery with a nominal capacity of 220 mAh [1]. This means the battery lasts for about 23,500 possible best case update runs. This should be acceptable for most development processes. Although these results show only the best case with 1 involved device and hence errors would decrease the number of possible updates accordingly. An error rate of 1% would increase the needed amount of packets at least to 273, more likely an even higher number of packets is needed due to the design of the error detection, but also increases the CPU active time and the LPM time. The maximum amount of packets (worst case) for a packet error rate of 1% is 285, every error occurred directly after the ack phase and therefore all other packets in this data round are lost too. This results in additional 3 more acks and 15 more packets, i.e. a total amount of $2.26 \cdot 10^{-7}$ Ah must be added to the power consumption.

5.3 Calculations - Time

The main objective during the development of the update protocols was to achieve a fast and reliable process and hence time evaluation of the update process is important. The time an update run needs can be calculated as follows:

$$\text{completionTime} = \text{Time}_{\text{discoveryPhase}}$$
$$+ \text{Time}_{\text{dataPackets}} + \text{Time}_{\text{TDMA/ACKphase}}$$

At present the user sets the time of the discovery phase. In this time slot each node has to complete its RFU communication and hence the more devices are updated the longer this time should be. Time needed for transmitting all the data packets depends on the size of the update. The usable flash memory of the device is 32 KB, which results currently, since the data payload of one packet is 100 bytes, in maximum 32 s. The TDMA/ACK phase of the update is calculated differently and dependent on the amount of sensor nodes which require an update. The first 10 devices can use the normal time between 2 data packets to transmit their acknowledgements. After that every 10 devices get an additional 100 ms time slot to transmit the ack packet. Thus, the TDMA time can be computed as follows:

$$\text{Time }_{\text{TDMA/ACK}} = (\#\text{devices} - 1) \; / \; 10 \cdot 100 \, \text{ms} \cdot \#\text{acks}$$

This time increases with growing amount of update devices and becomes the most important factor that determines how long an update run needs to be done. With, e.g., 1000 devices and an update size of 27 KB time spent in the TDMA phase is about 535 s, while the actual sending of the packets is 27 s. In later improvements of the update protocol the time spent in the TDMA windows should be minimized to get faster update results. The time to finish the update depends heavily on the error rate. The more errors, the more packets have to be sent. But with growing number of sensor devices the TDMA phase has the most impact on the finishing time. If we use again a small error rate of 1% different update times could be observed. The best case with regard of completion time are errors that are recognized immediately. With 3 additional sent packets, 273 in total, the TDMA/ACK phase length would be the same – still under the best case assumption. Since the last round is incomplete and if all 3 packets are received without errors the last TDMA phase is not started, leading to no additional time cost for the update process.

The worst case on the other hand is completely different. If an error occurs right after the ACK phase, the whole packet round is unusable and therefore, all packets are lost. As a result only 3 errors would cost another 3 additional TDMA rounds. While only one device is involved, only the additional 15 packets sent are relevant for the execution time of the update. Given the example of 1000 Devices, 3 more TDMA phases would mean: $99 \cdot 100 \, \text{ms} \cdot 3 = 29,7 \, \text{s}$ more time to complete the update for all devices. Thus, the exact time/place of the errors has a huge impact on the completion time of the process. Furthermore, with more devices an error becomes more and more important regarding the completion time.

6   Experiments

This section contains experiments we made with our available hardware. Not all introduced update protocols contain an evaluation of their methods on a real hardware environment, therefore we particularly want to describe our experiments we made. For all tests of the update process we considered all available nodes which need an update are in very close distance to the access point, i.e. max distance was 1 m in our test environment. The most important metric to measure quality of an update process in our scenario, i. e. the development of new software for sensor networks, is the update duration. Another top priority achievement is reliability. All devices must be updated completely and without

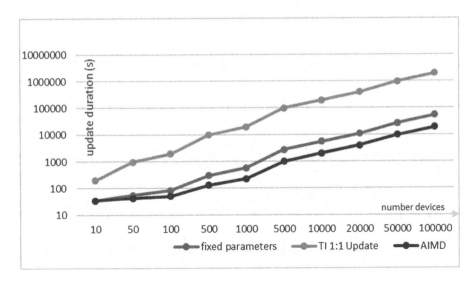

Fig. 5. Update duration with different number of devices [23].

errors. Although energy consumption is important in wireless sensor networks, it has a lower priority in this case. Otherwise the battery must be replaced very frequently and most benefits of an update process like fast and simple testing of new code would be lost.

Calculated best case results for updates are shown in Fig. 5. The x-axis (bottom) shows the amount of devices involved whereas on the y-axis (left side) the time to update this amount of devices is shown. The diagram is valid for an update size of 27 KB. The fixed parameters update process has an acknowledgement rate of 5. This means that after each 5 data packets there is a time window where all watches can reply with an ack packet. The number of ack phases can be reduced, if the radio channel is good and an error is unlikely. In this case we used a different approach for the ack phase. The AIMD and AIAD variant introduce easy mechanisms to respond flexible to the current radio channel and adapt the ack rate. AIMD start at the same ack rate and from there on the algorithm decides whether to increase or decrease the ack rate. The discovery phase was set to 7 s during all experiments. This was sufficient for our amount of sensor nodes, but must be adjusted if more nodes are updated simultaneously.

The acceleration factor between different update modes (TI 1:1, fixed, AIMD) is shown in Fig. 6. Because the TI update does only allow a 1:1 update, the 1:n update process is obviously faster. The factor does increase with growing number of sensor nodes but is kind of limited due to the acknowledgement phase of the update protocol. As shown before in Sect. 5.3 the ack phase becomes the bottleneck of the update process since every ack round needs significantly more time than sending the 5 data packets one after the other. In case the AIMD and/or AIAD implementation is used and the quality of the radio channel is good, the ACK phase does not trigger as often as before, thus saves a lot

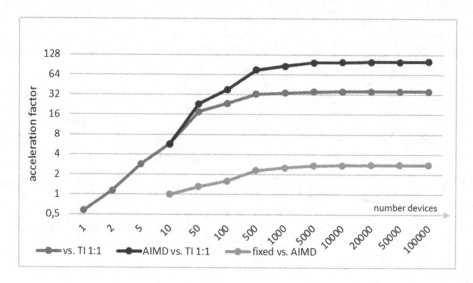

Fig. 6. Acceleration between the different update modes [23].

of time. These diagrams always show the best case, which means that no error occurs during the entire update time, hence are at this time only theoretical values. The experimental results, which will be presented in the next section will indicate how likely it is to achieve these values.

6.1   Results - Static Acknowledgement

Table 3 shows some actual results from experiments we made. These initial results were executed for all nodes within a small area and equipped with the fixed parameters software. One hundred of each test runs, i.e. in total 500 update runs were executed with several amount of sensor nodes. The table shows the amount of devices we used for one update run (up to 25), the time the experimental worst case (WC) run was longer than the best case (BC) calculation and the average and worst case PER (packet error rate). The entire column, i.e. the rate of successful updates gives an overview of how many of these firmware

Table 3. Measurements – static variant [23].

#devices	WC-BC	complete	avg.PER	max.PER
5	0.6 s	99.2%	0.12%	1.09%
10	2.5 s	99.8%	0.45%	3.75%
15	3.0 s	99.1%	0.66%	4.69%
20	4.2 s	99.8%	1.23%	7.76%
25	7.7 s	99.6%	2.92%	9.72%

updates were done totally without errors, meaning a runnable new software is stored in flash memory. PER is the packet error rate which indicates the channel quality between access point and watches during the software update.

These experimental results show, that completion rate does not correlate with amount of nodes which are updated. Through all test runs the completion rate was approximately the same with no spike in either one direction. In other words the mechanism does not become unreliable with more sensor nodes and hence, is able to scale with the problem size. The simple update protocol has a dependability over 99%. In the present implementation an error can occur in the final data round, the acknowledgement gets lost and therefore the update device can not complete the run.

A more sophisticated, explicit error handling like a two-way communication between the update device and the access point during or at the end of the update process could increase the percentage further. When both devices expect a validation packet the error is recognized for sure, therefore an explicit handling for this case could be created. Since in all experiments nodes where in a very dense formation, i.e. the average distance between the different nodes was about 1 cm, the PER does correlate with the number of nodes. This leads to the assumption that there is possible interference between the individual sensor nodes, which leads to corrupted packets.

The power consumption does increase over time since more CPU and radio activity is necessary. The calculation results shown in Fig. 5 for more devices will most likely not be reached since average PER is not near 0, but does vary between 0% and 3% during different update runs. The duration to finish the update on all watches goes up with the PER. As long as the number of devices is 10 or lower the TDMA has no influence on the update duration, as shown in the previous section in Sect. 5.3. The duration increases only due to packets which are sent again. In all other cases time increases not only by sending data packets again, but also with the additional time spent in the TDMA window. This behaviour was noticed in our experiments between 20 and 25 update nodes. In both specific worst cases the PER was high, but the actual completion time and its difference to the best case was significantly higher with 25 devices compared to 20 devices. The explanation for this is the acknowledgement phase. For every error that results in an additional ack window the update time increases by 200 ms with 25 devices instead of 100 ms with 20 devices. This also means, that for a large number of nodes an error is much more impactful than for a small amount of devices.

A further characteristic behaviour of the update protocol is based on the statically fixed acknowledgement state (in this specific case after every 5 data packets). A packet error can enlarge the number of packets necessary to be sent significantly and therefore the completion time for the update. This happens if an error occurred directly after the acknowledgement phase and is only recognized in the next phase. For this easy protocol it is not possible to detect this error otherwise than during the acknowledgement phase.

6.2   Results - AIMD and AIAD

The more sophisticated approach to get acknowledgement packets is to react to the current quality of the radio channel. Techniques used by our protocol to adjust are the AIMD and AIAD mechanisms. The initialization process and the message types are the same as before. The only difference to the previous mechanism is the rate at which the watches transmit their acknowledgement information. The acknowledgement rate starts again at 5. This means after 5 data packets the first TDMA is initialized. After this first ack phase the access point adapts the time for the next ack round. All other messages, timings and states are valid again. The results of these 150 (75 for each variant) update test runs with 25 sensor devices are shown in Table 4. The best case time calculation for both the AIMD as well as the AIAD mechanism is 38 s. This means that each single packet is transmitted without an error. This includes both data and ack packets. A non received positive ack, meaning an ack that would confirm that no error occurred is treated as an error. This minimal time can be reached by the update process as shown in Table 4, but the experimental evaluated average case is significantly higher. The average case still shows that the quality of the radio channel is sufficient to reach shorter completion times compared to the normal static mechanism. The best case of the first approach lies with 45 s higher than the average case of both the AIMD and AIAD protocols. However, with experiments evaluated we can show that the quality of the radio channel can go low enough that the update execution time is longer than with the static mechanism. The worst case execution time of the AIMD protocol is 55.9 s and with the AIAD 57.9 s. The worst case of the static method is with 52.2 s lower than both the AIMD and AIAD protocols. If a short, random error occurred than acks are not needed often, but if an error occurred and is detected rather late or the error is due to some radio interference and stays in the system a more often TDMA phase would be necessary.

Table 4. Measurements – AIMD/AIAD variant [23].

	avg.PER	avg.T	min.T	avg.#dataPackets
AIMD	1.49	43.6	38.4	287.75
AIAD	1.32	41.9	38.1	295.57

These algorithms have a delay to respond to both error cases. This fact can slow down the complete update process. The comparison between AIMD and AIAD is similar. Since the multiplicative decrease mechanism can react faster to errors which remain in the system, the worst case execution time with a high PER is shorter than the additive decrease mechanism. But if one random error occurred, the AIMD protocol needs a long time to recover before it is at the same ack rate as before the error, meaning it loses time compared to an additive decrease mechanism. The AIAD can react to such random errors much better.

As shown in the results, most of the time the quality of the radio channel is good enough to use the AIAD algorithm to get faster updates than AIMD. But as seen in Table 4 the AIAD needs in average more packets until the update is complete. However, as explained in Sect. 5.3 the TDMA/ACK phase is the update state where most of the time is spent. The number of data packets is not the crucial part of the completion time.

Since both the flexible ack mechanisms are faster than the previous one and the AIAD is faster than the AIMD, we learned that in general and over a lot of update runs the AIAD method gives the best results in terms of completion time and as previous explained this is the most important metric for the presented update scenario. The power consumption between the different protocols can be compared based on the average results shown in Table 4. The interesting part about the results is that the AIAD needs more radio transmission in general. Since more packets are sent during an average AIAD update run, the devices must be more often in RX mode. This results in higher power consumption for each sensor node. The LPM and radio-idle power consumption is lower than with AIMD as a result of the lower execution time of the update. The formula shown in Sect. 5.2 is now not exact enough to calculate the difference between the individual update mechanisms regarding the active CPU time. The active time with AIAD is still higher than in the AIMD process (in Sect. 5.2 this would be differently computed). The more packets are received the more the CPU is active. To calculate the exact differences between each update protocol a more specific CPU active formula would be needed. Since the power consumption was not the most important goal in the development, the power consumption is not significantly higher than in the static variant and the number of update runs should be sufficient for the software development, such exact computations were not done.

7 Conclusion and Further Work

We presented a fast and reliable but still simple update mechanism plus first improvements and their evaluation in this paper. This kind of an update protocol shows an easy way to update a large number of sensor nodes in parallel while keeping its effort manageable. Our approach could be used with a variety of different hardware. The co-development of a wireless updater during the development of software for the sensor network should be top priority since the benefit from such an update process is huge. The easy possibility to update all the nodes at the same time decreases the amount of time necessary to reprogram all sensor nodes and therefore, it is easy to test new code very quickly. An exactly shared time based protocol is not as hard as update mechanisms that come with multiple senders and/or multi-hop concepts. The power consumptions of this protocol is not problematic as calculations show that the update can be executed multiple times. The execution time is much less than in a 1:1 update/flash scenario and its scalability means it is usable with any amount of nodes. Improvements for the update protocol could be done by analysing the radio channel to reduce the ack phase frequency. A further improvement for the protocol is not only to make the ack phase adaptable, but also the size, i.e. the payload, of the packets. A good radio channel and 1.5 times larger packet size, the TDMA frequency would be reduced by the same factor. This would lead to an smaller execution time for the update due to higher throughput.

Acknowledgements. This work was supported by the research cluster for Robotics, Algorithms, Communication and Smart Grid (RAKS) of the OTH Regensburg. Further information under www.raks-oth.de. This work was also supported by the Regensburg Center of Energy and Resources (RCER) and the Technology- and Science Network Oberpfalz (TWO). Further information under www.rcer.de.

References

1. Datasheet lithium manganese dioxide battery cr2032 (2018). https://www.mouser.com/ds/2/315/panasonic-lithium-cr2032-datasheet-837927.pdf
2. Sinha, A., Chandrakasan, A.: Dynamic power management in wireless sensor networks. IEEE Des. Test Comput. **18**, 62–74 (2001)
3. Altmann, M., Schlegl, P., Volbert, K.: A low-power wireless system for energy consumption analysis at mains sockets. EURASIP J. Embed. Syst. **2017**(1), 18 (2017)
4. Schindelhauer, C., Volbert, K., Ziegler, M.: Geometric spanners with applications in wireless networks. In: Computational Geometry: Theory and Applications (CGTA 2007) (2007)
5. Sternecker, C.: Reprogrammierungstechniken fuer drahtlose sensornetzwerke. Seminar Sensorknoten - Betrieb, Netze und Anwendungen (2012)
6. Chong, C.-Y., Kumar, S.P.: Sensor networks: evolution, opportunities, and challenges. Proc. IEEE **91**, 1247–1256 (2003)
7. Sivrikaya, F., Yener, B.: Time synchronization in sensor networks: a survey. IEEE Netw. **18**, 45–50 (2004)
8. Akyildiz, I.F., Su, W., Sankarasubramaniam, Y., Cayirci, E.: A survey on sensor networks. IEEE Commun. Mag. **40**, 102–114 (2002)
9. Beutel, J., Dyer, M., Meier, L., Ringwald, M., Thiele, L.: Next-generation deployment support for sensor networks. Computer Engineering and Networks Lab; Swiss Federal Institute of Technology (ETH) Zurich
10. Edmonds, J.: On the competitiveness of AIMD-TCP within a general network. Theor. Comput. Sci. **462**, 12–22 (2012)
11. Hui, J.W., Culler, D.: The dynamic behavior of a data dissemination protocol for network programming at scale (2004)
12. Kenner, S., Thaler, R., Kucera, M., Volbert, K., Waas, T.: Comparison of smart grid architectures for monitoring and analyzing power grid data via modbus and rest. EURASIP J. Embed. Syst. **2017**(1), 5 (2017)
13. Stolikj, M., Cuijpers, P.J.L., Lukkien, J.J.: Efficient reprogramming of wireless sensor networks using incremental updates and data compression. Department of Mathematics and Computer Science System Architecture and Networking Group (2012)
14. Meyer-auf-der-Heide, F., Schindelhauer, C., Volbert, K., Grünewald, M.: Congestion, dilation, and energy in radio networks. Theory Comput. Syst. (TOCS) **37**, 343–370 (2004)

15. Levis, P., Patel, N., Culler, D., Shenker, S.: Trickle: a self-regulating algorithm for code propagation and maintenance in wireless sensor networks (2004)
16. Rickenbach, P., Wattenhofer, R.: Decoding code on a sensor node. In: 4th International Conference on Distributed Computing in Sensor Systems (DCOSS) (2008)
17. Schlegl, P., Robatzek, M., Kucera, M., Volbert, K., Waas, T.: Performance analysis of mobile radio for automatic control in smart grids. In: Second International Conference on Advances in Computing, Communication and Information Technology (CCIT 2014) (2014)
18. Wagn, Q., Zhu, Y., Cheng, L.: Reprogramming wireless sensor networks: challenges and approaches. IEEE Netw. **20**, 48–55 (2006)
19. Karp, R., Koutsoupias, E., Papadimitriou, C., Shenker, S.: Optimization problems in congestion control. In: Proceedings of FOCS 2000. IEEE Computer Society (2000)
20. Brown, S., Sreenan, C.J.: Software updating in wireless sensor networks: a survey and lacunae. J. Sens. Actuator Netw. **2**, 717–760 (2013). ISSN 2224–2708
21. Kenner, S., Volbert, K.: A low-power, tricky and very easy to use sensor network gateway architecture with application example. In: 10th International Conference on Sensor Technologies and Applications (SENSORCOMM 2016) (2016)
22. Lukovszki, T., Schindelhauer, C., Volbert, K.: Resource efficient maintenance of wireless network topologies. J. Univers. Comput. Sci. (J. UCS) **12**, 1292–1311 (2006)
23. Schwindl, T., Volbert, K., Bock, S.: Fast and reliable update protocols in WSNs during software development, testing and deployment. In: 7th International Conference on Sensor Networks (Sensornets 2018) (2018)
24. Stathopoulos, T., Heidemann, J., Estrin, D.: A remote code update mechanism for wireless sensor networks. Center for Embedded Networked Sensing (2003)
25. TI: CC430 family - user's guide (2013)
26. TI: MSP430^{TM} SoC with RF core (2013)
27. TI: MSP430F5510, MSP430F550X mixed-signal microcontrollers (2015)
28. TI: MSP gang programmer (MSP-GANG) (2017)
29. Jacobson, V.: Congestion avoidance and control. SIGCOMM Comput. Commun. Rev. **18**(4), 314–329 (1988)

Indoor Localization System Using Ultra Low-Power Radio Landmarks Based on Radio Signal Strength and Travel Time

Fabian Höflinger[1](✉), Joan Bordoy[2], Rui Zhang[2], Yitong Quan[1],
Amir Bannoura[1], Nikolas Simon[1], Leonhard Reindl[1], Christian Schindelhauer[2],
and Zhi Wang[3]

[1] Department of Microsystems Engineering, University of Freiburg,
Freiburg im Breisgau, Germany
`fabian.hoeflinger@imtek.uni-freiburg.de`
[2] Department of Computer Science, University of Freiburg,
Freiburg im Breisgau, Germany
[3] School of Control Science and Engineering, Zhejiang University, Hangzhou, China

Abstract. In this paper we present a novel indoor localization system to track the emergency responders using landmarks network. The low-power landmarks are small and cost-efficient and can be integrated into the building infrastructure, such as smoke detectors with very long operation duration thanks to radio wake-up technology. During the sleep mode the landmarks consumes only $66\,\mu\mathrm{W}$ and can maintain its operation up to 5 years. The positioning is achieved by combining the either the radio strength or UWB travel time and IMU based dead reckoning to overcome the disadvantages such as error due to multipath propagation and sensor drift. The experimental results show that the proposed system using either radio strength or radio travel time based ranging is able to outperform both standalone systems and meanwhile maintain the low power consumption.

Keywords: Indoor localization · Ultra-wideband · On-demand · Wake-up · Low power

1 Introduction

In the recent decade, a growing demand in precise wireless indoor locating systems could be observed [1,2] so that indoor location services, such as locating victims in avalanches or earthquakes, injured skier on ski slope, military personnel, fire fighters or lost children, can be delivered. However, in contrast to this increasing demand, the technology for reliable indoor navigation is still in its infancy, since these applications need very high accuracy requirements, low power consumption and low complexity. Nowadays most of indoor locating technologies can be divided into acoustic, optical, and radio frequency methods. The last type of methods can be divided into continuous wave, for example, WLAN

© Springer Nature Switzerland AG 2019
C. Benavente-Peces et al. (Eds.): SENSORNETS 2017/2018, CCIS 1074, pp. 98–117, 2019.
https://doi.org/10.1007/978-3-030-30110-1_6

or RFID, and impulse signals. Unfortunately, the above mentioned technologies either cannot fulfill the criteria of high accuracy or low power consumption required by indoor location service applications.

2   State-of-the-Art

Many non-GPS localization systems based on various technologies have been developed [3]. Most of them can be classified into absolute and relative localization systems.

Absolute localization systems normally require external references that consists of fixed landmarks such as Wi-Fi access points [4] or ultra-wide band systems [2] to determine the position by measuring the Received Signal Strength Indicator (RSSI) or the Time of Arrival (ToA)/Difference of Arrival (TDoA). Due to its high energy consumption, such systems are required either to be connected to the power grid or frequent battery charging/replacement. As a result, such system are not suitable for catastrophic scenarios due to its high installation costs and power consumption.

The most commonly used relative non-GPS indoor localization approach is inertial measurement units (IMU) based dead reckoning. The IMU can be attached to the body or mount on the shoe of the rescue forces [5–8]. In this approach, the relative positioning is obtained in a recursive manner, i.e. the direction and the distance relative to the initial state are calculated via integration of acceleration and gyroscope data. Therefore, no external reference or pre-installation is needed. The system can also be powered by small size batteries. The main drawback of such systems is that the error will be accumulated over time due to drift of the sensors. Therefore, several approaches have been developed [9–11] to minimize such error. Nevertheless, standalone IMU based localization systems are not capable of providing sufficient accuracy for long term measurements, especially if the nature of movements is unsteady, which is often the case during rescue operations.

In order to fulfill the requirements of the indoor location application such as very high accuracy requirements, low power consumption and low complexity, one should decrease the system energy consumption especially for absolute localization systems and increase the tracking accuracy of the system. By applying wake-up technology, the power consumption can be significantly reduced. By combining both absolute and relative localization systems, the tracking accuracy can be greatly enhanced.

3   Concept Overview

In this paper we present a indoor localization system using landmarks based on low-power wake-up nodes which can be integrated into smoke detectors. As a central component of this system we have developed a handheld device that serves as a master node to communicate with our landmarks. The difference between this study and our previous work [12] is that we have developed a new handheld device equipped with the Ultra-Wide-Band (UWB) transceiver and the new UWB landmarks. In this way, the handheld device broadcasts a wake-up message and measures not only the Received Signal Strength Indicator (RSSI) of each answer received from the previous landmarks but also the Round Trip Time (RTT) from the new UWB landmarks. Both measurement data will be used to calculate the current position of the handheld device by master node.

The advantage of UWB is that UWB signal can effectively penetrate through a variety of materials inside building, such as walls, doors and furniture. Due to its broad range of the UWB frequency spectrum including low frequencies as well. And these low frequencies signal have long wavelengths, allowing them to penetrate a variety of materials. Besides, UWB system uses carrierless, very short-duration-pulses (nanosecond) for information transmission and reception. The duration of pulses is so short that the reflected pulses have a very short time-window of opportunity to collide with the Line-of-Sight (LOS) signals, thus less likely to cause degradation. This property makes UWB system less sensitive to multipath propagation and make UWB a very good candidate for indoor localization using RTT measurements. For this study, although the radio RSSI based system has many similar advantages, the RSS values will significantly decrease if there is obstacles between handheld device and landmarks, resulting incorrect distance estimation. Moreover, RSS is much more sensitive to environmental changes than RTT, making RTT more reliable measurement for many localization applications.

Similar as our previous work, the handheld device is able to receive inertial sensor data of our wireless IMU which can be integrated in shoes. The additional information allows movement tracking between two wake-up events to increase localization accuracy. Moreover, due to the high short-distance accuracy of inertial data based localization, the number of wake-up events can be reduced and hence lifetime of the reference landmarks is increased.

4   Hardware Design

In the following section the main components of the hardware are described:

4.1   Handheld Device

The developed prototype of our new handheld devices also consists of two parts: The credit-card sized low-power computer BeagleBone Black with a compatible touchscreen and our developed expansion circuit board integrated with UWB transceiver module, as shown in Fig. 1.

As shown in Fig. 2 our developed expansion circuit board is made up of two wireless modules, a power management module, UWB module and an EEPROM. The UWB module DWM-1000 is operated to measure the distance based on RTT principle. One of the wireless modules communicates with our wake-up nodes by transmitting wake-up messages (wake-up message details see Gamm et al. [14]) if requested by the computer and receiving the answers of the landmarks. The other

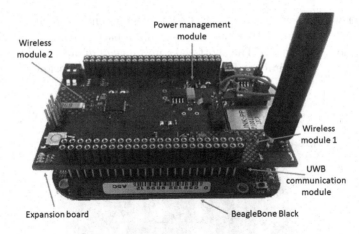

Fig. 1. Expansion board stacked on top of the credit-card sized low-power computer BeagleBone Black [13]. The UWB transceiver module is integrated on the back of the expansion board.

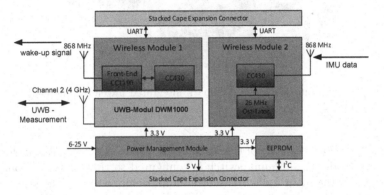

Fig. 2. Block diagram of the expansion board with its components for radio RSSI ranging and UWB RTT ranging. The board is stacked on the BeagleBone Black for communication and power supply.

one receives inertial sensor data from our wireless IMU. Both wireless modules use a CC430 low-power microcontroller from Texas Instruments to communicate on a frequency of 868 MHz with the appropriate component. To extend the wake-up range of the system an additional front-end amplifier CC1190 is used for the wireless module. Furthermore, each controller uses a separate UART connection to transfer the received data to the BeagleBone Black computer via the cape expansion connectors.

4.2   Low-Power Wake-Up Landmarks

Our developed landmarks, shown in Figs. 3 and 4 are based on a wake-up technology presented in Gamm et al. [14] which uses a 125 kHz wake-up receiver.

Low power wake-up receivers are used for keyless go entry systems in automotives. They are built to work a long time without a battery change and therefore operate at low frequencies. The short wake-up range of about 3 m due to inductive coupling is of no limiting factor for the keyless go application.

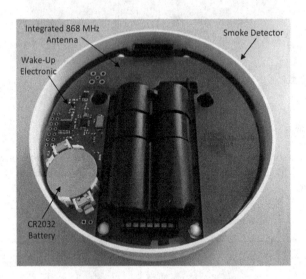

Fig. 3. Top view of our developed landmark integrated into a commercially available smoke detector [12].

In Fig. 5 a block diagram of the wake-up landmark is shown. When the node is in active mode, the antenna switch is configured so that all in and outgoing signals pass to the main radio transceiver chip. Before entering the sleep mode, the microcontroller toggles the antenna switch. All incoming signals during sleep mode are then routed to the analog circuit consisting of impedance matching, rectifying and low pass filtering. The incoming 868 MHz wake-up signal is passively demodulated by a rectifier and filtered. The passive demodulation and the analog path is an important factor in the performance of the wake-up receiver since non-ideal impedance matching will result in a shorter wake-up distance. The analog path of the presented node consists of a matching network, two demodulation diodes and a low pass filtering circuit. The RF Schottky demodulator diodes are connected as a typical voltage doubler circuit. Its purpose is to rectify the modulated RF carrier signal. Because of the OOK modulation of the carrier signal the rectifier charges a capacitor of a low pass filter up to a certain value during the ON period of the carrier. When the carrier is turned OFF the capacitor is discharged through a resistor. This way, a triangular signal is generated with a frequency of 125 kHz. Afterwards, the signal is coupled to the wake-up receiver through a capacitor in order to remove any DC offset.

The filtered signal is then passed to the input of the wake-up receiver IC. In our node we used the AS3932 wake-up receiver from Austriamicrosystems.

Fig. 4. Front and back view of the UWB prototype landmark. Notice that at the moment UWB landmark prototype is not yet integratable into the smoke detector. The integration will be conducted in the near future.

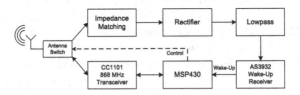

Fig. 5. Block diagram of the wake-up circuit in our landmarks [14].

It consumes in one channel listening mode 2.7 μA current and has a wake-up sensitivity of 100 μVRMS as well as a high input impedance of 2 MΩ. One of the main reasons for choosing the AS3932 is that it has an integrated correlator which compares the received signal to a byte pattern saved in a configuration register.

In case of a positive correlation of the incoming signal with an internal saved 16-Bit sequence the wake-up receiver changes the state of one of its output pins. This signal change is fed to an interrupt capable input port of the microcontroller. The generated interrupt triggers the controller from its sleep to active mode. When entering the active mode, the controller again toggles the antenna switch so that the main radio transceiver is connected to the antenna. The node can then establish a normal communication link, e.g. send an acknowledge or send a message for the RSSI-Measurement between landmark and the handheld device.

While listening for a wake-up packet the standby current of the node is about 2.78 μA which results in a standby power consumption of 5.6 μW. Using a CR2032 coin cell battery with a capacity Q_{Bat} of 230 mAh as power supply we have to take an additional self-discharge current of about 263 nA into account. Therefore, the overall current consumption of the node in sleep mode sums up to 3.044 μA. After the node has been in this mode for t_{sleep} the remaining charge of the battery Q_{Left} can be calculated with the following Eq. 1. Therefore, the theoretical maximum lifetime of the node without any wake-up is 8.62 years.

$$Q_{Left} = Q_{Bat} - t_{sleep} \cdot I_{sleep} \tag{1}$$

Assuming a maximum current consumption of 15 mA during a sending process which takes about 13 ms the theoretical maximum operating time of our landmarks after t_{sleep} can be calculated using Eq. 2.

$$T_{maxOp} = \frac{Q_{Left} \cdot T_{Wakeup}}{T_{Send} \cdot I_{Send} + (T_{Wakeup} - T_{Send}) \cdot I_{Sleep}} \tag{2}$$

Once the system is in operation the wake-up period T_{Wakeup} dominates the power consumption and thus the maximum life time of our nodes [14]. Figure 6 shows the negative linear behaviour of the remaining operating time for three different wake-up periods after the node has been sleeping for t_{sleep}.

As a guidance system for emergency responders the operating temperature range is an important criteria. Table 1 shows that our crystal is the most critical component which limits operation theoretically to a temperature range of $-10\,°C$ to $70\,°C$. However, our practical tests have shown that a successful communication with our nodes is possible within a temperature range of $-20\,°C$ to $115\,°C$ as shown in Fig. 7. Notice that the radio frequency from the quartz oscillator changes when the temperature varies. Beyond $100\,°C$ the reception bandwidth of receiver can not detect the transmitted radio frequency any more.

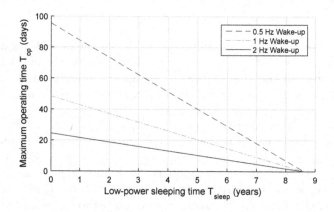

Fig. 6. This figure shows the maximum theoretical operating time of a landmark for different wake-up frequencies after it has been in its ultra-low power state for T_{sleep} [12].

With this technology we build a real-time capable low-power landmark with a theoretical maximum standby time which is comparable with the one of commercially available smoke detectors. Therefore, we adapted our circuit board design to be able to integrate the nodes in this existing infrastructure and hence ease the hardware setup to have a system which is ready-to-use in case of a catastrophic scenario (Fig. 3).

Table 1. Temperature range of critical components [12].

Component	Operating temperature	
	Min. (°C)	Max. (°C)
MSP430F2350	−40	85
CC1101	−40	85
ADG918	−40	85
AS3932	−40	85
HSMS285C	−65	150
Balun 868	−40	125
Crystal	−10	70

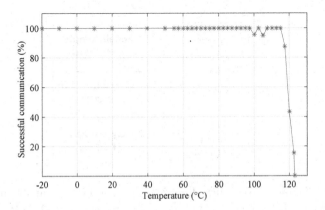

Fig. 7. Our measurements show a successful communication within a temperature range of −20 °C to 115 °C [12].

The sensitivity has been measured in by using a signal generator. A successful wake-up was observed up to an attenuation of −52 dBm [14]. Through improved impedance matching a wake-up distance of up to 80 m is possible at 20 dBm power output [15].

For landmark equipped with UWB technology, due to the additional UWB module integrated into the hardware, the energy consumption is different. The basic consumption of the node in standby mode for one day is about 0.48 mAh. If the system is operated with a LiPo battery with a capacity of 1200 mAh (80%), the battery life for a basic consumption of is about 5.5 Years. If 100 distance measurements are carried out in one day, it will decrease the battery life to 0.42 years.

4.3 Micro-Inertial Measurement Unit (IMU)

Our wireless micro-IMU V3 [16] used in this application, has already been successfully used for short-distance indoor motion tracking of pedestrians when mounted on a shoe [7]. With its small size of 22 mm × 14 mm × 4 mm the micro IMU is in this application mounted on a shoe and transmits its sampled sensor data wirelessly to our receiver, the handheld device. Concerning this, a CC430 microcontroller from Texas Instruments is used to transmit the data at 868 MHz. Besides the controller the micro IMU consists of a three-axis accelerometer, a three-axis gyroscope and a three-axis magnetometer as well as a voltage regulator (see Fig. 8). The raw data of the sensors can be sent with a maximum rate of 640 samples per second. Thereby, data post processing is done by the receiver to increase the performance of the IMU. More details about metrological characteristics can be found in Hoeflinger et al. [7].

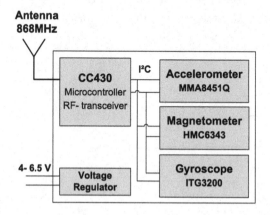

Fig. 8. Block diagram of the Micro-IMU V3 [17]. The IMU is capable of transmitting acceleration, magnetic field and angle velocity sensor data via its 868 MHz radio module.

Fig. 9. Topview of the micro-IMU V3 which is mounted on a shoe [12].

5 Localization

5.1 Problem Setting

The low power wake-up nodes are placed randomly at unknown stationary positions $\mathbf{S}_j$ $(1 \leq j \leq B)$. For simplicity, we assume they are located in a two-dimensional Euclidean space. The handheld device $\mathbf{H}$ moves in the two-dimensional Euclidean space, waking up the nodes and measuring the signal strength (RSSI) (Fig. 9).

5.2 Range Estimation

The handheld device is located at a distance d from the node j:

$$d = \|\mathbf{H} - \mathbf{S}_j\| \tag{3}$$

where $\| \cdot \|$ denotes the Euclidean norm.

RSSI Ranging. For radio RSSI based ranging, the relation between d and the RSSI measurements can be modelled as follows [18]:

$$P_R = \frac{G_t G_r}{4\pi} P_T \frac{g^2 \gamma}{d^n} \tag{4}$$

where P_T is the transmitted power, G_t and G_r are the transmitter and the receiver gains, respectively, n is the path loss exponent, and g and γ are the parameters that conform the Rayleigh/Rician and lognormal distributions, respectively.

Assuming the received signals are averaged over a certain time interval, the fast fading term can be eliminated. Thus, the logarithmic equation which relates the received signal strength and the distance can be formulated as follows [18,19]:

$$P_R(dBm) = \alpha - 10n \log_{10}(d) + \chi \tag{5}$$

where χ denotes a Gaussian random variable with zero mean caused by shadowing. The term α is a constant which depends on the averaged slow and fast fading, the transmitted power and the gains of the antennas. Figure 10 depicts the relation between received signal strength and the distance in this application.

The parameters of the theoretical model which relates the received signal strength and the distance (see Eq. (5)) are estimated by collecting measurements from 5 nodes in 7 different positions in a corridor. The best fit to the real measurements are a path loss exponent of 7.1 and a constant α equal to 89.7 (see Fig. 10).

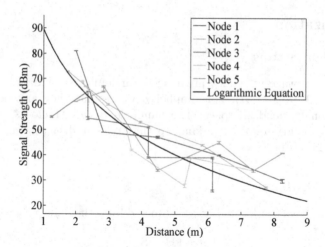

Fig. 10. Real and modeled relation between the received signal strength and the distance between the node and the hand-held device. The uncertainty bars show the standard deviation of the signal strength after the 5% highest and the 5% lowest RSSI signals for each distance have been rejected [12].

UWB RTT Ranging. For UWB RTT based ranging, the distance d is calculated using the signal travel time Δt between the sending time the receipt time, based on the relation:

$$d = \Delta t \cdot c, \qquad (6)$$

where c is the speed of the UWB signal, which is the speed of light, approximately equals to 3×10^8 m/s. In order to measure the above mentioned signal travel time, Time of Arrival (TOA) should be determined. However, TOA requires a precise time synchronization between each pair of mobile tag and anchor nodes, since the signal travel time is calculated base on the local timestamps of these devices.

To avoid the time synchronization, Round Trip Time (RTT) can be used. The principle of RTT is shown in Fig. 11. In this procedure, two messages are sent sequentially.

In this procedure, two messages are sent sequentially. The first message is sent from the anchor node to the mobile tag. Then the mobile tag reply to the anchor node after some delay, due to internal processing in mobile tag, or due to the purpose of making specified transmission time predictable and aligned with the transmit timestamp. In Fig. 11, t_0, t_3, t_2, t_1 are the timestamps of sending and receiving messages in anchor node mobile tag. After message 1 is received, mobile tag will send t_2, t_1 to anchor node through message 2. The distance can be calculated using these timestamps as (7).

$$d = \frac{(t_0 - t_3) - (t_2 - t_1)}{2} \cdot c, \qquad (7)$$

There are several implementation of RTT, in this UWB application, Double Sided Two Way Ranging (DSTWR) is used. Figure 12 illustrates the operation

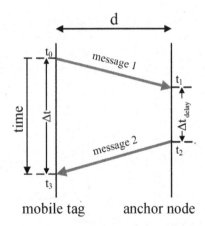

Fig. 11. Principle of RTT.

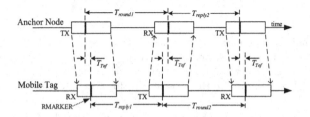

Fig. 12. Illustration of DSTWR.

of DSTWR. The mobile tag first sends a message to the anchor node. Then the anchor node responds back to the mobile tag with another message, which serves as the end of the first RTT measurement and the beginning of the second RTT measurement. Finally, the mobile tag sends back a third message to the anchor node and ends this ranging.

The TOA can be calculated by (8)

$$T_{TOA} = \frac{T_{round1} \cdot T_{round2} - T_{reply1} \cdot T_{reply2}}{T_{round1} + T_{round2} + T_{reply1} + T_{reply2}} \cdot c \tag{8}$$

DSTWR has the advantage of small error in calculating TOA in comparison to the process shown in Fig. 11, and the disadvantage of requiring multiplication and division operations.

5.3 Node and Standing Positions Localization

The continuous movement of the master device results in a system of equations which cannot be solved in closed form, as for every received measurement there are two new variables of position to estimate. Consequently, the equation system is under-determined and cannot be solved in closed form without further information or assumptions on the scenario. Therefore, we assume the master node stops in q different positions $\mathbf{H}_i$, then we have time to receive at least one signal from every node (*stop-and-go motion*). Doing this, it is only required to estimate one handheld device position (2 variables) for every B received signals, which makes possible an uniquely determined system of equations (cf. Fig. 13).

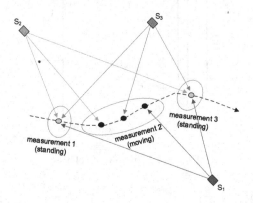

Fig. 13. Schematic of the under-determined equation system. If the firefighter moves continuously, for every new measurement there are two new variables to estimate only for its position. On the other hand, if he stops, his device receives one signal from every node (S_1, S_2 and S_3), leading to three constrains for every two position variables [13].

Then, we obtain a system of hyperbolic equations of the form:

$$f_{p,j} = \|\mathbf{H}_p - \mathbf{S}_j\| - z_{p,j} \tag{9}$$

where $1 \leq j \leq B$ and $1 \leq p \leq q$. The term $z_{p,j}$ is the measured distance between the sender j and the standing position p using either a RSSI measurement with Eq. (5) or RTT measurement.

The system of equations has now qB independent equations, which has to be higher than the number of variables:

$$qB \geq \underbrace{2q}_{\text{Handheld device}} + \underbrace{2B}_{\text{Nodes}} \tag{10}$$

Which means the system of equations can be solved in a closed form if the number of standing still positions q is higher than:

$$q \geq \frac{2B}{B-2} \tag{11}$$

Assuming the *stop-and-go* motion and having a number of standing positions and nodes fulfilling Eq. (11) the system of hyperbolic equations can be solved with local optimization algorithms. We use both the gradient descent and the Gauss-Newton method, the two are first-order methods that use the derivative of the system of hyperbolic error equations. The Eq. (9) results in a quadratic objective which can be formulated as follows:

$$\sum_{p=1}^{q} \sum_{j=1}^{B} \arg \min_{\mathbf{H}_p, \mathbf{S}_j} (f_{p,j})^2. \tag{12}$$

Which in vector notation is proportional to $w = \frac{1}{2}\mathbf{b}^T\mathbf{b}$ with $\mathbf{b} = (f_{1,1}, ..., f_{q,B})^T$. The operator $(\cdot)^T$ denotes the transposition.

We calculate the direction of the steepest ascent:

$$\nabla w = \nabla \left(\frac{1}{2}\mathbf{b}^T\mathbf{b}\right) = \mathbf{Q}^T\mathbf{b} \tag{13}$$

where $\mathbf{Q}$ is the Jacobian matrix:

$$\mathbf{Q} = \begin{bmatrix} \frac{\partial f_{1,1}}{\partial \mathbf{S}_1} & \cdots & \frac{\partial f_{q,B}}{\partial \mathbf{S}_1} \\ \vdots & \ddots & \vdots \\ \frac{\partial f_{1,1}}{\partial \mathbf{S}_B} & \cdots & \frac{\partial f_{q,B}}{\partial \mathbf{S}_B} \\ \frac{\partial f_{1,1}}{\partial \mathbf{H}_1} & \cdots & \frac{\partial f_{q,B}}{\partial \mathbf{H}_1} \\ \vdots & \ddots & \vdots \\ \frac{\partial f_{1,1}}{\partial \mathbf{H}_q} & \cdots & \frac{\partial f_{q,B}}{\partial \mathbf{H}_q} \end{bmatrix}^T \tag{14}$$

The partial derivative with respect to a vector is defined as the derivative with respect to each of its components:

$$\frac{\partial f_{p,j}}{\partial \mathbf{H}_i} = \left(\frac{\partial f_{p,j}}{\partial H_{p,x}}, \frac{\partial f_{p,j}}{\partial H_{p,y}}\right)^T \tag{15}$$

In our case the partial derivative with respect to the node position S_j is:

$$\frac{\partial f_{p,j}}{\partial \mathbf{S}_j} = -\frac{\mathbf{H}_p - \mathbf{S}_j}{\|\mathbf{H}_p - \mathbf{S}_j\|} \tag{16}$$

The partial derivative with respect to the handheld position is:

$$\frac{\partial f_{p,j}}{\partial \mathbf{H}_p} = \frac{\mathbf{H}_p - \mathbf{S}_j}{\|\mathbf{H}_p - \mathbf{S}_j\|} \tag{17}$$

All the variables which need to be estimated are components of the state vector $\mathbf{u}$:

$$\mathbf{u} = (\mathbf{S}_1^T, ..., \mathbf{S}_B^T, \mathbf{H}_1^T, ..., \mathbf{H}_q^T)^T \tag{18}$$

Every iteration the state vector is updated using $\mathbf{Q}$ and $\mathbf{b}$. The methods used are:

The Gradient Descent Method. In every iteration step l the Gradient Descent method updates the state vector in direction of the steepest descent. The adaptive factor λ sets the step width.

$$\hat{\mathbf{u}} = \lambda \nabla w = \lambda \mathbf{Q}^T \mathbf{b}$$
$$\mathbf{u}^{l+1} = \mathbf{u}^l - \hat{\mathbf{u}} \tag{19}$$

The Gauss-Newton Algorithm. Instead of relying on an adaptive factor γ it calculates the step size using the inverse $(\mathbf{Q}^T \mathbf{Q})^{-1}$ for every iteration:

$$\mathbf{u} = (\mathbf{Q}^T \mathbf{Q})^{-1} (\mathbf{Q}^T \mathbf{b}) \tag{20}$$

We calculate for higher numerical stability the pseudo-inverse with singular value decomposition instead of calculating the inverse.

This algorithm is faster, nevertheless it is very prone to divergence when applied to random initial positions. However, it can be used when the Gradient Descent error function has become steady to reduce notably the number of iterations [20].

5.4   Handheld Device Localization. Data Fusion

The IMU has been proved to be capable of tracking pedestrians in indoor areas showing a maximum deviation of $1\,\text{m}$ after a walk of $30\,\text{m}$ [7]. However, it cannot be used as the only source of information due to its accumulative error. In order to solve this, we combine the measurements of the IMU and the anchor nodes using an unscented Kalman filter (UKF). The UKF is a recursive state estimator which fulfils the bayesian filtering model and uses a set of sample points (*sigma points*) to linearise non-linear functions. Therefore, it is cheaper in computation than other similar algorithms like the particle filter, which requires evaluation of a large number of particles, or the extended Kalman filter, which requires calculation of the Jacobian matrix. More detailed information about it and its implementation can be found in [21]. In our case, the state vector $\mathbf{x}_t$ which contains the variables to estimate has the following components:

$$\mathbf{x}_t = \left(\mathbf{M}_t^T, \mathbf{V}_t^T, \mathbf{A}_t^T \right)^T \tag{21}$$

where $\mathbf{M}_t$ is the position of the target, $\mathbf{V}_t$ his velocity and $\mathbf{A}_t$ the acceleration. All of them in a two-dimensional euclidean space.

We use the Weiner process acceleration model [22] in two dimensions.

$$\begin{bmatrix} \mathbf{M}_t \\ \mathbf{V}_t \\ \mathbf{A}_t \end{bmatrix} = \Theta_{t-1} \begin{bmatrix} \mathbf{M}_{t-1} \\ \mathbf{V}_{t-1} \\ \mathbf{A}_{t-1} \end{bmatrix} + \Phi_{t-1} \qquad \Phi_{t-1} \sim \mathcal{N}(0, R_m) \tag{22}$$

where

$$\Theta_t = \begin{bmatrix} 1 & \Delta t & \Delta t^2 \\ 0 & 1 & \Delta t \\ 0 & 0 & 1 \end{bmatrix} \qquad R_m = \tau \begin{bmatrix} \frac{\Delta t^5}{20} & \frac{\Delta t^4}{8} & \frac{\Delta t^3}{6} \\ \frac{\Delta t^4}{8} & \frac{\Delta t^3}{3} & \frac{\Delta t^2}{2} \\ \frac{\Delta t^3}{6} & \frac{\Delta t^2}{2} & \Delta t \end{bmatrix} \tag{23}$$

where τ is a parameter that depends on the expected movement of the target.

In this case we assume each time the nodes are woken up the RSSI or UWB TOA measurements are received at the same position. Then, having RSSI or TOA measurements of N different nodes at time t, the first N components of the predicted measurement vector $\overline{z}_{t,1:N}$ fulfil the following sensor model:

$$\overline{z}_{t,i} = \alpha - 10n \log_{10}(\|\mathbf{M}_t - \mathbf{S}_i\|) + \varrho_t \qquad \varrho_t \sim \mathcal{N}(0, \sigma_r) \tag{24}$$

where σ_r is the expected standard deviation of the RSSI or TOA measurement noise. We combine these measurements with the foot-mounted IMU measurements. The sensors that we use are the accelerometer and the gyroscope.

We remove the effect of the gravity and extract the x and y components of the acceleration by combining the acceleration and the angular rate. More information about this transformation can be found in [23]. Then, the components $N + 1$ and $N + 2$ of the measurement vector are predicted as follows:

$$\overline{z}_{t,N+1:N+2} = \mathbf{A}_t + \nu_t \qquad \nu_t \sim \mathcal{N}(0, \sigma_q) \tag{25}$$

where σ_q is the expected noise of the acceleration measurement.

To reduce the drift of the IMU sensors, we detect when the human being is not moving and we set the velocity and the acceleration to zero, as it is done in [24]. As the IMU has a much higher sampling rate than the nodes, the sensor data fusion is only done when the velocity and acceleration are not set to zero and there is a RSSI measurement or TOA measurement available. In the other cases, the UKF estimates the values using only the IMU measurements.

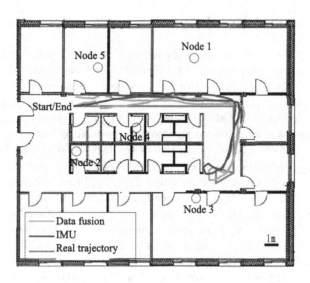

Fig. 14. Master node localization. A person moves continuously with the IMU attached to his shoe. Sensor data fusion is performed to combine the RSSI and the IMU data [12].

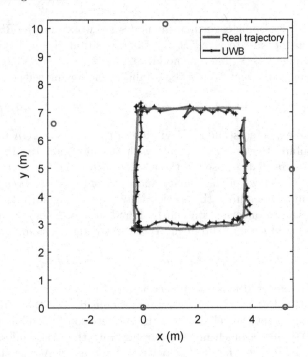

Fig. 15. UWB tracking. A person moves with a square form trajectory. 5 UWB land-marks are shown as red circles. (Color figure online)

6   Experimental Results

In order to test the performance of the sensor data fusion using radio RSSI and UWB RTT ranging, we perform two different experiments with different setup to bring out the best possible performances of both systems. The RSSI ranging experiment is held in narrower path in office building using the same path loss exponent and α mentioned above so that the ranging distance is not too large. The IMU device was attached to the foot of a person to monitor all the detail movement of the foot. The sampling rate of the IMU is 50 Hz and data from the wake-up nodes is received every 3 s. As having only one RSSI measurement can lead to high errors, the measurement noise of the RSSI measurements is increased in this case in order to reflect this uncertainty. In Fig. 14 we can see both the result of using only the IMU and sensor data fusion. The median error using only the IMU is 0.470 m with a standard deviation of 0.332 m while the median error using also the RSSI measurements is 0.276 m with a standard deviation of 0.229 m. Therefore, the error is notably reduced.

Another set of experiments are done with UWB radio signal with IMU in a larger experimental hall. Figure 15 illustrates the experiment setup, in which 5 UWB landmarks were placed in known positions. The wake-up rate and sampling rate of the UWB system are both 1.5 Hz. Figure 15 shows the result of using the UWB comparing to the ground true trajectory. The median error using the UWB is 0.20 m with a standard deviation of 0.090 m. This result shows that our UWB fusion system can achieve a better tracking than the RSSI does.

7   Conclusion and Future Work

In this paper, we have presented two novel indoor localization systems for emergency responders using either 868 MHz or UWB radio landmarks, combined with inertial sensor data. For this system we have developed new wireless landmarks using ultra low-power wake-up technology, which makes them ready-to-use for up to 8 years if powered by a coin cell. The nodes are integrable into building infrastructures like smoke detectors. Moreover, a handheld device has been developed to send initial wake-up calls to the landmarks, measure the RSSI or UWB RTT of the response, and use this data to estimate and display the current position of the firefighter. Additionally, our handheld device is able to receive inertial sensor data by a body-mounted micro-inertial measurement unit (IMU) to increase localization accuracy. The data is fused with an Unscented Kalman filter.

The experimental results demonstrate that using the obtained relation of signal strength and distance the RSSI based system is able to track the handheld device with a median error of 27.6 cm in an indoor environment. While using the Ultra-Wide-Band (UWB) technology, the system is able to locate our moving target with a median error of 20 cm, which is about 25% less than the one using RSSI. Therefore, we will focus more on developing UWB technology based tag and landmark and integrating UWB landmark inside the smoke detector housing.

In addition, it can be clearly seen that UWB based trajectory is less smooth than the one using RSSI. It might be due to the fact that the algorithm still has difficulty to detect the UWB RTT outliers. Notice that the algorithm will put less weight on IMU during fusion when UWB RTT is not considered as outlier. As mentioned in the previous study, we plan in the future to investigate and adapt more reliable estimators that explicitly consider outlier error mitigation and detection, e.g. RANSAC [1], or robust regression [25] for the proposed system so that system robustness can be further enhanced.

Acknowledgements. This work has partly been supported by the German Federal State Postgraduate Scholarships Act (Landesgraduiertenförderungsgesetz - LGFG) within the cooperative graduate school "Decentralized sustainable energy systems".

References

1. Bordoy, J., Wendeberg, J., Schindelhauer, C., Höfflinger, F., Reindl, L.M.: Exploiting ground reflection for robust 3D smartphone localization. In: 2016 International Conference on Indoor Positioning and Indoor Navigation (IPIN), pp. 1–6. IEEE (2016)

2. Kuhn, M., Zhang, C., Lin, S., Mahfouz, M., Fathy, A.E.: A system level design approach to UWB localization. In: IEEE MTT-S International Microwave Symposium Digest, MTT 2009, pp. 1409–1412. IEEE (2009)

3. Fischer, C., Gellersen, H.: Location and navigation support for emergency responders: a survey. IEEE Pervasive Comput. **9**, 38–47 (2010)

4. Bahl, P., Padmanabhan, V.N.: RADAR: an in-building RF-based user location and tracking system. In: Proceedings of INFOCOM 2000: Nineteenth Annual Joint Conference of the IEEE Computer and Communications Societies, vol. 2, pp. 775–784. IEEE (2000)

5. Hoeflinger, F., Mueller, J., Zhang, R., Reindl, L.M., Burgard, W.: A wireless micro inertial measurement unit (IMU). IEEE Trans. Instrum. Meas. **62**, 2583–2595 (2013)

6. Zhang, R., Hoeflinger, F., Reindl, L.: Inertial sensor based indoor localization and monitoring system for emergency responders. IEEE Sens. J. **13**, 838–848 (2013)

7. Hoeflinger, F., Zhang, R., Reindl, L.M.: Indoor-localization system using a micro-inertial measurement unit (IMU). In: European Frequency and Time Forum (EFTF), 2012, pp. 443–447. IEEE (2012)

8. Nilsson, J.O., Rantakokko, J., Händel, P., Skog, I., Ohlsson, M., Hari, K.: Accurate indoor positioning of firefighters using dual foot-mounted inertial sensors and inter-agent ranging. In: Proceedings of the Position, Location and Navigation Symposium (PLANS), 2014. IEEE/ION (2014)

9. Zhang, R., Hoeflinger, F., Gorgis, O., Reindl, L.: Indoor localization using inertial sensors and ultrasonic rangefinder. In: 2011 International Conference on Wireless Communications and Signal Processing (WCSP), pp. 1–5. IEEE (2011)

10. Fang, L., et al.: Design of a wireless assisted pedestrian dead reckoning system-the navmote experience. IEEE Trans. Instrum. Meas. **54**, 2342–2358 (2005)

11. Zhang, R., Reindl, L.: Pedestrian motion based inertial sensor fusion by a modified complementary separate-bias Kalman filter. In: 2011 IEEE Sensors Applications Symposium (SAS), pp. 209–213. IEEE (2011)

12. Hoeflinger, F., et al.: Localization system based on ultra low-power radio landmarks. In: Proceedings of the 7th International Conference on Sensor Networks, vol. 1, pp. 51–59 (2018)

13. Simon, N., et al.: Indoor localization system for emergency responders with ultra low-power radio landmarks. In: International Instrumentation and Measurement Technology Conference (I2MTC) (2015)

14. Gamm, G., Kostic, M., Sippel, M., Reindl, L.M.: Low power sensor node with addressable wake-up on demand capability. Int. J. Sens. Netw. **11**, 48–56 (2012)

15. Gamm, G., Sester, S., Sippel, M., Reindl, L.M.: SmartGate - connecting wireless sensor nodes to the internet. J. Sens. Sens. Syst. **2**, 45–50 (2013)

16. Fehrenbach, P.: Entwicklung einer inertialsensorik zur analyse von schwimmbewegungen (2014)

17. Fehrenbach, P.: Entwicklung einer inertialsensorik zur analyse von schwimmbewegungen. Master's thesis, University of Freiburg (2014)

18. Qi, Y.: Wireless geolocation in a non-line-of-sight environment. Ph.D. thesis, Princeton University (2003)

19. Mazuelas, S., et al.: Robust indoor positioning provided by real-time RSSI values in unmodified wlan networks. IEEE J. Sel. Top. Signal Process. **3**, 821–831 (2009)

20. Wendeberg, J., Höflinger, F., Schindelhauer, C., Reindl, L.: Calibration-free TDOA self-localization. J. Locat. Based Serv. **7**, 121–144 (2013)

21. Thrun, S., Burgard, W., Fox, D.: Probabilistic Robotics. MIT Press, Cambridge (2005)

22. Bar-Shalom, Y., Li, X.R., Kirubarajan, T.: Estimation with Applications to Tracking and Navigation. Wiley-Interscience (2001)
23. Kuipers, J.: Quaternions and Rotation Sequences. Princeton Paperbacks, Princeton (2002)
24. Woodman, O., Harle, R.: Pedestrian localisation for indoor environments. In: Proceedings of the 10th International Conference on Ubiquitous Computing, pp. 114–123. ACM (2008)
25. Bordoy, J., Schindelhauer, C., Zhang, R., Höflinger, F., Reindl, L.M.: Robust extended Kalman filter for NLOS mitigation and sensor data fusion. In: 2017 IEEE International Symposium on Inertial Sensors and Systems (INERTIAL), pp. 117–120. IEEE (2017)

Promoting Exercise in Wheelchairs Through Wireless Sensing and Computing in a Mobile App

James Sunthonlap, Kevin Monsalvo, James Velasco, Jackson Tu,
Christine Ong, Omar Ochoa, James Enciso, Isaac Bowser, Amit Pal,
Ray D. de Leon, Roxanna Pebdani, Christine Dy, Stefan Keslacy,
and Deborah S. Won[✉]

Department of Electrical and Computer Engineering,
California State University, Los Angeles, CA 90032, USA
dwon@calstatela.edu

Abstract. Individuals with lower mobility impairment face many barriers to regular, appropriately intense exercise. To combat these barriers and the resulting cardiometabolic disease risk, we are developing a mobile fitness system to promote and facilitate exercises which can be done in wheelchairs in the convenience of one's home. This mobile fitness system exploits computing and wireless sensing to promote exercise in a number of ways: (A) monitoring a fitness metric which users find a reliable and trustworthy; (B) gamifying exercises; (C) healthy, friendly competition with other users; and (D) providing text notifications as reminders to exercise.

Keywords: Activity monitor · Fitness monitor · Exergaming · EMG ·
Wireless sensors · METS estimation

1 Benefits of and Barriers to Exercise for Individuals in Wheelchairs

Individuals with lower mobility impairment, due to injury or disease, are at a much higher risk of cardiometabolic disease and suffer other physical and mental health issues which result in lower quality of life measures; in particular, those with spinal cord injury are 2.7 times more likely to have cardiovascular disease than healthy controls [1–5]. Exercise has been shown to combat all these factors in quality of life [5–8]. The barriers to regular exercise at prescribed quantities and intensity levels are numerous, ranging from limited access to adapted gyms, to the expense of regular professional physical therapy, the inconvenience of transportation to gyms or clinics, to large and expensive equipment that is not practical for everyday home use [9–12]. We address these issues by developing

Supported by Department of Education, NIDILRR grant #90IFS0001-01-00.

C. Benavente-Peces et al. (Eds.): SENSORNETS 2017/2018, CCIS 1074, pp. 118–134, 2019.
https://doi.org/10.1007/978-3-030-30110-1_7

a mobile app system which is designed to promote and facilitate exercise and overcome the limitations which hamper motivation to exercise [10,13–15]. This system development is part of a larger project called the DREAM project at California State University, Los Angeles (Disability, Rehabilitation, Engineering Access for Minorities Project), in which the goal is to promote cardiovascular health and an active lifestyle, and consequently quality of life, for those with mobility impairment. Thus, we have named our mobility fitness system DREAM Moblie Fitness.

2   System Design Overview

The DREAM Mobile Fitness system conveniently consists of multiple body-worn wireless sensors and a mobile phone app (Fig. 1). In Fig. 2, a DREAM Fitness user can be seen donning the sensors and performing resistance arm band exercises from the wheelchair while playing one of the exergames on the DREAM mobile app.

Fig. 1. System components of the DREAM exercise monitor [16]: (A) Dynofit's Flexdot wireless EMG sensor; (B) the DREAM mobile app; (C) the custom packaged wireless IMU board; (D) Mio Global's Alpha 2 heart rate monitor (Mio Global, Vancouver, British Columbia).

The design of our system architecture, as described above and shown in Fig. 3, include a number of features which are expected to achieve the goal of promoting and facilitating exercises from a wheelchair. These features and the rationale for including them in the design are given here:

– Mobile platform - allows user to exercise any where, and in particular at home. Exergaming on a mobile app at home without needing assistance is expected to give the user a sense of independence in daily activities.
– Real-time wireless sensing of energy expenditure - allows for exercises to control game outcome so that the user will achieve greater fitness levels just by playing the game, and aiming for a higher score.

- Multi-modal sensing - overcomes limitations of unreliability of accelerometry alone or heart rate alone, and incorporating EMG allows isometric contractions to still count toward caloric expenditure metric. Essentially allows for a more accurate model of energy expenditure from practical, available wireless sensors, so that user actually trusts in the game score, which consequently, provides more motivation to achieve a high score, and therefore to exercise more. Encouraging feedback.
- User profiles and cloud communication - allows for social engagement and another way to motivate the user to exercise. The app has the capability to access individual's data during exercises and creates a leaderboard as well as play back saved data to simulate a multiplayer game or to play a live multiplayer game (see Sect. 5).
- Cloud storage of user data - communicate long-term trends to encourage feedback to the user.

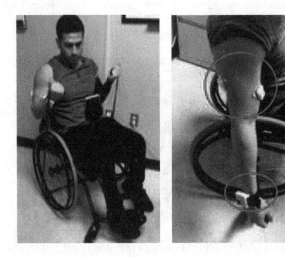

Fig. 2. Physical setup of the DREAM mobile fitness system. User dons wireless sensors (EMG Flexdots and custom IMU device) and exercises in wheelchair while monitoring progress on DREAM mobile app.

Table 1. Performance specifications.

	EMG	HR	IMU
Output metric	Integrated envelope	Heart rate	Wrist acceleration
Units	% of max. isometric	Beats per minute	m/s^2
Sampling rate (samples/sec)	60	1	4
Input range	$\pm300\ \mu V$	0–200 bpm	±8 g
Resolution	440 μV (12-bit)	1 bpm	940 μg (14-bit)
Current consumption (active mode)	3 mA	<1 mA	12.5 mA
Battery life (hrs of active use)	73 h	300 h	41 h
Cost	$100 per unit	$50	$38

The performance specifications of the DREAM mobile system are provided in Table 1.

3 Sensor Characterization and Testing

The DREAM Mobile Fitness app can communicate with a heart rate monitor, multiple EMG sensors, and a custom accelerometer. In order to determine the most suitable fitness metric, the system was designed to acquire heart rate, end-point acceleration, and EMG, the former two being prevalent already in fitness trackers, the latter being a novel signal to include in a fitness tracker.

The DREAM app works with one of two commercial heart rate monitors: the wristworn Alpha 2 (Mio Global, Vancouver, British Columbia) or the Tikr (Wahoo Fitness, Atlanta, GA). These off-the-shelf heart rate monitors can be used in the DREAM development platform because the Tikr transmits data via the ANT+ wireless protocol. Thus, the DREAM app can communicate directly with the Tikr without need for any proprietary information. However, the top-of-the-line accelerometers that are most often used in activity monitoring in the literature pose the same issues that the wireless EMG did; namely, they require connection to a PC and proprietary software. From preliminary data, we had already seen that accelerometry alone would not provide sufficiently accurate feedback about energy consumption. Therefore, we custom built a wearable BLE-based wireless inertial monitoring unit module, and incorporated a novel EMG sensor. We describe these latter two sensors here.

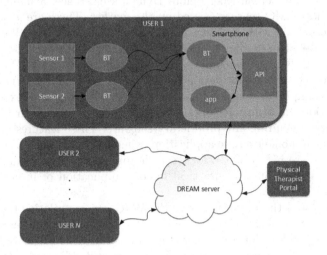

Fig. 3. Schematic system diagram of DREAM mobile fitness system architecture [16]. The physical therapist portal will be included in the next generation of the DREAM mobile fitness system.

3.1 Standalone EMG Sensor

A novel standalone sensor, fully packaged with analog front end board, Bluetooth
Low Energy transceiver, and coin cell battery (Dynofit, Inc. Carrollton, TX),
measures muscle activity (or EMG) and is pictured in Fig. 4.

Fig. 4. Flexdot components [16]: the plastic housing for the signal processing circuitry,
with 3 female snap connections, a 3V-coin cell battery, and the disposable snap electrodes (Medtronic Covidien PLC, Minneapolis, MN).

We selected the Flexdot based on a trade analysis shown in [16]. At the time
of developing the DREAM fitness system, Dynofit's Flexdots were a completely
novel EMG sensor. In fact, the sensors we incorporated into our design were
Dynofit's first commercial sale. Before Dynofit's existence, a number of commercial wireless EMG sensors existed on the market. These are generally high
performance sensors with excellent noise cancellation, motion artifact suppres-
sion, and overall signal to noise ratio. However, to the authors' knowledge, all of
these wireless EMG sensors require a receiver base station and a PC workstation
with proprietary software for data acquisition. We selected the Dynofit Flexdot
for EMG sensing because of its standalone capability; i.e., the Flexdot requires
no base station but transmits data wirelessly through Bluetooth Low Energy
(BLE) without requiring any proprietary software. These features make it well
suited for our in-home exercise application, whereas the other high performance
EMG systems are better suited for research applications or patient assessment
in a clinical setting but not practical for our application of in-home exercise
monitoring.

We also tested the performance of the EMG sensors relative to one of the
top-of-the-line wireless EMG commercial systems, which we treat as our experimental control. A Flexdot was adhered to the muscle belly of the right bicep; a
control sensor was adhered to the muscle belly as well, adjacent to the Flexdot.
EMG was acquired from both systems for 60 s during bicep curl exercises and
isometric contractions. The EMG envelope was obtained by full-wave rectifying
the raw EMG, and then applying a moving average filter with a rectangular window of 100 ms. Figure 5 illustrates that the envelope was appropriately obtained
from the raw EMG. Both envelope amplitudes were normalized to range between
0 and 1 (Fig. 6).

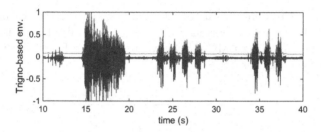

Fig. 5. EMG envelope superimposed on the raw EMG acquired from the Trigno sensor [16].

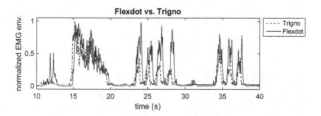

Fig. 6. Comparison of EMG envelope acquired from the Dynofit Flexdot by the DREAM app and the EMG envelope obtained from Delsys Trigno [16].

The envelope obtained from each of the sensors were compared, as shown in Fig. 4. The Flexdots provided the necessary information we needed with sufficient accuracy and temporal precision for our application.

To help confirm that the differences were more likely due to differences in post-processing schema than to physical characteristics, such as size and location of the electrodes, we conducted another test. This time, the subject performed bicep curls with elastic arm bands (TheraBand, Akron, OH) at 3 levels of increasing resistance. Recordings were taken from a Trigno sensor placed on the left arm slightly proximal to the center of the muscle belly, and a Flexdot sensor placed just distal to the Trigno sensor, such that they both overlapped with the center of the muscle belly. On the right arm, we had the converse placement of sensors, as seen in Fig. 7.

Fig. 7. Placement of wireless EMG sensors. Left arm: Trigno sensor placed more proximally, Flexdot sensor more distally. Right arm: Flexdot sensor placed more proximally, Trigno more distally [16].

Five bicep curls were conducted at each resistance level. To increase the resistance level, we merely shortened the theraband to fixed lengths (of 80, 60, and 40 cm). The resulting EMG envelopes are shown in Fig. 8 for the left arm, and Fig. 9 for the right arm.

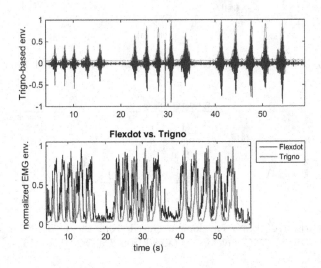

Fig. 8. Comparison of Trigno-derived vs. Flexdot-derived EMG envelopes (from left arm) with Trigno sensor more proximal, Flexdot more distal [16].

The increasing amplitude of the Trigno envelope corresponds with the increasing resistance of the arm bands. It is possible that the Flexdot envelope

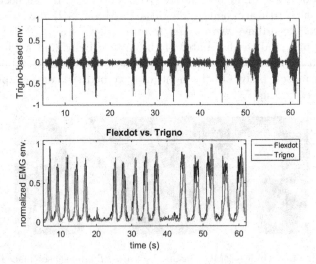

Fig. 9. Comparison of Trigno-derived vs. Flexdot-derived EMG envelopes (from right arm) with Trigno sensor more distal, Flexdot more proximal [16].

has an adaptive gain that was designed to maximize use of the dynamic range at all times. The Flexdot performs very well in terms of temporal resolution, which in our application is critical. How accurate the amplitude needs to be in order to provide a motivating, reliable fitness metric to potential DREAM app users has yet to be researched. Adjustment of the EMG envelope amplitude is expected to require a straightforward adjustment of low-pass filtering parameters applied to compute the envelope.

3.2   Wearable IMU Module

Because of the proprietary software and prohibitive expense of the commonly used accelerometers on the market, we designed and built a custom inertial measurement (IMU) device. The central component in our custom IMU device is the BNO055, an intelligent 9-axis orientation MEMS sensor, with a UART interface. The ATMega 328P microcontroller, on board an Arduino Pro Mini, controls the UART communication interface between the BNO055 and a UART wireless adapter board (Bluefruit, Adafruit Industries). The Bluefruit board is a UART wireless adapter that establishes serial communication with the BNO055 and then transmits this data through the Bluetooth Low Energy (BLE) transmitter to the mobile smart phone. This IMU module is powered by two 3.7V Li-ion Polymer batteries in series, and fits in a custom housing unit that can be worn via velcro strap around the wrist, as shown in Fig. 2.

The system components and IMU module design are provided in the board schematic in Fig. 10. This custom PCB board consists of an IMU IC, BLE-UART wireless adapter, and Arduino microcontroller board. The BNO055 is an intelligent 9-axis orientation MEMS sensor with a UART interface. We use only the accelerometry measurements. In order for our mobile app to acquire acceleration data wirelessly from the BNO055, we interface the BNO055 with a BLE transmitter on board the Bluefruit LE-UART Friend (Adafruit Industries). The Bluefruit board is a UART wireless adapter that establishes serial communication with the BNO055 and then transmits this data through the BLE transmitter to the mobile smart phone. The ATMega 328P microcontroller, on board an Arduino Pro Mini, controls the UART communication between the BNO055 and Bluefruit board.

This IMU module is powered by two 3.7V Li-ion Polymer batteries in series, and fits in a custom housing unit that can be worn via velcro strap around the wrist. The Solid Works CAD drawing for the housing unit is provided in Fig. 11. The package has slots for the velcro strap and space for a power switch. The housing is approximately 4 cm × 4 cm × 2 cm.

Magnitude of 3D acceleration recorded during wheelchair pushes, tricep extensions, and lat rows for approximately 30 s bouts, with 30 s rest intervals, is shown in Fig. 12. The DREAM IMU module appears to record similar magnitude as Actigraph, but the Actigraph shows less high frequency noise. We plan to implement low-pass filtering in the DREAM IMU module to obtain acceleration waveforms which even more closely match Actigraph's.

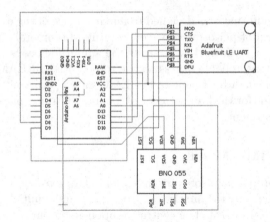

Fig. 10. Circuit schematic of IMU module [16].

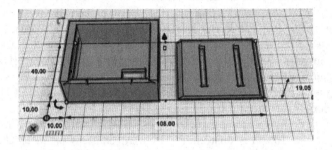

Fig. 11. CAD design for the IMU module housing unit, 3D-printed in ABS plastic. Dimensions are provided in mm [16].

4   Exergaming

Our primary strategy to increase likelihood of greater activity levels and compliance with physician-recommended workout protocols is to gamify them so that the user will be focused on winning the games and in doing so, burn more calories. The score will be designed to reflect the user's level of effort and energy expenditure, and ultimately cardiovascular fitness. The development of a reliable metric for use in these wheelchair-based exergames is described in Sect. 6.

The exergames were designed to engage users in an exercise protocol developed loosely based on Nash et al.'s circuit resistance training protocol [17,18]. The protocol consists of three exercises: (1) spinning or rolling; (2) shadow boxing or ball exchange, and (3) resistance arm bands.

For the spinning activity, the user would mount their wheelchair onto a stationary roller (Invictus® Roller) which permits the wheelchair to roll without moving forward. Subjects would continuously roll their wheels at increasing intensity levels, as defined by their heart rate as a percentage of their

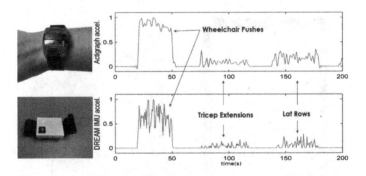

Fig. 12. Endpoint acceleration magnitude acquired by Actigraph sensor vs. DREAM IMU module.

maximum resting heart rate. The angular speed of the car around the elliptical track is controlled by the activity level, according to Eqs. 1–3

$$x = k_1 + r \cdot \cos\left(\theta \cdot \frac{\pi}{180^o}\right) \tag{1}$$

$$y = k_2 + r \cdot \sin\left(\theta \cdot \frac{\pi}{180^o} \cdot k_3\right) \tag{2}$$

$$\frac{d\theta}{dt} \propto A \tag{3}$$

where (x, y) are the coordinates of the car around the ellipse defining the perimeter of the track; k_1, k_2, and k_3 are constants that are callibrated according to the phone screen size and track dimensions; and A is the user's activity level computed from the sensor signals. θ is the angular position of the car relative to the center of the ellipse. The position is updated using 1st order Euler's method.

Figures 13 and 14 illustrate the screens the user would see when choosing to play the "Racing" game. Before the game begins, the user will be asked to input minimum and maximum values of heart rate, EMG, and the number of laps they desire to reach. A set of instructions on how to play and win the game are provided for the user before starting the game. Once the user has completed initalization, the user will click "start" and a sound of an engine will play indicating that the race has begun.

While the game is played, the user interface includes a heart rate label, an EMG progress bar, the laps left to complete, the time duration, and target zones of the heart rate and EMG. An additional motivating feature of the displayed user interface is the EMG progress bar. The progress bar provides real-time feedback to the user on their effort level relative to their max effort and encourages them to sustain their efforts. When the user has completed the set number of laps desired, a message will appear to the user and display "Game over. You win" as well the time duration it took to complete laps and the highest EMG amplitude achieved. Results of the data will be saved under the session name for users to check back and keep progress of achievements.

Fig. 13. Racing game setup: User sets min and max expected EMG and heart rate levels, and target number of laps. User is provided with instructions before starting the game.

The primary muscle targeted during the spinning exercise is the tricep muscle. Therefore, for the racing game, the EMG sensor is placed on the triceps muscle body. The heart rate sensor is used to display the user's heart rate while the game is in progress to ensure that the user's heart rate stays within the acceptable range. The objective of the game is to complete the desired number of laps around the race track set in the beginning of the game in the shortest amount of time as possible. The speed of how fast the car moves around the track is determined by how much muscle activity is detected. As long as the app receives input from the sensors, the game character will continue moving forward and will stop when no activity is detected. The harder the user works out, the faster the car will move on the screen to complete the game.

For the exchange exercise routine, subjects were instructed to pass a medicine ball back and forth to a trainer standing in front of them for 7 min. Then, the medicine ball was held in front of the subject to be punched at a rate that maintained their heart rate within the heart rate zone. Another way to get a similar form of physical exercise is to do rapid repeated punches in the air or at a stationary object. The boxing game was created to emulate this type of repetitive exercise. In this game, the user tries to again complete 3 levels of increasing difficulty by achieving 5 stars at each level. Each star represents a fixed number of detected punches. A larger amount of force must be used for each punch to be detected at the next level.

5   Multi-player Gaming

In addition to wireless sensing, we also exploit cloud service to motivate users to exercise. We store user data on the cloud and exchange data between users in order to create a multiplayer game environment. Multiplayer gaming is expected

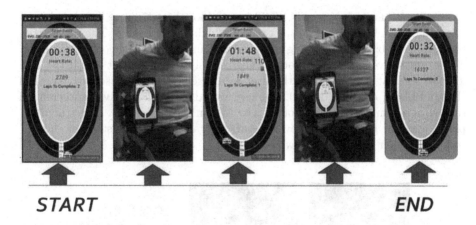

Fig. 14. Sequence of racing game: Upon start, car sprite (or fragment) appears at starting line, with lap counter on target number of laps. As the user spins their wheelchair, the car moves, and the speed of the car depends on the user's activity level. The lap counter counts down as the car completes a lap, while a live reading of the heart rate is displayed as text, and a live reading of the EMG amplitude is displayed as a progress bar, as a percentage of the max EMG.

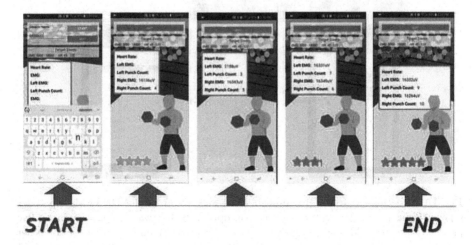

Fig. 15. Sequence of boxing game: Screenshots of mobile app game at the start and as the user would advance to each of the 3 levels. Game ends when user has performed enough punches to reach the end of the 3rd level.

to provide social interaction and healthy competition to increase motivation to exercise. Each user has their own account and their sensor data and summary statistics can be saved to their account. Then these statistics can be used to view trends and track long-term progress in fitness levels. The data can also be played back as a "ghost" player in a multiplayer game mode, as described here (Fig. 15).

The multiplayer functionality is illustrated for the resistance arm band exercise game, loosely modeled on the carnival "high striker" game. The player tries to fill in their bar by expending more calories until the bar is completely filled. There are 3 levels, and it becomes progressively more difficult to fill the bar. To play against a live player, the user would select the exercise activity, then the multiplayer option (Fig. 16). The user would then select "Live" and create a session name and wait for the other user to join the gameroom. Once the other player joins the game room, they can start the game. In this illustration, "user3" completed their bars first and won the game.

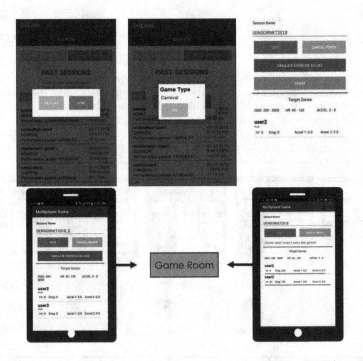

Fig. 16. Creating a virtual live multiplayer game room in the DREAM app: User selects the exercise activity, then multiplayer option. If they want to play against a live player, the user would select "Live", then create a session name and wait for the other user to join the gameroom. Once the other player joins the game room, they can start the game. In this illustration, "user3" completed their bars first and won the game.

If no other users are online and available to play, or the user just wishes not to play against a live player, the user may still play in multiplayer mode against a "ghost" player. The user simply selects "Replay" instead of "Live", then selects a user in the system against whom to play, and selects one of the past sessions from which data for that game was already recorded (Fig. 17). The selected session data will then be replayed as if it was a live player.

6 Fidelity of Fitness Metric

Many fitness trackers measure step counts, which for obvious reasons, would not apply for our user population. A widely accepted recommendation for reducing cardiovascular disease risk has been to increase average daily energy expenditure by 300–350 kilocalories [19]. The gold standard used in the literature and by the American College of Sports Medicine to quantify energy expenditure is the MET (or metabolic equivalent) which is directly related to VO_2 (or volume of oxygen consumption). In order to implement a game which is driven by the user's actual achievement in cardiovascular fitness, we desired to implement a method for reliably quantifying the amount of energy expended in Calories (kcal) from the physiological sensors we practically have at our disposal. Caloric expenditure will serve as a useful, relevant, motivating metric to feedback to users about their progress during a workout as well as over a long-term period. Caloric expenditure is most directly measured through whole-body calorimetry, which is not feasible during real-time exercises at home. Similarly, measuring VO_2 requires wearing a respiratory mask attached to specialized equipment, often in a

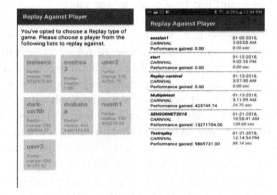

Fig. 17. Creating a virtual ghost multiplayer game room in the DREAM app.

Fig. 18. The "Leaderboard" showing the ranking of DREAM app users, ranked according to a fitness metric; and a log of stored data from past exercise sessions, all accessible from the DREAM cloud server.

controlled, clinical setting. This imposes a limitation of directly recording energy expenditure in a portable manner; therefore, a method must be derived to indirectly estimate absolute VO_2 from easily accessible sensors. Therefore, we are developing a metric of energy expenditure which can be derived from wearable sensor signals: heart rate, EMG, and acceleration sensors (Fig. 18).

Heart rate monitors are commonly used in fitness tracking devices, from which an estimate of VO2 can be obtained. However, there are a few main limitations in relying on heart rate monitors for our exergaming system. The top-of-the line Polar heart rate monitors would not be as practical for use in our DREAM Mobile Fitness System because they are not standalone, wireless devices. Rather, they require a receiver which connects to a computer with software which can read in the heart rate signal. Of the wireless standalone heart rate monitors, the ones worn on a chest strap provide the most accurate measures of heart rate, but because exercises in a wheelchair tend to move the torso more and require more bending at the waist or with arms moving across the chest, the chest strap tends to move, and motion artifact is detrimental to accurate heart rate monitoring. We also hypothesized that due to a condition, called autonomic dysreflexia, which leads to aberrant spikes in heart rate activity in individuals with SCI, heart rate would not be a reliable sole metric to use.

We performed single linear regression between VO_2 and heart rate, and found that VO_2 could be predicted from heart rate alone with an average accuracy, as measured by the coefficient of determination, of $R^2 = .31$ overall, despite using the high-end Polar heart rate monitor. The predictions could reach a maximum R^2 of .694, but this was only for the spinning exercise which is the most aerobic exercise of the 3 prescribed exercises. Another problem was that while the prediction could capture the low-frequency trends in VO_2 quite well, it did not accurately track the temporal dynamics that occurred on a shorter time scale (on the order of 10 s of seconds). This means that when a user is putting in spurts of high intensity effort, they would observe the same caloric expenditure, or METS level, as when they are cruising just before or after at a much lower effort level. In an attempt to get the VO_2 estimate to better match the effort level and temporal dynamics of actual caloric expenditure, we have attempted optimal linear filtering and artificial neural networks, the results of which are not published here. With the multiple linear regression, the max R^2 was .773. We also attempted other methods (including logistic regression, optimal linear filtering, and artificial neural networks), but thus far, none has reliably outperformed the multiple linear regression.

7 Conclusions

Decreased mobility leads to physical and psychological health problems, thereby affecting quality of life. Individuals with spinal cord injury and other forms of lower limb mobility impairment suffer limitations to exercise. We, therefore, developed a mobile exergaming and fitness tracking system for individuals who use wheelchairs due to mobility impairment. Increasing and encouraging regular cardiovascular exercise can prevent long term health risks and give patients a better quality of life by encouraging a more active lifestyle. Our goal is to promote an active lifestyle and to facilitate exercises at home even in the absence of a physical trainer or adapted gyms. Current activity monitors and fitness trackers have limitations as far as accurately monitoring fitness, and to our knowledge, none have been customized to appropriately incentivize exercise for individuals in wheelchairs. We are therefore developing a multi-modal energy expenditure metric, derived from multiple body-worn sensors, that will drive mobile app games.

References

1. Selassie, A., Snipe, L., Focht, K.L., Welldaregay, W.: Baseline prevalence of heart diseases, hypertension, diabetes, and obesity in persons with acute traumatic spinal cord injury: potential threats in the recovery trajectory. Top. Spinal Cord Inj. Rehabil. **19**, 172–182 (2013)
2. Garshick, E.E.A.: A prospective assessment of mortality in chronic spinal cord injury. Spinal Cord **43**, 408–416 (2005)
3. Abel, T., Platen, P., Vega, S.R., Schneider, S., Strüder, H.: Energy expenditure in ball games for wheelchair users. Spinal Cord **46**, 785 (2008)
4. Blair, S.: Effects of physical inactivity and obesity on morbidity and mortality: current evidence and research issues. Med. Sci. Sports Exerc. **31**, S646–S662 (1999)
5. Jacobs, P.L., Nash, M.S.: Exercise recommendations for individuals with spinal cord injury. Sports Med. Auckl. NZ **34**, 727–751 (2004)
6. Hicks, A.L., Martin Ginis, K.A., Pelletier, C.A., Ditor, D.S., Foulon, B., Wolfe, D.L.: The effects of exercise training on physical capacity, strength, body composition and functional performance among adults with spinal cord injury: a systematic review. Spinal Cord **49**, 1103 (2011)
7. Ditor, D.S., Latimer, A.E., Martin Ginis, K.A., Arbour, K.P., McCartney, N., Hicks, A.L.: Maintenance of exercise participation in individuals with spinal cord injury: effects on quality of life, stress and pain. Spinal Cord **41**, 446 (2003)
8. Martin Ginis, K.A., Jörgensen, S., Stapleton, J.: Exercise and sport for persons with spinal cord injury. PM& R **4**, 894–900 (2012)
9. Kehn, M., Kroll, T.: Staying physically active after spinal cord injury: a qualitative exploration of barriers and facilitators to exercise participation. BMC Public Health **9**, 168 (2009)
10. Semerjian, T., Montague, S., Dominguez, J., Davidian, A., de Leon, R.: Enhancement of quality of life and body satisfaction through the use of adapted exercise devices for individuals with spinal cord injuries. Top. Spinal Cord Inj. Rehabil. **11**, 95–108 (2005)
11. Levins, S.M., Redenbach, D.M., Dyck, I.: Individual and societal influences on participation in physical activity following spinal cord injury: a qualitative study. Phys. Ther. **84**, 496–509 (2004)
12. Löfgren, M., Norrbrink, C.: "But i know what works" - patients' experience of spinal cord injury neuropathic pain management. Disabil. Rehabil. **34**, 2139–2147 (2012). PMID: 22512334

13. Martin Ginis, K.A., Latimer, A.E., Arbour-Nicitopoulos, K.P., Buchholz, A.C., Bray, S.R., Craven, B.C., Hayes, K.C., Hicks, A.L., McColl, M.A., Potter, P.J., Smith, K., Wolfe, D.L.: Leisure time physical activity in a population-based sample of people with spinal cord injury Part I: demographic and injury-related correlates. Arch. Phys. Med. Rehabil. **91**, 722–728 (2010)

14. Sluijs, E.M., Kok, G.J., van der Zee, J.: Correlates of exercise compliance in physical therapy. Phys. Therap. **73**, 771–782 (1993)

15. Williams, T.L., Smith, B., Papathomas, A.: The barriers, benefits and facilitators of leisure time physical activity among people with spinal cord injury: a meta-synthesis of qualitative findings. Health Psychol. Rev. **8**, 404–425 (2014). PMID: 25211208

16. Pal, A., Monsalvo, K., Sunthonlap, J., Arguelles, P., Adame, A., Tu, J., Tjara, E., Velasco, J., Sarmiento, T., Pebdani, R., et al.: Wheelchair exercise monitor development platform-an application for wireless EMG sensors. In: SENSORNETS, pp. 67–73 (2018)

17. Nash, M.S., Jacobs, P.L., Mendez, A.J., Goldberg, R.B.: Circuit resistance training improves the atherogenic lipid profiles of persons with chronic paraplegia. J. Spinal Cord Med. **24**, 2–9 (2001). PMID: 11587430

18. Le, L.N., Keslacy, S., Ramirez, J., de Leon, R.d., Dy, C.: Feasibility and effectiveness of circuit resistance training using eleastic bands for individuals with spinal cord injury. In: Southwest Amercian College of Sports Medicine (2017)

19. Paffenbarger Jr., R., Hyde, R., Wing, A., Lee, I., Jung, D., Kampert, J.: The association of changes in physical-activity level and other lifestyle characteristics with mortality among men. N. Engl. J. Med. **328**, 538–545 (1993)

Bayesian Target Identification and Classification: Application of AIS, GMTI and BFT in Command and Control Systems

Albert Bodenmüller[✉]

Airbus Defence and Space GmbH, 89077 Ulm, Germany
albert.bodenmueller@airbus.com

Abstract. The Identification and classification of targets is one of the key capabilities of Ground based C4ISR systems, military Command and Control Systems and Combat Management Systems. It is a precondition for situational awareness and supports operational users in decision making. A correct identification is an important prerequisite to prevent fratricide and civilian collateral damages and to complete the Situational Awareness. Modern Combat Management and Surveillance systems deal with thousands of tracked objects and such an operator is unable to handle the huge amount of targets and data in an operationally acceptable timeline. Therefore an automated identification and classification process is integrated in such military systems. Typical sensors used for this task are radars, IFF and ESM sensors complemented by sources like Tactical Data Links, civil and military Airspace Control Means and flight plans.

In today's naval combat ships and surveillance systems various additional sensors and sources like Automatic Identification System (AIS), Automatic Target Recognition (ATR), GMTI Radar and Blue Force Tracking system are available to support identification, classification and decision making. This paper gives an overview of our solution for the extension of the Bayesian identification process.

Keywords: Military target identification and classification ·
Situation Awareness · Bayes decision theory · AIS · GMTI · NFFI

1 Introduction

In the first section of this paper the current existing military standard of target identification and classification will be described. This standard fusion process uses Bayes decision theory as described by [1, 2]. It has already been implemented in airborne reconnaissance systems and different naval and ground based Air Defense Systems, but it is not limited to military systems; it may be used for any identification and categorization problem.

Future systems will use the principle also for renegade detection and more granular rating of various kinds of suspicious behaviour. The implementation of this standardized fusion process ensures the comparability of results and the exchange of source data in future.

© Springer Nature Switzerland AG 2019
C. Benavente-Peces et al. (Eds.): SENSORNETS 2017/2018, CCIS 1074, pp. 135–150, 2019.
https://doi.org/10.1007/978-3-030-30110-1_8

Section 2 will give an overview of the principles of Bayesian Fusion for target identification and classification, Sect. 3 will detail the proposed source processing of some non-standardised sensors and sources in a Command and Control (C2) system. The paper describes our approach for some additional sensors which were not yet considered in the identification standard. For each of the described sources the sensor's provided source information and the required data for the processing is indicated.

2   Principles of Bayes Fusion

2.1   Source Processing

The identification process consists of two main processing parts: The first step is a source processing component, which provides the source specific processing, which is unique for each source type (Fig. 1), and the second step is the fusion component, which has the task to combine and fuse all contributing sources of information and to assign the final decision for the identification and classification. Such multiple instances of source processing are implemented (e.g. for each type of sensor or source), whereas one fusion process is sufficient for identification or classification.

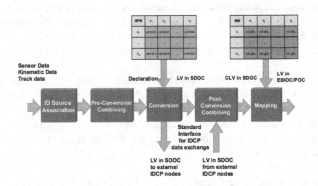

Fig. 1. Identification source processing (from [13]).

Following the flow of information the initial step is to establish an unique association between a sensor or source information and a system track. When no related existing system track can be found, a new track based on the kinematic data of the sensor will be initiated. This will be performed for those sensors or sources, which provide positional and/or kinematic data, e.g. a Blue Force Tracking/Friend Force Information system will normally provide the actual own position information. During this process the results of sensors like Electronic Support Measure (ESM) or Ground Moving Target Indicator (GMTI) Radar including the contributing collateral data is assigned to a track. For many sensors the association process and the pre-conversion combining are an integrated process making a final hard decision, if a source declaration is made or not.

In some cases the periodical association match analysis is input into a pre-conversion combining step, which uses a hysteresis or stochastic mean of several association attempts to make the final declaration hard decision. Also combinations of an integrated process making the association attempts based on a hysteresis function and stochastic output of the result are applied in some systems. The stochastic output finally has to be compared with a threshold for a final hard decision.

The source processing is specific for each kind of sensor and such the determined declarations are not in a form which is appropriate for fusion. Hence they are converted into a Likelihood Vector (LV), which is a set of probabilities related to appropriate types of object classes. The standard proposes for this conversion the application of a Source Probability Matrix, which represents the probability of the source to make these source specific declarations given a known object type. The Source Probability Matrix (SPM) contains for each possible declaration, which can be made by a source, the related likelihoods. Different qualities or confidences related to the association process are considered by different SPMs.

Given a determined source declaration and a priori determined source probabilities in the SPM the conversion step is performed by selection of the related row of the source specific SPM. The result of the conversion step is a Likelihood Vector (LV) in the Source Discrimination Object Class (named LV in SDOC) to which additional collateral information, which is required for the mapping stage, is attached.

The result of this conversion of a declaration D_i is a source specific Likelihood Vector LV_i which can be written in the following way:

$$LV_i = \left(p(D_i|O_1),\ p(D_i|O_2),\ \ldots,\ p\left(D_i|O_j\right) \right) \tag{1}$$

where $p(D_i|O_j)$ denotes the probability of declaration D_i given Object property O_j (from [13]).

The LV in SDOC expresses the performance of that particular source to make this declaration.

There exist also types of sources where the application of pre-calculated SPMs is not suitable. In such cases a dynamic determination of the LV in SDOC may be applied. For instance the dynamic evaluation of Electronic Support Measure sensors (ESM) requires for each emitter and emitter mode an emitter related SPM. This is not feasible in that way. One possibility is to calculate dynamically from the emitter characteristics and comparison with an emitter database the SPM values.

Also for very dynamic sources where the kinematic behaviour of target is compared with extreme kinematic characteristics, a dynamic SPM calculation is the better solution. For instance when the actual target kinematics is compared with operator defined extreme kinematic thresholds the a priori SPM values cannot be pre-calculated, because they change depending on the criteria and target characteristic. This kind of processing requires a specific database and collateral data.

There are different possibilities to exchange identification information between different identifying and classifying systems or nodes. One possibility is to exchange final identification and classification results as this is performed via Tactical Data Links e.g. Link-16 or Link-22. The disadvantage is that only the final result is available such that receiving nodes are not able to assess what the basis of this assessment had been.

Several surveillance systems also use the Variable Message Format (VMF) to exchange tactical data and the situational picture. These systems also have to deal with the disadvantage that only the final decision is available.

So the comparability of final results is often a problem when different systems interact in a joint combined mission. Therefore the exchange of identification source data is preferred. The exchange of Likelihood Vectors or references on harmonized pre-defined LVs enables a standardized identity information exchange between fusion nodes. By this way the source information and the confidence of the information is transferred, but the information has not yet been interpreted, i.e. the allegiance, the distinction of civil/military targets or the platform data has not been derived.

When more than one sensor or source of the same type (i.e. using the identical SDOC) of either several own sensors or by receiving data from other identification nodes contribute to one track, the combination of these LVs is performed by column wise multiplication in the Post Conversion Combination step according the following formula:

$$CLV = \left(\prod_{i=1}^{N} p(D_i|O_j) \right)_{j=1,...,M} \tag{2}$$

with $CLV = (p(D_{1,...},D_N|O_1), \ldots, p(D_{1,...},D_N|O_M))$ (from [13]).

The Combined Likelihood Vector (CLV) is determined by a column multiplication of the single contributing LVs, and is still in form of the source specific SDOC. Such a CLV in SDOC contains the complete information of one source type which contributes to the final result of the identification/classification. But still this first combination/fusion step is in a format which is not suitable for fusion with other source specific information.

2.2 Mapping Processing

A Likelihood Vector or Combined Likelihood Vector in SDOC is a source specific representation of information and such different LVs in SDOC cannot be fused directly without a conversion into a common format. In the Mapping stage the LVs/CLVs in SDOC are mapped in such a common information representation which allows for fusion.

This common information format is called Output Object Class (OOC). The OOC shall be defined according the operational needs to distinguish object categories, e.g. when only a distinction of civil and military targets is needed, the OOC may contain only the members:

- Military Target;
- Civil Target.

When a distinction of basic allegiances is needed the OOC contains for example the members:

- Own Forces (OF);
- Enemy Forces (EF);
- Non-Aligned (NA).

And a basic distinction of air platform categories can be defined for example as:

- FIGHTER;
- BOMBER;
- HELICOPTER;
- UAV;
- AEW AIRCRAFT;
- SAR AIRCRAFT;
- PATROL AIRCRAFT;
- FREIGHT AIRCRAFT;
- GLIDER;
- BALLOON;
- MISSILE;
- OTHER AIR TARGET.

Also combinations of basic OOC for certain applications are reasonable and hence an OOC using members like friendly fighter, hostile fighter, own forces civil helicopter etc. may be used. A very common composite OOC is the Extended Basic Object Class (EBIOC) using the combinations of basic allegiances and civil/military targets, e.g. Own Forces Civil (OFC) and Own Forces Military (OFM). Depending on the discriminating capabilities of the contributing sensors/sources and the user's operational requirements any kind of Platform Object Class (POC) can be defined as OOC for target classification applications. In any case the OOC members shall be mutually exclusive and the OOC has to be exhaustive.

The mapping is calculated according the formula:

$$p_{OOC}(D_i|B_j) = \sum_{k=1}^{M} p(D_i|O_k) \cdot P_{MM}(O_k|B_j) \tag{3}$$

where $p(D_i \mid O_k)$ denotes the CLV in SDOC and $P_{MM}(O_k \mid B_j)$ denotes the Mapping Matrix (MM) (from [13]).

The mapping values are stored in a source specific Mapping Matrix, which is defined specifically for each corresponding source type and SDOC. In cases where different operational facts or constraints have to be considered (e.g. a radar may be currently jammed) different MMs can consider such circumstances by different mapping values. After the mapping stage the LV in OOC is normalized and then passed to the conflict detection and fusion process.

2.3   Conflict Recognition on Basis of Source Information

The next step now is to check if there exist source inconsistencies and contradictions. The identification source information after the mapping step is available in a common normalized format which enables the recognition of potentially contradicting information. The inconsistency/conflict recognition is performed in the following way:

When an element of a LV in OOC indicates that one object class is very likely and the same element of the compared second LV in OOC indicates that this object class is very unlikely, this test indicates a possible information inconsistency/conflict.

When an element of a LV in OOC indicates that one object class is very likely and another element of the compared second LV in OOC indicates that this different object class is very likely, this test indicates a further possible information inconsistency/ conflict.

Finally an information content distance measure between two LVs indicates a possible information inconsistency when the distance exceeds a certain threshold:

$$d = \sum_{i=1}^{M} |x_i - y_i| \tag{4}$$

where x and y represent the two LVs to be tested (from [13]).

This test makes sense particular for large LVs with many elements. The statistical information distance between two LVs is a measure for inconsistency.

The inconsistency/conflict recognition tests are performed for each combination of two contributing LVs in OOC and the results are summarized for display purposes to the operational user.

Figure 2 illustrates the following processing steps including conflict detection, fusion and final category decision.

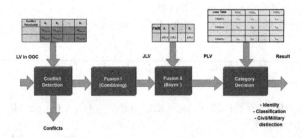

Fig. 2. Bayesian identification fusion and decision (from [13]).

2.4   Fusion

In the first step of the fusion process a combination of all determined contributing LVs/CLVs in OOC is calculated by a component wise multiplication of all contributing LVs, building the Joint Likelihood Vector (JLV). The JLV is a probability distribution over all members of the OOC. The elements of the calculated JLV contain the probability that a target may have these associated declarations given that the target belongs to that respective OOC (from [13]):

$$JLV = \left(\prod_{i=1}^{N} p_{OOC}(D_i|B_j) \right)_{j=1,...,M} \qquad (5)$$

In the second step the Posterior Likelihood Vector (PLV) is calculated from the JLV by application of Bayes' Theorem according the following formula:

$$p(B_j|D_i) = \frac{p(D_i|B_j) \cdot p(B_j)}{\sum\limits_{j=1}^{N} p(D_i|B_j) \cdot p(B_j)} \qquad (6)$$

where p(B$_j$ | D$_i$) denotes the PLV, p (D$_i$ | B$_j$) denotes the JLV and p(B$_j$) denotes the required a priori information called Force Mix Ratio (FMR) (from [13]).

The FMR is a priori information and it quantifies the relative expectation that a member of that object class could be found in the area of interest. When using this processing for target classification analogously a Platform Mix Ratio is required. The elements of the calculated PLV contain the posterior probability that the target belongs to that respective OOC given the considered declarations.

2.5 Conflict Recognition on Basis of Combination/Fusion Result

The declaration combination result JLV can be used additionally to detect possible information inconsistencies.

When an element of the JLV indicates that one object class is very likely and the same element of the a priori FMR indicates that this object class is very unlikely this test indicates a possible information inconsistency.

When an element of a JLV indicates that one object class is very likely and another element of the a priori FMR indicates that this different object class is very likely this test indicates a further possible information inconsistency.

The inconsistency/conflict recognition is performed on each update of the JLV and the result is used for display purposes or alerting the operational user.

Generally it depends on the operational application and required depth of information level, which inconsistency information shall be indicated to an operational user, and if such consistency tests are performed. In larger C2 systems (e.g. frigates) or Command and Reporting Centers (CRC) normally the operator has more time to investigate problematic targets for inconsistencies and his operational task requires as detailed information from the automatic system as possible. But if a similar identification software is running in a small tank or shelter with minimum staff (e.g. 1 to 2 persons) there is no need for such detail of information nor the capability to investigate such cases. Possibly he has only few seconds to decide to execute an engagement of a target and any detail of information delays the decision process.

2.6   Final Identity Decision Process

The PLV contains the fusion result and such it can be displayed to operators to support the further decision process. A final identity decision could be realized by a simple thresholding function based on the most likely element. But usually this result is translated into a recommendation, which regards the user's needs and operational aspects [3]. In the domain of target identification the operational user expects an identity category according to NATO STANAG 1241 or MIL-STD 6016 and a civil/military target assessment. In the case of target classification a platform type or platform specific type according to military Data Link standards STANAG 5516 or STANAG 5522 is required.

The decision process is based on a loss function which uses a set of loss values (see Fig. 3), which define the operational risk when making a wrong decision.

Loss Table	OFC	OFM	EFC	EFM	NAC	NAM
UNKNOWN	$L_{1,1}$	$L_{1,2}$	$L_{1,3}$	$L_{1,4}$	$L_{1,5}$	$L_{1,6}$
ASSUMED FRIEND	$L_{2,1}$	$L_{2,2}$	$L_{2,3}$	$L_{2,4}$	$L_{2,5}$	$L_{2,6}$
FRIEND	$L_{3,1}$	$L_{3,2}$	$L_{3,3}$	$L_{3,4}$	$L_{3,5}$	$L_{3,6}$
NEUTRAL	$L_{4,1}$	$L_{4,2}$	$L_{4,3}$	$L_{4,4}$	$L_{4,5}$	$L_{4,6}$
SUSPECT	$L_{5,1}$	$L_{5,2}$	$L_{5,3}$	$L_{5,4}$	$L_{5,5}$	$L_{5,6}$
HOSTILE	$L_{6,1}$	$L_{6,2}$	$L_{6,3}$	$L_{6,4}$	$L_{6,5}$	$L_{6,6}$
...						
KILO	$L_{M,1}$	$L_{M,2}$	$L_{M,3}$	$L_{M,4}$	$L_{M,5}$	$L_{M,6}$

Fig. 3. Identification loss table (from [13]).

The decision process determines for each decision alternative a specific risk value by weighting the loss values of that category (decision alternative) by the posterior probabilities of the fusion result:

$$\text{Risk} = p(OOC_1) * L_{ID,1} + p(OOC_2) * L_{ID,2} + \ldots + p(OOC_N) * L_{ID,N} \quad (7)$$

where $p(OOC_n)$ represents the nth element of the PLV, $L_{ID,m}$ the loss value related to that evaluated identity (ID) and OOC element m (from [13]).

The decision alternative comprising the lowest risk is proposed as final decision result. In those cases were ambiguous risk values prohibit a decision based on the risk values a final decision applying a rule based approach is advised.

If during the identification process additional operationally important information is attained, which is not suitable for fusion but relevant for the decision, this information is incorporated in the decision process. For instance when the operational alert state changes from peace to tension or a target violates a self-defence safety zone this has to be considered for the identity decision. For all these cases a set of dedicated loss tables has to be provided, which contain modified loss values regarding operational facts and target relevant criteria.

3 Novel Source Types for Identification and Classification

The following section describes our solution for some additional sources and sensors which were not yet covered by the identification standard. Hence we enhanced the standard and introduced capabilities like Automatic Identification System (AIS), Automatic Target Recognition (ATR), Ground Moving Target Indicator (GMTI) Radar and Blue Force Tracking systems. For some of these the implemented solution is presented in the following sections. Normally only the source processing has to be extended for new sources, i.e. further SDOCs have to be introduced and additional a priori conditioning data (SPMs, MMs) have to be designed and implemented. The generic approach of combining, fusion, and final category decision is not affected and keeps unchanged as described in the previous chapter.

3.1 Automatic Identification System

The Automatic Identification System (AIS) is originally a radio-based collision avoidance system for ships. AIS has the main requirements to

- Support the avoidance of collisions by enabling an efficient navigation of vessels;
- Support the protection of the environment by providing information about the ship's cargo;
- Actively support Vessel Traffic Systems (VTS) by providing static, dynamic and voyage data.

Besides that port authorities use AIS to warn ships about hazards, low tides and shoals that are commonly found at sea. In open sea AIS-enabled distress beacons are used to signal and locate men who have fallen overboard [5].

Several state-of-the-art surveillance satellites are now equipped with AIS [6], thus the fused information from dual sensors Radar and AIS contributes to global maritime surveillance. But also naval ships like corvettes and frigates are going to exploit received AIS data for the improvement of the maritime picture and tactical situation in real-time. The information extracted from AIS radio broadcast data includes:

- Static ship data: Maritime Mobile Service Identity (MMSI), i.e. the vessels unique identification number, International Maritime Organization (IMO) ship identification number, radio call sign, name of the vessel, type of ship;
- Dynamic ship data: navigation status, position of the vessel, time of position, course over ground, speed over ground, true heading, rate of turn;
- Further voyage data: current maximum draught of ship, hazardous cargo, destination, estimated time of arrival (ETA) at destination.

In a first step the received positional data of a vessel are used for the association of the AIS data with existing system tracks, which is part of the source data association. If no matching system track is available a new AIS based system track will be initiated and the track is updated with the AIS position data.

For the evaluation of AIS data for military target purposes it is important to recognize that AIS message content can be spoofed easily, so that the manipulated result of the data association process or from the information exploitation may be erroneous. Besides the intentional manipulation also any kinds of intentional and unintentional interference of the AIS signals or the improper setup of AIS devices may cause problems in the evaluation.

The AIS is a civilian system, hence no primary military information is transmitted by default. For military purposes also dedicated variants (NATO STANAG 4668 WARSHIP - AUTOMATIC IDENTIFICATION SYSTEM (W-AIS) and NATO STANAG 4669 - AUTOMATIC IDENTIFICATION SYSTEM (AIS) ON WAR- SHIPS) exists, which are not handled here in this paper. In order to use the civilian AIS data for military identification and classification purposes a further processing is nec- essary. In the optimal case a database providing military and intelligence information is available, such that the received AIS data can be compared with it and the stored (military) information can be retrieved to support the tactical interpretation. The database content provides information like ship type, specific type, platform class and platform name, allegiance, civil/military information and of course data like sensor equipment, weapon systems and further tactical intelligence information.

But usually on board of a ship this intelligence database is not available and such a more pragmatic solution was additionally necessary. In this case the broadcasted MMSI number is exploited, because the MMSI number uniquely identifies a vessel. The MMSI is not an identity in the military sense, where a distinction between civil and military objects and the membership to either a friendly, neutral or hostile allegiance is required. Thus the Identification Digit (MID), which is part of the MMSI number, is extracted from the MMSI. The MID is a 3 digit number and defines uniquely the country, where the vessel is registered.

A simple repository then is used to determine the allegiance of the country. A civilian/military distinction is determined from a simple MMSI repository. When this repository information is not available for a received MMSI, the civilian/military distinction is derived from the AIS message content "type of ship".

AIS is handled as a new source type and hence a new AIS specific SDOC definition and related SPM and MMs were introduced:

- Surface vessel with an operating AIS transponder is sending data 'x';
- Surface vessel with an operating AIS transponder is sending data different from 'x';
- Surface vessel is not fitted with a transponder or the surface vessel is fitted with an AIS transponder and the transponder is not operating.

The source type AIS provides the following declarations:

- AIS (data) received;
- AIS (data) not received.

The related SPM has therefore the following format as given in Table 1.

Table 1. AIS Source Probability Matrix (from [13]).

AIS SPM	AIS SDOC		
	Fitted and operating sending data x	*Fitted and operating, sending data different x*	*Fitted and NOT operating or NOT Fitted*
AIS received	A	B	C
AIS not received	1-A	1-B	1-C

Such the related Mapping matrices have the following format as indicated in Fig. 4.

AIS MM SDOC → EBIOC	OFC	OFM	EFC	EFM	NAC	NAM
Fitted and operating sending data x	A_1	A_2	A_3	A_4	A_5	A_6
Fitted and operating, sending data different x	B_1	B_2	B_3	B_4	B_5	B_6
Fitted and NOT operating or NOT Fitted	$1-A_1-B_1$	$1-A_2-B_2$	$1-A_3-B_3$	$1-A_4-B_4$	$1-A_5-B_5$	$1-A_6-B_6$

Fig. 4. AIS Mapping Matrix (from [13]).

One problem in the military identification using AIS data arises from the ability to manipulate the transmitted AIS data easily. Additional threats arise from triggering SAR alerts to lure ships into navigating to hostile, attacker-controlled sea space or spoofing collisions to possibly bring a ship off course. Hence a possibility to detect spoofing targets is required [7].

Evaluation of historic satellite AIS data worldwide showed, that more than 30% of AIS data are not quite correct; either due to operating failures, problems with the handling the AIS devices or spoofing.

In our system we implemented a multitude of consistency checks for the AIS data, were we compare the received data with repository and intelligence information for plausibility. When this check indicates a sufficient discrepancy the operator is alerted and he has the possibility either to suppress the generation of a declaration and the usage of the AIS data or to declare this vessel as a spoofing target. This knowledge is then used in the mapping process for the selection of dedicated mapping values for the spoofing case or in the final identity decision processing to assign special identity categories respectively.

3.2 Automatic Target Recognition

For our naval and ground based Command and Control Systems (C2 Systems) we are using (different types of) Daylight/Infra-Red cameras with Automatic Target Recognition (ATR).

ATR has become increasingly important in modern defense systems, because it permits precision strikes against certain tactical targets with reduced risk and increased efficiency [8]. ATR helps to minimize collateral damages to civilian persons and objects (like cars, vessels, planes and buildings). The main advantage is that ATR systems connected and fed by sensors can detect and recognize targets automatically so that the workload of an operator can be reduced and the accuracy and efficiency of the complete C2 System can be improved.

For the detection and recognition of tactical relevant objects and their more or less coarse classification different algorithms are known, e.g.:

- Pattern recognition;
- Detection theory;
- Artificial Neural Network;

- Model-based target recognition;
- Artificial intelligence and model-based methods.

In our system we implemented a combination of model-based target recognition and Artificial Neural Network for detection and classification of target objects. The result of this processing is already in the form of a probability distribution over the discriminated object attributes (object classes), so it can be processed and fused directly in our identification and classification processing.

An interface for sensors and sources, which provide results in a form which is suitable for fusion, has been introduced and allows for the fusion of the image processing result, because the ATR result is already a probability distribution over platform categories, which correspond to a LV in POC (see Fig. 5). The detection of conflicts with other sensor results, the combining, Bayes' processing and final category decision are performed as described in Sect. 2.

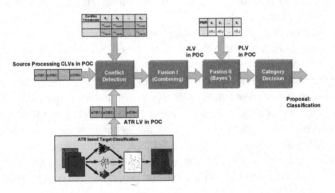

Fig. 5. Extension of Bayesian classification fusion with ATR interface (from [13]).

3.3   Ground Moving Target Indicator (GMTI) Radar

Usually GMTI Radars are mounted on reconnaissance aircrafts and UAV which operate in high altitudes above the normal height of civil aircrafts. The observed area has a large extend and allows for the observation of many ground and maritime moving targets [9].

The NATO Standard Agreement [10] provides a generic and complex GMTI radar interface standard which describes the data encoding. Sometimes problems occur by different interpretation and implementation of the format description and such a robust interface connection is necessary [11].

STANAG 4607 GMTI target reports provide an enumeration field denoting the classification of the target. The classification types include e.g. wheeled vehicles, non-wheeled vehicles, helicopters, fixed-wing air targets, rotating antenna, maritime etc., for both live and simulated targets. Additionally an optional Target Classification Probability (TCP) may be transmitted.

The classification result set is relative coarsely, but it is sufficient to perform a target classification based on it. In order to achieve a good classification result the interpretation of STANAG 4607 GMTI target report classification and probability results shall be clarified with the vendor such that the GMTI source processing can be optimized for that sensor and the related mapping values can be adapted accordingly.

A pre-conversion is not necessary when the GMTI radar provides the result of the most actual integrated assessment. Otherwise a temporal integration using adequate methods like a hysteresis function or a probabilistic logic using a running mean $p = \Sigma$ TCP_i/n, where TCP_i is the received Target Classification Probability, and a threshold function are used to make a declaration.

The integrated assessment is converted into a proper related normalized LV in OOC using the Target Classification Probability for the proper OOC element, the residual R (R = 1-TCP) is equally distributed on the remaining OOC components. The normalized vector is then input into the fusion process analogously to ATR (Fig. 5). In cases where no TCP is transmitted a proxy LV in OOC is determined using experience or analytic measures.

3.4   Blue Force Tracking/Friend Force Tracking Information

For multi-national operations with forces of coalition partners a state-of-the-art Combat Management System requires Network Enabled Capabilities (NEC) for exchange of blue force information to avoid possible blue-on-blue situations. Several incidents during the past NATO missions are pointing out the importance of a positive friend identification and classification to prevent fratricide and fatal collateral damages. Therefore NATO has specified a format for exchange of Friendly Force Tracking (FFT) information of ground targets called NATO Friendly Force Information (NFFI). The specification includes an XML schema to allow the exchange of blue force tracking information using a Web service [12].

The participants in a NFFI network report their position and further information to other units via NFFI message information. The self-generated messages are either encrypted or sent via a secure network, so they are a cooperative source of high confidence.

The information extracted from NFFI data includes as relevant data:

- Positional Data: position coordinates in latitude/longitude/altitude including accuracy data, target speed, bearing, time of measurement, source identifier, reliability;
- Identification Data: identity, classification category encoded as military symbol.

It is important to note, that there are currently specific restrictions and constraints concerning the usage of NFFI, which have to be regarded in the system design and implementation/integration of NFFI:

- Military allegiance: the provided affiliation code, which contains information about the object's hostility, is normally fixed to indication of "friendly" targets, because the usage of NFFI is specified for friendly forces. But there exists no hard restriction thus principally any military allegiance can be derived from NFFI;
- Tactical environment information: the provided Battle Dimension code is usually restricted to ground, since NFFI tracks usually identify mobile objects, in particular land-based objects;

- The track data received by NFFI are non-real-time track data and thus special care has to be taken in the association process.

For association of the extracted FFT data with existing tracks the included positional data and time of measurement is used. Further non-kinematical criteria support the association process.

The military unit symbol code is the main identification and classification information content of FFT.

Taking the specific characteristic of NFFI into account a new FFT specific SDOC definition and a related SPM and MMs were introduced. The SDOC consists of the following elements:

- object is generating this FFT message;
- object is not generating this FFT message (no knowledge, intent or capability).

The source type provides the following declarations:

- FFT message received;
- FFT message not received.

The related SPM has therefore the following format as indicated in Table 2.

Table 2. FFT Source Probability Matrix.

FFT SPM	FFT SDOC	
	Object is generating this FFT message	*Object is not generating this FFT message*
FFT message received	A	B
FFT message not received	1-A	1-B

For each encoded affiliation in the military unit symbol code one related Identification MM is necessary for mapping into the identification related Output Object Class. Such the related Mapping matrices have the following format as indicated in Fig. 6.

FFT MM SDOC → EBIOC	OFC	OFM	EFC	EFM	NAC	NAM
object is generating this FFT message	A_1	A_2	A_3	A_4	A_5	A_6
object is not generating this FFT message	$1 - A_1$	$1 - A_2$	$1 - A_3$	$1 - A_4$	$1 - A_5$	$1 - A_6$

Fig. 6. FFT identification Mapping Matrix.

Analogously for each relevant encoded target category one related Classification MM is needed to map from the SDOC into the POC. The classification related Mapping matrices have the following principal format, depending on the applied Platform Object Class, as illustrated by example in Fig. 7.

FFT MM SDOC → POC	Car	Armoured vehicle	...	Tank	Truck	Train
object is generating this FFT message	M_1	M_2	...	M_{n-2}	M_{n-1}	M_n
object is not generating this FFT message	$1 - M_1$	$1 - M_2$	...	$1 - M_{n-2}$	$1 - M_{n-1}$	$1 - M_n$

Fig. 7. FFT classification Mapping Matrix.

4 Conclusions

In Sect. 2 an overview on the principles of Bayesian identification and classification information fusion has been given. The necessary processing steps like association, conversion, mapping, combining, fusion, Bayesian inference and risk assessment have been detailed.

In Sect. 3 this paper explained further sensor and sensor-like sources which complete the Situation Awareness of Combat Management Systems today. The data provided by AIS is not only a very important source for Vessel Traffic Systems and maritime surveillance but can also be evaluated for an enhanced identification and classification. Also the processing of daylight or infra-red pictures and video applying ATR algorithms supports the object classification. A quite novel information source for Situation Awareness and classification of ground objects is provided by GMTI Radars, which are mounted on reconnaissance aircrafts and UAV operating in high altitudes above the normal height of civil aircrafts. Finally the information provided by Blue Force Tracking/Friend Force Tracking Information system, which may be received via radio communication means or secure networks, is a very valuable cooperative source for identification and classification and means to prevent fratricide.

In our implemented systems we could prove that the identification results were complying with the expectations of the military operators and the adherence of identification doctrines and operational rules succeeds very well. Significant simulation or just real results cannot be published without disclosure of restricted information.

References

1. Desbois, M.: Sensor data fusion & sensor management in the NATO AIR C2 SYSTEM (ACCS). In: RADAR 2009 International Radar Conference, Bordeaux, France, 12–16 October 2009 (2009)
2. Stroscher, C., Schneider, F.: Comprehensive approach to improve identification capabilities. In: RTO IST Symposium on 'New Information Processing Techniques for Military Systems', Istanbul, Turkey, 9–11 October 2000, ser. RTO Meeting Proceedings RTO-MP-049. NATO Research & Technology Organization, April 2001 (2000)
3. Krüger, M., Kratzke, N.: Monitoring of reliability in Bayesian identification. In: 12th International Conference on Information Fusion, Seattle, WA, USA, 6–9 July 2009 (2009)
4. Bodenmüller, A.: Method and device for monitoring target objects. Patent application European Patent Office, Pub. No. EP2322949, Publication Date: 09.11.2010, EADS Deutschland GmbH (2010)

5. Balduzzi, M., Wilhoit, K.: A security evaluation of AIS. Trend Micro Forward-Looking Threat Research Team, A Trend Micro Research Paper (2014). https://www.trendmicro.de/cloud-content/us/pdfs/security-intelligence/white-papers/wp-a-security-evaluation-of-ais.pdf

6. Høye, G.K., Eriksen, T., Meland, B.J., Narheim, B.T.: Space-based AIS for Global Maritime Traffic Monitoring. Norwegian Defence Research Establishment (FFI), NO-2027 Kjeller, Norway (2007)

7. Katsilieris, F., Braca, P., Coraluppi, S.: Detection of malicious AIS position spoofing by exploiting radar information. NATO STO Centre for Maritime, Research and Experimentation, La Spezia, Italy (2013)

8. Dudgeon, D.E., Lacoss, R.T.: An overview of automatic target recognition. Linc. Lab. J. 6(1) (1993). https://www.ll.mit.edu/publications/journal/pdf/vol06_no1/6.1.1.targetrecognition.pdf

9. Austin, R.: Unmanned Aircraft Systems. UAVS Design, Development and Deployment. Wiley, Chichester (2010)

10. NATO STANAG 4607: NATO Ground Moving Target Indicator Format (GMTIF) STANAG 4607 Implementation Guide (2013). http://nso.nato.int/nso/zPublic/ap/aedp-7(2).pdf

11. Dästner, K., von Hassler zu Roseneckh-Köhler, B., Opitz, F.: GMTI radar data analysis and simulation. In: 19th International Conference on Information Fusion, Heidelberg, Germany, 5–8 July 2016 (2016)

12. Porta, R.: Friendly force information sharing, lessons learned and way towards NNEC. In: 7th NATO CIS Symposium, Prague, CZE, 15 October 2008 (2008)

13. Bodenmüller, A.: Bayesian multi-sensor data fusion for target identification. In: 7th International Conference on Sensor Networks, Funchal, Madeira, Portugal, 22–24 January 2018 (2018)

An Effective Satellite Remote Sensing Tool Combining Hardware and Software Solutions

Francesco Gugliuzza[1(✉)], Alessandro Bruno[1,2], Edoardo Ardizzone[1], and Roberto Pirrone[1]

[1] Dipartimento dell'Innovazione Industriale e Digitale (DIID), Università degli Studi di Palermo, Viale delle Scienze Ed. 6, 90128 Palermo (PA), Italy
{francesco.gugliuzza,alessandro.bruno15,edoardo.ardizzone, roberto.pirrone}@unipa.it
http://www.diid.unipa.it/cvip
[2] INAF-IASF Palermo Istituto Nazionale di Astrofisica, Istituto di Astrofisica Spaziale e Fisica Cosmica, Via Ugo La Malfa 153, 90146 Palermo (PA), Italy
bruno@iasf.inaf.it
http://www.iasf-palermo.inaf.it

Abstract. In this paper we propose a new effective remote sensing tool combining hardware and software solutions as an extension of our previous work. In greater detail the tool consists of a low cost receiver subsystem for public weather satellites and a signal and image processing module for several tasks such as signal and image enhancement, image reconstruction and cloud detection. Our solution allows to manage data from satellites effectively with low cost components and portable software solutions. We aim at sampling and processing of the modulated signal entirely in software enabled by Software Defined Radios (SDR) and CPU computational speed overcoming hardware limitation such as high receiver noise and low ADC resolution. Since we want to extend our previous method to demodulate signals coming from various meteorological satellites, we propose a new high frequency receiving system designed to receive and demodulate signals transmitted at 1.7 GHz. The signals coming from satellites are demodulated, synchronized and enhanced by using low level image processing techniques, then cloud detection is performed by using the well known K-means clustering algorithm. The hardware and software architecture extensions make our solution able to receive and demodulate high frequency and bandwidth meteorological satellite signals, such as those transmitted by NOAA POES, NOAA GOES, EUMETSAT Metop, Meteor-M and FengYun.

Francesco Gugliuzza and Alessandro Bruno contributed equally to this work.

A. Bruno—The contribution of Alessandro Bruno falls within the activities of the current project titled "I telescopi Cherenkov per lo sviluppo tecnologico e culturale della Sicilia" at INAF-IASF Palermo, under the scientific supervision of Researcher Dr. Anna Anzalone.

C. Benavente-Peces et al. (Eds.): SENSORNETS 2017/2018, CCIS 1074, pp. 151–175, 2019.
https://doi.org/10.1007/978-3-030-30110-1_9

Keywords: Remote sensing · Satellite communication ·
Signal processing · Cloud detection

1 Introduction

Remote sensing techniques allow us to measure information about an object without touching it. In the last decades remote sensing has been used in various applications such as Earth observation, weather and storm predictive analysis, atmospheric monitoring, climate change, human-environment interactions. Sensors on airborne and satellites have been recording signals from space for many years, giving rise to a huge amount of data. Some data are processed on-board but others are treated and post-processed in ground stations. Signal and image processing are widely applied on data coming from satellite to extract meaningful information for the aforementioned tasks. Satellites and ground stations communicate with each others by using several transceivers and techniques; for instance communication is the largest sector of satellite services. Since the cold war a lot of scientific progress has been made both in navigation and in signal communication and processing. We are interested in communicating with satellites equipped with Advanced Very High Resolution Radiometer (AVHRR). The AVHRR is a cross-track scanning system allowing the acquisition of signals by using five spectral bands having a resolution of 1.1 km and a frequency of two Earth scans per day. NOAA weather satellites broadcast an APT (Automatic Picture Transmission) and a HRPT (High Resolution Picture Transmission) signal containing a live weather image of the area overflown by the satellite. The scanning lines are oriented perpendicular to the motion of the sensor platform. By using a system that includes a rotating mirror each line is scanned from one side of the sensor to the other. As the platform moves forward over the Earth, successive scans build up a two-dimensional image of the Earth's surface. As said before, AVHRR scanning system acquires signal by using five spectral bands and, for instance, the visible light image and one of the infrared images are combined in a row vector; the combination is performed using the Automatic Picture Transmission system (APT).

Despite many scientific progresses over last few years, many scientific issues still affect NOAA satellites: information calibration, physical layer, synchronization, data detection, channel coding. Several scientific experiments are ongoing to overcome those issues, and we focused our efforts to propose a new effective satellite remote sensing tool for signal processing. In greater detail the tool consists of a low cost receiver subsystem for public weather satellites and a signal and image processing module for several tasks such as signal and image enhancement, image reconstruction and cloud detection. Our solution allows to manage data from satellites effectively with low cost components and lightweight computations. As we will show in the experimental results section the overall performances are very promising in terms of signal quality and image reconstruction. The rest of the paper is organized as it follows: in Sect. 2 we describe the state of the art methods for satellite signals modulation and imagery, in Sect. 3 we show in greater detail our proposed platform for the reception of satellite signals, in

Sect. 4 we show the experimental results for the reconstructed images and the Sect. 5 ends the paper with conclusions and future works.

In this paper we propose the extension of our previous work [1] as an effective tool for satellite data elaboration: the signals coming from satellites are demodulated, synchronized and enhanced by using low level image processing techniques, then cloud detection is performed by using the K-means clustering algorithm [2]. Also, we propose a new hardware and software architecture able to receive and demodulate high frequency and bandwidth meteorological satellite signals, such as those transmitted by NOAA POES, NOAA GOES, EUMETSAT Metop, Meteor-M and FengYun.

2   State of the Art

In this section we give an overview of the widely adopted techniques for the demodulation of signals coming from satellites. Since we perform cloud detection on remote sensing imagery, we give a brief description of techniques of the state of the art for cloud detection.

2.1   Satellite Communications and Signal Reception

In this section it is our interest to give the reader a brief description of some aspects related to our research with respect to the satellite communications and signal reception systems. In the last decades satellites have played a critical role interconnecting mankind through complex antennas and receiving systems. Scientific literature shows many technical solutions for antenna elements, sensors, array types, hyperspectral cameras. Depending on the satellite, we can find a low bandwidth communication system (VHF/UHF) or a high bandwidth communication system (more recent solutions have been dealing with communications by using arrays of high bandwidth microwave transponders with the purpose to offer multimedia services [3]). Scientific community has paid particular attention to reconfigurable antennas and ground receiving station, focusing the efforts towards user demands [4]. In this respect, several studies have been conducted to assess such aspects as signal propagation, tracking control, higher frequencies, arrays and reflectarrays, mechanical aspects, frequency selective surfaces [4].

Modern communication systems allow satellites to receive and transmit simultaneously thousands of signals: radiometers and hyperspectral cameras have been widely used to analyze Earth's visible and infrared radiation from the spacecraft, Synthetic Aperture Radars (SAR) have been used to map surface features and texture, even through dense cloud cover. Due to the aforementioned reasons, we are able to analyze soil/vegetation moisture (to detect anomalies and risks) [5] or produce 3D models of remote ares of the Earth (up to 1 m of spatial resolution). Noise and distortions in raw sensor data are usually linked to the sensor nonlinearities. As a general rule they are usually corrected by using classification or regression methods [6].

The APT format (Fig. 1) was developed around 1960 by U.S. National Aeronautics and Spatial Administration (NASA) as a communication system enabling

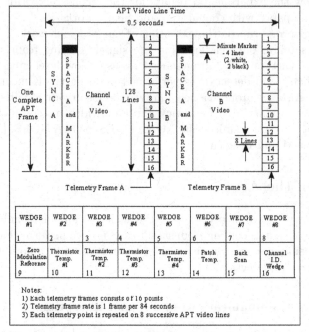

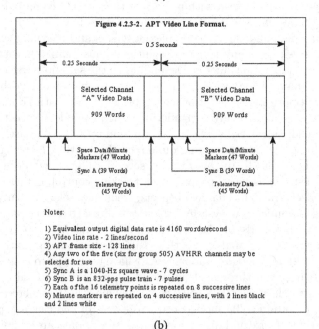

Fig. 1. (a) APT frame and (b) row format.

weather satellites to take pictures over wide areas and transmit them to ground stations on Earth [7,8]. From that time on, APT has been slightly modified and many stations still keep using analog radio equipment designed in the 1980s or the 1990s. The APT signal is formed by amplitude modulating a 2400 Hz carrier with each line of pixel data obtained by merging two images and calibration data, and then frequency modulating the result; the ease of building a basic receiver composed of a FM demodulator followed by an AM demodulator and an analog-to-digital converter has sparked the interest of researchers, scientists and radio operators. Several aspects such as Doppler effects, free space attenuation (varying with the distance from the satellite) make the reception and demodulation challenging tasks for signals coming from non-geostationary satellites. Furthermore, due to satellite's variable rotation relative to Earth's axis, linearly polarized antennas become unsuitable. For this reason circularly polarized antennas are used to fix the problem, assuring reliable and effective demodulation and synchronization, as well as a good quality output image. Other than demodulation and frequency tracking, image synchronization and calibration are usually performed by means of software solutions rather than hardware systems [9] because they are non-real time tasks that require some CPU power; it is also important to say that it would be somewhat challenging to implement those tasks in hardware (at least for non-experts). Sensor data can then be further corrected to compensate small sensor alignment errors, orbit uncertainty and on-board clock offset, by comparing expected and measured emissivity over land and sea and binning results into a high-resolution grid [10]. Over the last years several researchers have dealt with satellite remote sensing tools addressing the issue of affordability of hardware components and software solutions, to accomplish the tasks mentioned in the Introduction section of the paper. The authors of [11] designed a land station receiving through the combination of a software-defined radio (SDR), adaptive antennas on VHF band and FTP servers for the remote analysis of the obtained images. A satellite receiver was designed by Mahmood et al. [12] with the help of Realtek Software Defined Radio (RTL-SDR), Quadrifilar Helicoidal Antenna (QHA) and Trifilar Balun. QHA and Balun were designed and constructed under a precise and controlled environment. The signals were fed to SDR Sharp (generic SDR software) and were decoded to receive the latest weather image using WXtoImg. In [13] the authors proposed an experimental kit where a radio signal is received into the computer via the digital TV tuner that operated with the custom driver called RTL-SDR, and then the received signal is processed with a Python signal processing script. In [14] a low cost alternative to USRP (Universal Software Radio Peripheral) was proposed using RTL-SDR (Realtek Software Defined Radio) which is only used for reception. Furthermore a mixer circuit maps the baseband signal to the band that can be received by RTL-SDR.

2.2 Cloud Detection

Cloud properties such as cloud top height, temperature, infrared radiance have big impact on atmospheric monitoring results (forecasting of meteorological phenomena) [15]. Because of the aforementioned reasons cloud detection in remote sensing imagery is a very critical step. It is not straightforward to extract cloudiness mask from a given image from satellite because of several issues with surface properties such as reflectance and emissivity. Since many satellite missions are involved into atmospheric monitoring, achieving good results in terms of detection accuracy is quite important for improving the quality of successive steps of image analysis. Depending on the satellite product we find several features to analyze to detect cloud from an image. In this section we give a brief overview of the state of the art methods focused on cloud detection in satellite imagery. Heidinger et al. in [16] performed a naive Bayesian approach for cloud detection. This kind of methodology has been adopted for cloud detection on NOAA AVHRR data. In [17] the authors used the region growing method for dust cloud segmentation. The authors of [18], in order to accomplish the task of cloud detection, proposed an automatic supervised approach based on the scene-learning scheme. In greater detail, they simulate a kind of cubic structural data by considering different image features such as color, statistical information, texture, and structure. In [19] the authors of the document described the methods used to perform cloud detection in MODIS imagery. Lin et al. [20] proposed a radiometric normalization step to perform cloud detection in optical satellite images using invariant pixels. In [21] the authors examined two probabilistic methods for cloud masking of images from NOAA satellites, obtained with the Advanced Very High Resolution Radiometer. Simpson and Gobat in [22] used AVHRR Split-and-Merge Clustering (ASMC) for cloud detection to overcome the problem of spatially and temporally varying land surface reflectance and emissivity. Split-and-merge clustering allows to segment the scene in its natural groupings and label them as cloud, cloud-free land, uncertain. Gonzàlez et al. in [23] performed cloud classification by using watershed image segmentation, this method has been tested on images from MSG-SEVIRI (Meteosat Second Generation-Spinning Enhanced Visible and Infra-red Imager). The idea behind the method is to segment multispectral images using order-invariant watershed algorithms computed by a multi-dimensional morphological operator. In [24] after a super-pixel segmentation step, the authors accomplish the cloud detection task through bag-of-words and object classification methods. Several approaches have been adopted to perform cloud detection on remote sensing imagery, Foga et al. [25] compared many state of the art methods with respect to Landsat imagery. Bai et al. [26] performed cloud detection with machine learning and multi-feature fusion based on a comparative analysis of typical features such as spectral and texture [27]. A supervised approach using a neural network is proposed in [28] for detecting clouds over the ocean using AVHRR data. Other than the aforementioned methods there are deep learning based techniques such as [29], in which the authors used Convolutional Neural Networks (CNNs) consisting of four convolutional layers and two fully-connected layers, which can mine the deep features of clouds.

3   Proposed Method

Our method focuses on the possibility of directly sampling and processing of the modulated signal entirely in software enabled by recent breakthroughs on Software Defined Radios (SDR) and CPU computational speed. Our objective was achieving good results with low cost SDR hardware like RTL-SDR [14] (a repurposed DVB-T USB dongle) or LimeSDR: in particular, we had to overcome hardware limitations present in the RTL-SDR receiver: high noise figure and low ADC resolution. We also dealt with the inherent drawbacks caused by frequent tuner saturations. We developed an integrated hardware and software system able to perform the following steps: satellite pass prediction, time scheduling, signal demodulation, image cropping and filtering, and implemented two image processing algorithms to perform cloud detection.

3.1   APT Signal

The APT was introduced in 1960s and it shows its age in some respects: it is a mixed modulation signal (AM+FM) carrying a completely analog payload. The standard APT format consists of around 2080 pixels row, which is divided in two sub-rows of 909 pixels each belonging to two different sub-images (A and B) and then padded with synchronization and diagnostic information words. Images A and B during daytime are recorded in the visible range and in the infrared range of the electromagnetic spectrum respectively. At night-time, image A is replaced with one recorded at an infrared wavelength different from that of B. Rows can be grouped logically in frames of 128 lines each: a complete frame contains image calibration data and dynamic range references (wedges) [8]. The payload is used to amplitude modulate a 2400 Hz carrier according to (1) (as in [1])

$$s(t) = [1 + m(t)] \; A \; \cos(2\pi f_c t) \tag{1}$$

where m(t) is the modulating signal, A the carrier's amplitude and fc the carrier's frequency. The amplitude modulated signal is then frequency modulated with a frequency deviation of about 18–20 kHz and transmitted in the 137 MHz band at about 5 W EIRP (36.99 dBm) and 4160 sym/s symbol rate. Right hand circularly polarized (RHCP) antennas transmit the signal, so particular care had to be taken when choosing which antenna type to use in the receiving station.

3.2   Hardware

NOAA weather satellites require a circularly polarized antenna: the "turnstile" crossed-dipoles design was chosen because of its simplicity and the good performance provided when placed over a ground plane. Ease of construction, durability and suitability of common materials (which can be bought in hardware store) compensate the drawbacks of the system: the medium gain offered (6 dBi) and many nulls present in such a design [30]. In particular, the antenna shown here (Fig. 2a) has been built exclusively off PVC pipes, threaded bars as dipole

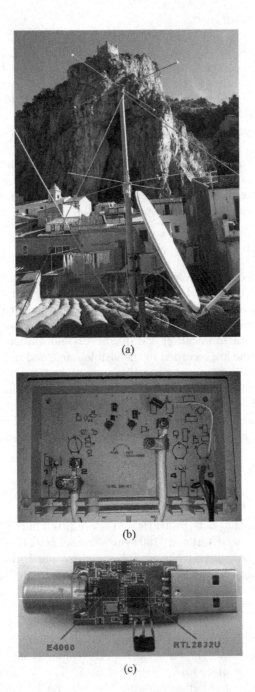

(a)

(b)

(c)

Fig. 2. (a) The turnstile antenna built for 137 MHz reception, (b) the modified TV amplifier, (c) a RTL2832U-based DVB-T dongle with an Elonics E4000 tuner.

elements, nuts and bolts and 75 Ω generic coaxial cable. The antenna is directly connected to a repurposed old TV amplifier (SIEL .269 01) (Fig. 2b), modified to behave like a wide-bandwidth amplifier. The input variable attenuator and high-pass filter have been removed, and the RF output has been separated from DC power path, allowing power without a bias tee. The amplifier uses two active components:

- BFR90A - 16 dB gain, 1.8 dB NF
- BFR91A - 14 dB gain, 1.6 dB NF

The results are 30 dB gain and ~1.83 dB NF (calculated using Friis' formula).

Ignoring noise introduced by amplifier's passive components, and considering room temperature of 290 K and 40 kHz bandwidth, the noise output of the amplifier can be calculated with formula (2) (as in [1]).

$$N_{in} + g + NF \tag{2}$$

N_{in} is the input noise (-127.95 dBm), g the gain (30 dB) and NF the total noise figure (1.83 dB). The result is a noise output of -96.12 dBm. Input noise has been calculated using formula (3) (as in [1]).

$$10\log_{10}(kTB) + 30 \tag{3}$$

k is the Boltzmann constant, T is absolute temperature and B is signal bandwidth, while $+30$ has been added to convert results from dBW to dBm. Considering NOAA satellites transmit at 5 W EIRP, when they are at receiving station's zenith the signal power at the receiver's input can be calculated as follows (as in [1])

$$36.99 \text{ dBm} - 133.34 \text{ dB} + 6 \text{ dBi} - 3 \text{ dB} + 30 \text{ dB} = -63.35 \text{ dBm} \tag{4}$$

133.34 dB is free space loss and 3 dB is the estimated loss due to cable and connectors. Output SNR in best-case conditions is then 32.77 dB, more than enough to ensure good image quality. The amplifier's output is connected to a SAW filter (Tai-Saw TA1581A) centered on 137.5 MHz to attenuate out-of-band signals and reduce the severe distortion caused by high-power FM broadcast stations and GSM signals. The TA1581 is a 50 Ω device, but an impedance matching circuit has not been installed because of the low mismatch loss (0.177 dB from antenna to filter and another 0.177 dB from filter to next RF device, which has 75 Ω impedance) compared to filter's 3.5 dB insertion loss. We added a standard ferrite bead near the receiver to shield common-mode interference caused by high-frequency equipment (PC, lab instruments, electronic ballasted lamps, etc.). The SDR hardware is widely available at a very low cost and is built around two chips: a RF tuner and an ADC/COFDM demodulator combo chip. The first used to be an Elonics E4000 (zero-IF), but has been replaced on new models with two superheterodyne alternatives, the Rafael Micro R820T and R820T2. The demodulator chip, a Realtek RTL2832U, is commonly used to demodulate the QPSK or QAM DVB-T signal into a MPEG stream and send it to a PC via an USB interface, but has a hidden passthrough mode which allows passing the ADC sample stream instead. The samples are internally filtered by a 32 coefficients FIR filter. For this study a dongle containing an E4000 tuner has been used (Fig. 2c).

3.3 High Frequency High Bandwidth Hardware

Our new high frequency receiving system is designed to receive and demodulate the signals of various meteorological satellites (not only NOAA) transmitting at 1.7 GHz. At this band the signals can have a larger bandwidth and convey data from multiple sensors at higher resolution (e.g. High Resolution Picture Transmission - HRPT [8]).

Antenna. The system has been designed around an offset parabolic antenna having a diameter of 1.3 m an efficiency factor of 0.75 (Fig. 3a). Because traditional systems have been built using prime-focus dishes having an efficiency of 0.6, our dish can actually have the same performance of a 1.5–1.6 m prime-focus dish, while being lighter and putting less stress on the antenna rotators. As it can be calculated using formula (5), where k is the efficiency factor, D the diameter and λ the signal wavelength, our antenna has a theoretical gain of 26 dB at 1.7 GHz (Fig. 3b).

$$10 \log_{10} \left[k \left(\frac{\pi D}{\lambda} \right)^2 \right] \tag{5}$$

The antenna's structure holds a helical feed designed for a dish having a focus/diameter (f/D) ratio of 0.8 (Fig. 4).

Antenna Rotator. In order to rotate and keep the antenna pointed towards the satellites, a Yaesu G-5500 rotator has been chosen for its durability and reliability, as it has been observed by various amateur radio operators. It can be controlled by the computer via the Yaesu GS-232A interface, which also allows to change azimuth rotation speed to ensure better satellite tracking.

Low Noise Amplifier. In order to amplify the received signal power to an easily demodulable level, we designed and built a dedicated LNA board. It has two stages: the first stage uses an ATF-36163 pHEMT transistor having a very high gain (>20 dB) and low noise figure (<0.5 dB) at 1.7 GHz. The second stage further boosts the signal and is based on a more traditional GaAs MESFET, the ATF-13284, which offers a 16 dB gain and 0.6 dB noise figure ad 1.7 GHz. Because those are high frequency and high gain components, PCB design was very critical and we had to take various approaches to avoiding unwanted emissions, instabilities and impedance mismatch. The design has also been optimized for minimum noise figure (0.5 dB) at 1.7 GHz, while also keeping a very high gain (>35 dB) and being easily reconfigurable by simply changing discrete inductors

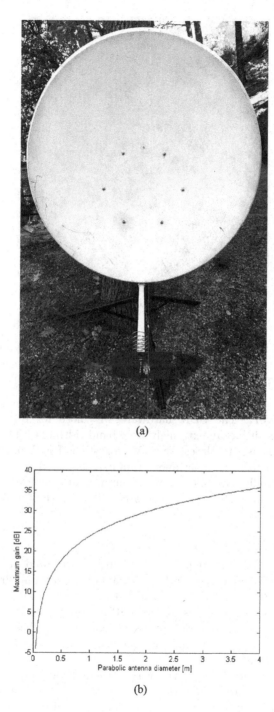

(a)

(b)

Fig. 3. (a) The offset parabolic antenna, (b) theoretical gain vs. diameter of a parabolic antenna having an efficiency of 0.75.

Fig. 4. The helical feed.

and capacitors. The circuit schematic can be seen in Fig. 5a, while a simulation of its performance is reported in Fig. 5b. Finally, the final version of the PCB after it has been populated with components is in Fig. 5c.

SDR Transceiver. The SDR hardware we chose for our system is the LimeSDR, because it has an extremely wide bandwidth of 61.44 MHz, it is fully open source and it uses the latest Lime Microsystems RF chip, the LMS7002M. The LimeSDR is capable of continuous tuning from 100 kHz to 3.8 GHz and its digital design will allow to offload the computational complexity of the demodulation task from the CPU to the integrated FPGA in the future.

3.4   Software

The RTL2832 and the tuner require specific initialization and tuning commands, so we decided to rely on a third-party hardware abstraction library coded by the RTL-SDR team [31], used by the official Mathworks RTL-SDR support package [32]. The latter allows easy access to the SDR hardware directly from MATLAB and Simulink environments. As a consequence, this study has been focused on the development of DSP algorithms on Simulink, taking advantage of its model-to-code conversion functionality.

We originally decided to use the very efficient Kyle Keen's rtl_fm [33] FM demodulator, but we later found that it was very easily saturated probably due to some issues in its integer math calculations. Therefore, it was necessary to implement a simple FM demodulation algorithm directly in the Simulink model.

The software we developed consists of the following parts:

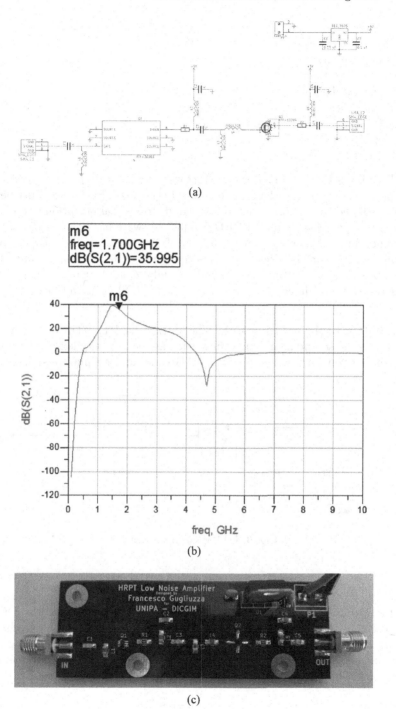

(a)

(b)

(c)

Fig. 5. (a) The amplifier's schematic, (b) its gain vs. frequency plot, (c) the populated PCB.

- satellite pass predictor
- digital down-converter
- FM demodulator
- FIR low-pass filter
- AM demodulators
- synchronization block
- pixel dynamic range calibration block
- model's parameters generator.

Satellite Pass Predictor. Because most weather satellites follow a polar orbit, they periodically pass on the same regions of the Earth. Each pass must be precisely predicted to schedule when to start and stop signal reception and demodulation, so John Magliacane's PREDICT [34] software has been used to predict start/end times and maximum elevations of the next satellite passes. In our system this software is called from a script and configured via command line parameters, and its output gets parsed to make it compatible with Microsoft Windows' task scheduler or, in the future, Linux/UNIX's cron scheduler.

RTL-SDR Library for Simulink. The Mathworks RTL-SDR library we used includes all the secondary required files, such as the precompiled low-level hardware abstraction library, sample MATLAB code and a Simulink signal source block.

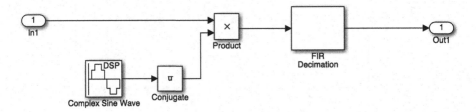

Fig. 6. Digital down-converter.

Digital Down-Converter. In order to mitigate the effects of the DC offset present in the Zero-IF tuner, we implemented an offset tuning mechanism (Fig. 6): the tuner is set 500 kHz lower than the real signal frequency, and circular frequency shift is performed to shift the satellite's signal back to baseband in software. This mechanism is mathematically explained in (6) (as in [1]).

$$e^{-j\Omega_0 n} = e^{\frac{-j2\pi f_0 n}{f_s}} \tag{6}$$

FM Demodulator. The original implementation of our system included a non-CPU intensive FM demodulator with automatic output amplitude rescaling (to compensate input amplitude fluctuations) [35], but it was prone to uncontrolled phase shifts in the demoduled output which heavily corrupted the 2400 Hz AM carrier. Therefore a traditional arcotangent-based FM demodulator [36] with amplitude rescaling was used in our work (Fig. 7a).

Low-Pass FIR Filter. The high frequency noise present in the FM demodulator output is filtered with a linear phase FIR filter designed using a Kaiser window and having a cutoff frequency of 5000 Hz. The latter has been tweaked experimentally by studying receiver and FM demodulator behavior and output frequency content.

AM Demodulators. In our system two AM demodulators are present: the first (Fig. 7b) is based on a discrete-time PLL followed by a low-pass filter with a cutoff of 1500 Hz to attenuate $2\pi f_c$ frequency components. Being a PLL-based receiver, the choice of K_i and K_p coefficients influences heavily its stability, performance and frequency tracking capability, especially when demodulating low SNR signals. We initially considered the delay of the FIR filter when tweaking the coefficients, as in [37], but the demodulator was still plagued by frequent losses of lock and low output SNR. The best results were obtained with the values reported in atpdec's [38] code.

The second demodulator (Fig. 7c) is based on an envelope detector, similar to analog diode detector demodulators: the absolute value function rectifies the signal and is followed by a linear-phase FIR filter having steep frequency characteristics. This filter greatly attenuates the f_c component while leaving the modulating signal intact and having lower computational complexity than a PLL-based approach. Thanks to the steep characteristics, demodulation is very satisfactory when the input signal has high SNR; when its SNR degrades (as at the start or the end of a satellite pass) it is recommended to switch to the PLL-based demodulator, which is also capable to compensate the Doppler effect to a certain extent.

Synchronization Block. APT format is equipped with two synchronization pulses: horizontal synchronization (sync A) is used as a boundary between video lines and inter-channel synchronization (sync B) is used as a boundary between the two video channels [8]. Our system includes a DSP block that detects synchronization pulses and splits the input signal in image lines composed by 2080 pixels; the image is further decomposed in two sub-images later in the Image Processing code.

The synchronization block requires that the input signal is sampled at a multiple of the symbol rate (4160 symbols/s) and downsamples it by selecting the median of an array of N samples, therefore filtering the signal and rejecting impulse noise.

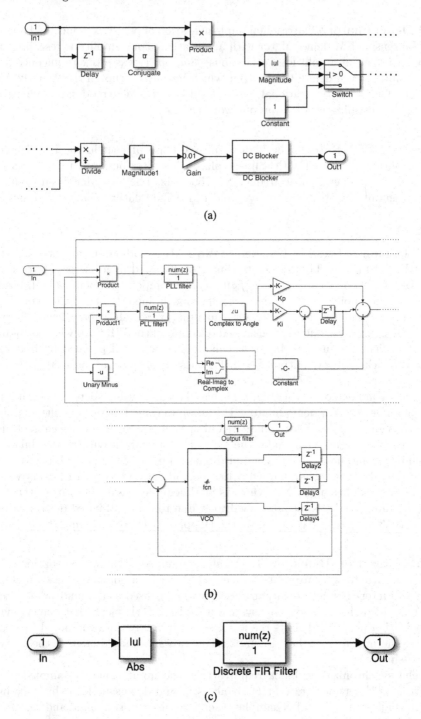

Fig. 7. (a) FM demodulator, (b) PLL-based AM demodulator, (c) Envelope detector AM demodulator (as in [1]).

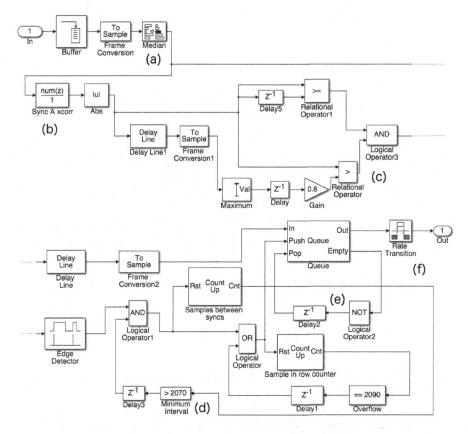

Fig. 8. Synchronization block (as in [1]).

During the experimental stage we also tested a simple interpolation algorithm for signal sampling, but this solution introduced excessive smoothing to the image and therefore we preferred the median algorithm solution.

Part (a) of Fig. 8 down-samples the signal, while (b) correlates previous part's output with a pattern of sync A; synchronization pulses are detected comparing local correlation peaks with maximum correlation in the last 3/4 s (c) (time during which one and a half video lines get transmitted). If correlation at discrete instant k-1 is a local peak and is greater than 80% of maximum correlation in said interval, it is considered as a synchronization pulse and a row formed by the last 2080 samples is inserted as a new element at the end of queue (e). Sometimes, however, synchronization pulses are lost or are erroneously detected due to signal fading or noise, so a filtering technique was devised (d): it filters pulses detected less than 2070 samples after last one. If a pulse has not been detected after 2090 samples the line is inserted at the end of the queue anyway and the 2090 samples counter is reset; the 2070 samples counter is not reset not to interfere with subsequent synchronization pulses. Finally, the Rate Transition block (f) outputs two lines of 2080 pixels each per second.

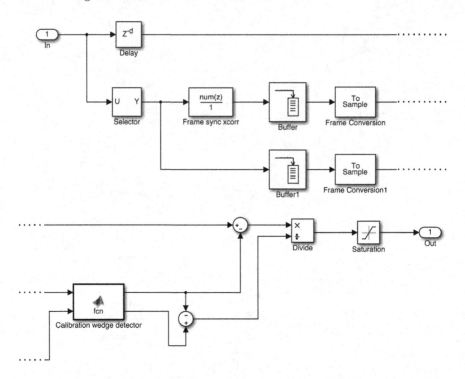

Fig. 9. Pixel dynamic range calibration block.

Pixel Dynamic Range Calibration Block. Each frame, composed of 128 rows, contains 16 "wedges": the first nine carry data about the image dynamic range (wedges 1–8 represent values from 1/8 to 8/8, while 9 is the zero reference). Our calibration block (Fig. 9) correlates a column of pixels of the wedge region with an example pattern, and then finds the exact position of each wedge. The values of wedges 8 and 9 are sampled and intensity offset and dynamic range are calculated. Offset is subtracted from pixel values and the result is divided by the detected dynamic range to normalize pixel values to the [0 1] interval: values outside this range are considered noise or saturation and clipped to 0 or 1.

This block outputs a stream of rows composed of 2080 pixels, which are later processed using Image Processing algorithms.

3.5   New Software

MathWorks Simulink is not optimized for real-time processing of high bandwidth signals, so we chose a different and more appropriate framework: GNU Radio [39]. GNU Radio offers a flowgraph representation of signal processing algorithms and its blocks are written in Python or C++. Blocks can take advantage of fast and efficient low level math functions via CPU abstractions (VOLK machines [40]) or, using third-party libraries, they can directly use GPU acceleration.

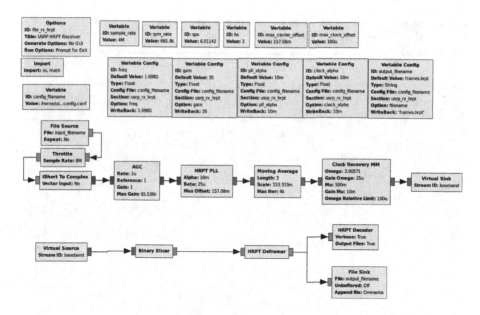

Fig. 10. Example flowgraph for HRPT reception in GNU Radio [41].

Many SDR transceivers and signal processing blocks are already supported in GNU Radio.

Flowgraphs for APT or HRPT signal decoding are already available on the Internet [42,43] or in the official libraries [41] (Fig. 10). Our objectives include adding support for other signal types, as Color HRPT (CHRPT), Advanced HRPT (AHRPT), Meteor-M HRPT, High Rate Information Transmission (HRIT), GOES Variable (GVAR) and GOES Rebroadcast (GRB).

Some parts of the legacy software solution, like the satellite pass predictor, are general purpose and can be reused.

Fig. 11. AVHRR image after automatic cropping (as in [1]).

Fig. 12. Disk filtered remote sensing image from NOAA (as in [1]).

4   Experimental Results

Our system generates a 2080 × 2*T image, where T is running time in seconds. Background white noise or artifacts caused by low signal SNR, fading, interferences and out-of-band intermodulation (Fig. 11) are cropped out by an algorithm using pixel variance in calibration wedges to estimate row reception quality. Only rows whose calibration wedges have an entropy below a certain threshold are kept. To further enhance image quality, various Image Processing filters have been applied to the output images and objective metrics (PSNR, RMSE, SNR_{rms} and SSIM) have been used to compare the results, which are reported in Table 1. The disk filter is shown to be achieving the best results (Fig. 12).

After image denoising we tried two classical approaches to image segmentation, in order to isolate cloud pixels both from land pixels and the rest of the image: the first approach uses the Otsu method [44] (as in [1]), a global thresholding based on spatial clustering: the one dimensional version of the method

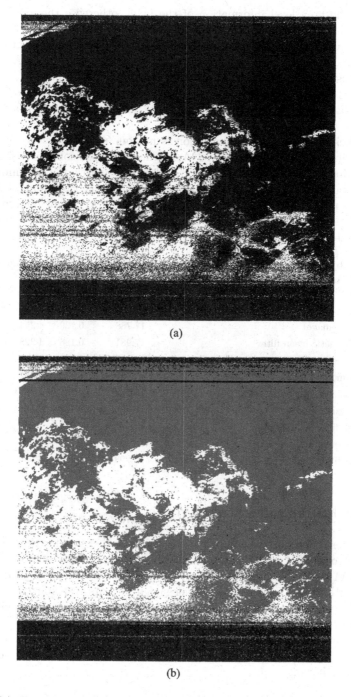

(a)

(b)

Fig. 13. (a) Cloud segmentation obtained with Otsu method (as in [1]) and (b) cloud segmentation achieved using the K-means algorithm (K = 3).

uses only the grey level information of the pixel, otherwise the 2D version of the method uses both the grey level information of the pixel and the spatial correlation within the neighbourhood. It is widely used for its simpleness and effectiveness, and is a good solution for images coming from NOAA satellites because it is robust against noise (usually present in APT images). The results are satisfactory and are shown in Fig. 13a. The second approach is based on K-means segmentation [2] with K = 3, and its results are also satisfactory and are shown in Fig. 13b.

That being said, cloud segmentation is not our main objective: we built a new accessible platform to receive NOAA signals, we used some new signal processing techniques for the demodulation and synchronization of the information coming from satellites, and finally we adopted some Image Processing techniques to enhance noisy images and achieve better results in terms of remote sensing imagery. We also show the results of cloud segmentation achieved using the Otsu method and K-means segmentation.

Table 1. Objective metrics results for image enhancement filtering (extended version of the table reported in [1]).

Method	PSNR [dB]	RMSE	SNR_{rms}	SSIM
None (raw image)	17.788	0.129	4.253	0.557
3 × 3 arithmetic mean filter	17.981	0.126	4.228	0.606
3 × 3 geometric mean filter	13.655	0.208	2.488	0.472
3 × 3 harmonic mean filter	13.295	0.216	2.357	0.449
3 × 3 contraharmonic mean filter with Q = 1	18.023	0.126	4.499	0.625
3 × 3 gaussian filter	18.485	0.119	4.551	0.609
3 × 3 disk filter	18.590	0.118	4.570	0.634
Adaptive median filter (min: 3 × 3 − max: 5 × 5)	18.444	0.120	4.586	0.622
Adaptive filter 3 × 3	16.298	0.153	3.550	0.563

5   Conclusion and Future Works

In this paper we proposed a complete system for weather satellite data reception. It is able to predict and track satellite passes, receive and demodulate both legacy NOAA APT signals (thanks to our previous work reported in [1]) and high resolution data contained in newer signal formats transmitted by various satellites. Despite the new system being still a work in progress, its specifications already match or exceed those of commercially available solutions [45], while being very easily reconfigurable to support new signal and data formats. In our future works we want to improve our solution with modular upgrades, thus adding the following:

- Multiple feeds and LNAs for multiple frequency bands;
- Support for various meteorological signal and payload formats;
- Support for error correction codes (where available)

– An algorithm for thermal maps generation based on the analysis of multi-spectral infrared images;
– Noise profiling based on long time analysis of the radio frequency interferences when the interferences are located near the receiver.

We aim to develop a modular solution for the prediction of atmospheric phenomena, based on the analysis of the images retrieved from several satellites (each one transmitting at its own frequency and with its own modulation scheme) at different times of the day. As far as it concerns cloud detection we proposed a solution that is mainly based on a simple and straightforward clustering method, that is, K-means. The method performs well with $K = 3$ but, generally speaking, the performance of a segmentation method based on clustering depends on the elements inside the image. We think that a fixed number $K = 3$ for K-means algorithm could not be sufficient for cloud detection whether the image contains elements such as soil, sea, cirrus, aerosols and clouds as well. In future works we want K cluster number to be adaptive with respect to the image we deal with. We could analyze the histogram of a patch to count the number of distribution modes, trying to establish a correspondence with the number of elements inside the image.

References

1. Ardizzone, E., Bruno, A., Gugliuzza, F., Pirrone, R.: A low cost solution for NOAA remote sensing. In: Proceedings of the 7th International Conference on Sensor Networks (SENSORNETS 2018), SCITEPRESS - Science and Technology Publications, Lda. All rights reserved, pp. 128–134 (2018)
2. MacQueen, J., et al.: Some methods for classification and analysis of multivariate observations. In: Fifth Berkeley Symposium on Mathematical Statistics and Probability, Oakland, CA, USA, vol. 1, pp. 281–297 (1967)
3. Farserotu, J., Prasad, R.: A survey of future broadband multimedia satellite systems, issues and trends. IEEE Commun. Mag. **38**(6), 128–133 (2000)
4. Rahmat-Samii, Y., Densmore, A.C.: Technology trends and challenges of antennas for satellite communication systems. IEEE Trans. Antennas Propag. **63**(4), 1191–1204 (2015)
5. Al-Moustafa, T., Armitage, R.P., Danson, F.M.: Mapping fuel moisture content in upland vegetation using airborne hyperspectral imagery. Remote Sens. Environ. **127**, 74–83 (2012)
6. Camps-Valls, G., Benediktsson, J.A., Bruzzone, L., Chanussot, J.: Introduction to the issue on advances in remote sensing image processing. IEEE J. Sel. Top. Signal Process. **5**(3), 365–369 (2011)
7. Barnes, J.C., Smallwood, M.D.: TIROS-N series direct readout services users guide. National Earth Satellite Service, NOAA (1982)
8. Wallach, J.: User's Guide for Building and Operating Environmental Satellite Receiving Stations. National Environmental Satellite, Data, and Information Service, NOAA (1997)
9. Benabadji, N., Hassini, A., Belbachir, A.H.: Hardware and software consideration to use NOAA images. Revue Internationale des Energies Renouvelables, CDER **7**(01), 1–11 (2004)

10. Moradi, I., Meng, H., Ferraro, R.R., Bilanow, S.: Correcting geolocation errors for microwave instruments aboard NOAA satellites. IEEE Trans. Geosci. Remote Sens. **51**(6), 3625–3637 (2013)

11. Bosquez, C., Ramos, A., Noboa, L.: System for receiving NOAA meteorological satellite images using software defined radio. In: ANDESCON, 2016 IEEE, pp. 1–4. IEEE (2016)

12. Mahmood, S., Mushtaq, M.T., Jaffer, G.: Cost efficient design approach for receiving the NOAA weather satellites data. In: 2016 IEEE Aerospace Conference, pp. 1–6. IEEE (2016)

13. Uengtrakul, B., Bunnjaweht, D.: A cost efficient software defined radio receiver for demonstrating concepts in communication and signal processing using Python and RTL-SDR. In: 2014 Fourth International Conference on Digital Information and Communication Technology and its Applications (DICTAP), pp. 394–399. IEEE (2014)

14. Sruthi, M., Abirami, M., Manikkoth, A., Gandhiraj, R., Soman, K.: Low cost digital transceiver design for Software Defined Radio using RTL-SDR. In: 2013 International Multi-Conference on Automation, Computing, Communication, Control and Compressed Sensing (iMac4s), pp. 852–855. IEEE (2013)

15. Feidas, H., Cartalis, C., Cracknell, A.: Use of Meteosat imagery to define clouds linked with floods in Greece. Int. J. Remote Sens. **21**(5), 1047–1072 (2000)

16. Heidinger, A.K., Evan, A.T., Foster, M.J., Walther, A.: A naive Bayesian cloud-detection scheme derived from CALIPSO and applied within PATMOS-x. J. Appl. Meteorol. Climatol. **51**(6), 1129–1144 (2012)

17. Alkhatib, M.Q., Cabrera, S.D., Gill, T.E.: Automated detection of dust clouds and sources in NOAA-AVHRR satellite imagery. In: 2012 IEEE Southwest Symposium on Image Analysis and Interpretation (SSIAI), pp. 97–100. IEEE (2012)

18. An, Z., Shi, Z.: Scene learning for cloud detection on remote-sensing images. IEEE J. Sel. Top. Appl. Earth Obs. Remote Sens. **8**(8), 4206–4222 (2015)

19. Ackerman, S., et al.: Discriminating clear-sky from cloud with MODIS algorithm theoretical basis document (MOD35). ATBD Ref. ATBD-MOD-06, version 4 (1997) 115p MODIS Cloud Mask Team. University of Wisconsin, Cooperative Institute for Meteorological Satellite Studies (1997)

20. Lin, C.H., Lin, B.Y., Lee, K.Y., Chen, Y.C.: Radiometric normalization and cloud detection of optical satellite images using invariant pixels. ISPRS J. Photogrammetry Remote Sens. **106**, 107–117 (2015)

21. Karlsson, K.G., Johansson, E., Devasthale, A.: Advancing the uncertainty characterisation of cloud masking in passive satellite imagery: probabilistic formulations for NOAA AVHRR data. Remote Sens. Environ. **158**, 126–139 (2015)

22. Simpson, J.J., Gobat, J.I.: Improved cloud detection for daytime AVHRR scenes over land. Remote Sens. Environ. **55**(1), 21–49 (1996)

23. González, A., Pérez, J.C., Muñoz, J., Méndez, Z., Armas, M.: Watershed image segmentation and cloud classification from multispectral MSG-SEVIRI imagery. Adv. Space Res. **49**(1), 135–142 (2012)

24. Yuan, Y., Hu, X.: Bag-of-words and object-based classification for cloud extraction from satellite imagery. IEEE J. Sel. Top. Appl. Earth Obs. Remote Sens. **8**(8), 4197–4205 (2015)

25. Foga, S., Scaramuzza, P.L., Guo, S., Zhu, Z., Dilley, R.D., Beckmann, T., Schmidt, G.L., Dwyer, J.L., Hughes, M.J., Laue, B.: Cloud detection algorithm comparison and validation for operational Landsat data products. Remote Sens. Environ. **194**, 379–390 (2017)

26. Bai, T., Li, D., Sun, K., Chen, Y., Li, W.: Cloud detection for high-resolution satellite imagery using machine learning and multi-feature fusion. Remote Sens. **8**(9), 715 (2016)
27. Ardizzone, E., Bruno, A., Mazzola, G.: Scale detection via keypoint density maps in regular or near-regular textures. Pattern Recogn. Lett. **34**(16), 2071–2078 (2013)
28. Yhann, S.R., Simpson, J.J.: Application of neural networks to AVHRR cloud segmentation. IEEE Trans. Geosci. Remote Sens. **33**(3), 590–604 (1995)
29. Shi, M., Xie, F., Zi, Y., Yin, J.: Cloud detection of remote sensing images by deep learning. In: 2016 IEEE International Geoscience and Remote Sensing Symposium (IGARSS), pp. 701–704. IEEE (2016)
30. Griffiths, M.: Turnstile design — DigitalHam (2014). http://www.digitalham.co.uk/design
31. Osmocom: rtl-sdr - OsmoSDR (2012). http://sdr.osmocom.org/trac/wiki/rtl-sdr
32. Sergienko, A.B.: Software-defined radio in MATLAB simulink with RTL-SDR hardware. In: 2014 International Conference on Computer Technologies in Physical and Engineering Applications (ICCTPEA), pp. 160–161. IEEE (2014)
33. Keen, K.: Rtl_fm Guide: Updates for rtl_fm overhaul (2013). http://kmkeen.com/rtl-demod-guide
34. Magliacane, J.: PREDICT - A Satellite Tracking/Orbital Prediction Program (2001). http://www.qsl.net/kd2bd/predict.html
35. Lyons, R.G.: Understanding Digital Signal Processing, 3/E. Pearson Education India (2004)
36. Shima, J.M.: FM demodulation using a digital radio and digital signal processing. Master's thesis, University of Florida (1995)
37. Wilson, J., Nelson, A., Farhang-Boroujeny, B.: Parameter derivation of type-2 discrete-time phase-locked loops containing feedback delays. IEEE Trans. Circuits Syst. II Express Briefs **56**(12), 886–890 (2009)
38. Leconte, T.: ATPDEC Home Page (2003). http://atpdec.sourceforge.net
39. The GNU Radio Foundation: GNU Radio (2001). https://www.gnuradio.org
40. The GNU Radio Foundation: Vector-Optimized Library of Kernels (2015). http://libvolk.org
41. The GNU Radio Foundation: NOAA POES HRPT receiver (2009) https://github.com/gnuradio/gnuradio/tree/master/gr-noaa
42. Csete, A.: NOAA Weather Satellite Reception with GNU Radio and USRP (2010). http://oz9aec.net/radios/gnu-radio/noaa-weather-satellite-reception-with-gnu-radio-and-usrp
43. Bülo, M.: A Simple GnuRadio HRPT Decoder (2018). https://tynet.eu/hrpt-decoder
44. Zhang, J., Hu, J.: Image segmentation based on 2D Otsu method with histogram analysis. In: 2008 International Conference on Computer Science and Software Engineering, vol. 6, pp. 105–108. IEEE (2008)
45. Dartcom Systems Ltd.: HRPT/AHRPT System (2018). https://www.dartcom.co.uk/products/hrpt-ahrpt-system

Multi-channel Communication Analysis of Industrial Wireless Sensor Networks in Outdoor Environments

Ruan D. Gomes[1(✉)], Emerson B. Gomes[2], Iguatemi E. Fonseca[2],
Marcelo S. Alencar[3], and Cesar Benavente-Peces[4]

[1] Federal Institute of Paraíba, Campina Grande 58432-300, Brazil
ruan.gomes@ifpb.edu.br
[2] Federal University of Paraíba, João Pessoa 58058-600, Brazil
emersonjpa@gmail.com, iguatemi@ci.ufpb.br
[3] Federal University of Campina Grande, Campina Grande 58401-490, Brazil
malencar@dee.ufcg.edu.br
[4] Universidad Politecnica de Madrid, 28031 Madrid, Spain
cesar.benavente@upm.es

Abstract. This paper describes a set of experimental studies, which investigates relevant properties of multi-channel wireless communications in outdoor industrial environments. Two different testbeds of IEEE 802.15.4 radios were employed in two different outdoor environments in order to evaluate the performance of the 16 channels defined by the standard. In the first environment the characteristics of the 16 channels were analyzed for 8 nodes simultaneously, and in the second environment the characteristics of the 16 channels were analyzed for 3 nodes in different positions, and in different times. From the collected data, some relevant facts are discussed, such as the spatial variations in channel quality, the differences in the characteristics of different channels, the link asymmetry, and the non-stationary characteristics of the channel. The possible problems that can arise in the deployment of industrial wireless sensor networks, based on the characteristics of the standards developed for this type of network, are described, as well as some possible solutions.

Keywords: Industrial wireless sensor networks ·
Multi-channel communication · Wireless channel characterization ·
Outdoor industrial environment

1 Introduction

The use of Industrial Wireless Sensor Networks (IWSN) to implement monitoring and control systems has some advantages, such as low cost and high flexibility to reconfigure the network. However, it is necessary to deal with typical problems of wireless networks, such as noise, electromagnetic interference, fading and high

C. Benavente-Peces et al. (Eds.): SENSORNETS 2017/2018, CCIS 1074, pp. 176–195, 2019.
https://doi.org/10.1007/978-3-030-30110-1_10

attenuation, due to the presence of many objects and obstructions. Many industrial environments also present characteristics that make the wireless channel non-stationary for long time periods [1].

Another problem is the link asymmetry. Some protocols use acknowledgement per packet and, in this case, it is necessary to guarantee a good quality of communication in the two directions of the link. Spatial variations in the channel quality can also occur in IWSN. In [17], a coherence length of 5.5 cm was found for IEEE 802.15.4 radios operating in the 2.4 GHz band. Hence, two nodes positioned at a distance more than 5.5 cm apart from each other, and using the same channel, can be considered uncorrelated, and thus the channel can present a high quality for one node, and a low quality for the other.

Some standards have been proposed in the last years with a focus on industrial applications, such as the WirelessHART and the ISA100.11a, which are based on the physical layer of the IEEE 802.15.4 standard, but define their own MAC layer based on Time Division Multiple Access (TDMA), to avoid collisions, and reduce the power consumption. They also use frequency hopping and blacklisting, to mitigate the problems related to interference and fading.

More recently, the IEEE 802.15.4e standard was released, which proposes solutions for applications that require high reliability (e.g. industrial applications) [10]. Five modes of operation are defined, but only the Time-Slotted Channel Hopping (TSCH), Deterministic and Synchronous Multi-Channel Extension (DSME), and Low Latency Deterministic Network (LLDN) modes have been explored in the literature, until now. In general, the modes are based on TDMA or frequency hopping to reduce collisions and mitigate the effects of interference and fading.

Even these new protocols define mechanisms to deal with the unreliability problems of IWSN, it is necessary to analyze the characteristics of the multi-channel communication in such environments, in order to properly deploy the network. For example, when using channel hopping, the nodes usually switch to a new channel before each transmission. However, if a proper management of the blacklist is not made, the network performance can be significantly degraded [12]. Problems due to the spatial variations in channel quality can also affect the performance of beacon-based protocols.

In this paper, the characteristics of the 16 channels, defined by the IEEE 802.15.4 standard, are analyzed, in two different outdoor industrial environments. Based on the experimental results, possible problems that can arise in the deployment of IWSN, and some possible solutions are described. For the first environment, where an experiment using eight nodes in different positions was performed, the parameters of the log-normal shadowing model were determined. Through the experiments in the second environment, it was possible to evaluate the influence of the modifications that occurred in the topology of the environment in the characteristics of the different channels, due to the movement of metallic structures around the nodes. The results highlighted the need of dynamically reconfigure the channels used in the network to guarantee a good quality of service in such environments. Some other studies have been performed in outdoor industrial environments [4] to analyze the impact of environmental aspects (e.g. temperature) on link quality. The novel contribution of this paper is the detailed analysis of the multi-channel communication in two different outdoor industrials environments, which may be important to design new techniques and protocols, as well as, more accurate simulation and theoretical models.

2   The Wireless Channel in Industrial Environments

The industrial environment usually contains metallic and mobile objects, such as robots, cars and people. This influences both the large-scale and small-scale fading. The power of the received signals depends on the transmission power, the antennas gains, the distance between transmitter and receiver and the effects caused by the environment. Even with the same values for the aforementioned parameters, there is a variation in the mean received power, depending on the place where the measurement is performed, which is known as log-normal shadowing. The log-normal shadowing model has been used to model the large-scale path loss and the shadowing in industrial environments [11,15]. Using this model, the path loss ($L(d)$) at a distance d is expressed according to

$$L(d) = L(d_0) + 10n \log \left(\frac{d}{d_0} \right) + X_\sigma, \tag{1}$$

in which n is the path loss exponent, d_0 is the reference distance, and $X\sigma$ is a Gaussian distribution with zero mean and standard deviation σ, and the two parameters are represented in dB. Besides the variation in the received power considering different locations, but with the same distance between transmitter and receiver, there are also variations when considering the transmission in different channels, even with the transmitter and receiver placed in fixed locations.

Besides path loss and shadowing, it is also necessary to analyze the small-scale channel fading due to rapid changes in the multipath profile of the environment, which is caused by the movement of objects around the receiver and transmitter. Experiments demonstrated that, in industrial environments, the temporal attenuation follows a Rice distribution, and the K factor of the Rice distribution has a high value. For the experiments described in [15], in industrial environments, K presented values between 4 dB and 19 dB, while in office environments, values between -12 dB and -6 dB. This can be explained by the open nature of industrial buildings and the large amount of reflective materials. Thus, there are many time-invariant rays and only a small part of the multipath profile is affected by moving objects.

It is also important to consider the non-stationary characteristics of the wireless channel for long periods of time. Experiments described in [1,8] showed that abrupt changes can occur in the link characteristics over time. Thus, the Rice distribution only fits the received power for small periods, in which the mean value of the received power remains constant. For example, the movement of a big metallic structure can change the multipath profile related to a set of rays that remained invariant for a long term, which causes differences on the mean value of the received power, although the transmitter and receiver remain static.

The IEEE 802.15.4 standard defines sixteen channels in the 2.4 GHz band, with 2 MHz of bandwidth, and channel spacing of 5 MHz. Thus, the channels are highly uncorrelated. Experiments described in [2] have found that changing the communication channel can lead up to 30 dB difference in the received power, in an office environment. Varga et al. [16] performed experiments for a short range, in an environment without multipath, and with line-of-sight. In that experiment, differences up to 10 dB were observed for some channels. Thus, besides the variation in shadowing observed depending on the place where the nodes are positioned, there is also a variation in shadowing regarding the different channels. In the experiments described in [7], differences of up to 15 dB were found for different channels in an indoor industrial environment, but only one link, and nine channels were analyzed.

In this paper, the aspects that influences the channel characteristics are discussed, based on experiments performed in two outdoor industrial environments with different characteristics, to analyze the temporal, spatial, and frequency variations in channel quality.

3   Experiment Methodology

In this paper, the experiments performed in two different outdoor industrial environments are described. The first one is a static environment, in which there are almost no movement of structures and people around the nodes. The results for this first environment were first described in our conference paper [6]. The second one is a dynamic environment, in which huge metallic structures move along the day, causing variations in the quality of the wireless channels over time. The results obtained in this second environment are novel.

The sensor nodes used in all experiments include an IEEE 802.15.4 transceiver (the MRF24J40MA from Microchip), with a transmission power of 0 dBm, a PCB antenna with a gain of 2.09 dBi, and a PIC18F46J50 microcontroller. In the following sections the specific details of each experiment are described.

3.1   Environment 1 – Water Treatment and Injection Station

In the experiments performed in the Environment 1, eight sensor nodes (1 to 8), and a coordinator (9), were placed in an outdoor industrial environment (Fig. 1(a)), according to the schematic shown in Fig. 1(b). The industrial unit is a water treatment and injection station, which treats the water that comes together with the oil from onshore oil fields and send it, pressurized, to a group of platforms placed about 25 km from the station. During the experiments, the station was operating normally, and the sensor nodes were placed alongside wired sensors that are currently installed in the unit.

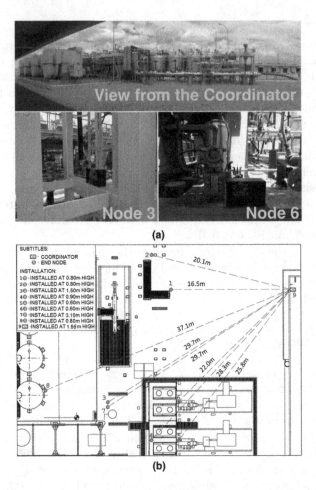

Fig. 1. (a) Environment 1 where the experiments were performed. (b) Schematic [6].

To allow the nodes to communicate using all channels, and without collisions, a protocol based on TDMA and channel hopping was implemented. In the protocol, the medium access occurs based on a slot-frame structure, which repeats continuously, similar to the slotframe defined on the TSCH protocol, but with the use of beacons, transmitted by the coordinator to synchronize the end-nodes in each cycle. The temporal structure of the slotframe is shown in Fig. 2.

The slotframe repeats continuously and is composed by 10 slots. In the first slot the coordinator transmits the beacon in broadcast, and waits to receive data packets that are transmitted by the end-nodes in the following eight time slots (*S1* to *S8*). There is an inactive interval in the end of the slotframe, that is used by the nodes to switch the channel and wait the next slotframe.

When an end-node receives a beacon from the coordinator, it waits until the time interval allocated to it and performs the transmission of a data packet to

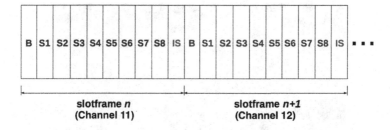

Fig. 2. Slotframe structure of the implemented protocol [6].

the coordinator. Each slot has a duration of 100 ms. This protocol was developed to allow the characterization of the multi-channel communication for multiple links simultaneously, but it was not developed taking under consideration any particular application.

In each *slotframe* a different channel is used, sequentially. To accommodate the use of channel hopping in the transmission of the beacons, it is necessary to have a mechanism to maintain the network synchronized in case of failures during the reception of a beacon. To do this, a timer is used in the end-nodes to identify that a beacon has been lost. The coordinator sends a new beacon for each 1 s, thus the timer is configured to expire after 1.1 s. If a node receives a new beacon before the timer expires, the timer is reseted. Otherwise, the node switches the channel, and waits for the next beacon, which maintains the synchronization.

After the reception of a beacon, the end-nodes obtain the Received Signal Strength Indication (RSSI) of the beacon, and transmit it back to the coordinator. For each received packet at the coordinator, the RSSI of the packet, as well as the RSSI of the beacon, sent by the end-node, are uploaded to a computer through a serial port. Thus, it is possible to analyze the spatial variations in the channel quality, and asymmetry, for all links. Even the individual RSSI samples are obtained in different moments for the different nodes and channels, due to the TDMA protocol, with the acquisition of many samples over time, it is possible to obtain the mean received power and the standard deviation, and compare the characteristics of the different channels for the different links.

In the Environment 1, two experiments were performed, in two days, with the nodes positioned in the same place. The network operated for about 3 h and 10 h, in the first and second days, respectively. The values of RSSI provided by the MRF24J40 transceiver varies between 0 and 255. For packets received with power between −94 dBm (transceiver sensitivity) and −90 dBm, the RSSI is equal to zero. However, despite this limitation, it was possible to analyze the differences in the characteristics of all channels, the spatial variations, and the non-stationary behavior of the wireless channel, and drawn remarkable conclusions about the multi-channel communication in outdoor industrial environments.

Fig. 3. The second environment where the experiments were performed.

3.2   Environment 2 – Solar Heating System

In the experiments performed in the second outdoor industrial environment
(Fig. 3) only two sensor nodes were used, an end-node and a coordinator. Three
replications were made with the coordinator at the same place, and the end-node
positioned in three different positions, at different distances and positioned in
places with different characteristics, according to the schematic shown in Fig. 4.

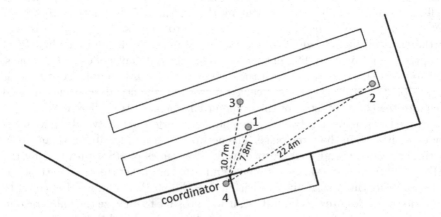

Fig. 4. Solar plant schematic, with the three different positions of the sensor-node.

The experiments were performed at a pilot solar heating system, which is an
industrial unit that consists of a field of solar parabolic troughs which converts
incident solar energy into heat for thermal oil. The nominal capacity of the

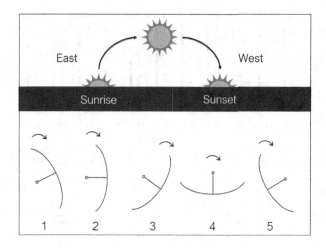

Fig. 5. Parabolic troughs tracking the sun.

system is 250 kW thermal, and in the normal condition, raises the temperature of the thermal oil from 80 °C to 120 °C. A solar parabolic trough is a long, trough-shaped reflector that has a parabolic cross-section with a slope affected by the rim angle. The trough focuses the reflected sunlight radiation along the trough.

The solar parabolic troughs have a tracking system, which are usually adjusted with their long axes from north to south and they are mounted on structural supports, made of aluminium, that allow them to track the sun from east direction to west direction during the day, as shown in Fig. 5. In the same figure, some inclinations of the parabolic troughs are shown, numbered from one to five. The Inclination 1 is equal to $-118°$, the Inclination 2 is equal to $-90°$, the Inclination 3 is equal to $-45°$, the Inclination 4 is equal to $0°$, and the Inclination 5 is equal to $45°$. Thus, during approximately 10 h of normal operation, the parabolic troughs start from Inclination 1 and reach the Inclination 5. After reaching the Inclination 5, the troughs return to the initial position with the Inclination 1. This movement causes temporal variations in the quality of the wireless channels, as shown in the results of this paper.

In the experiments performed in the Environment 2, the same protocol described in Sect. 3.1 was used, but with only three time-slots per slotframe (B, S1, and IS), since only one end-node was used in each replication. Three experiments were performed in three different days, with the end-node positioned in three different positions. In the first day (Position 1) the network operated for about 23 h, in the second day (Position 2) the network operated for about 18 h, and in the third day (Position 3) the network operated for about 12 h. Through these experiments, it was possible to observe the influence in the long term of the movement of the solar parabolic troughs in the quality of the 16 channels defined by the IEEE 802.15.4 standard for the three different positions.

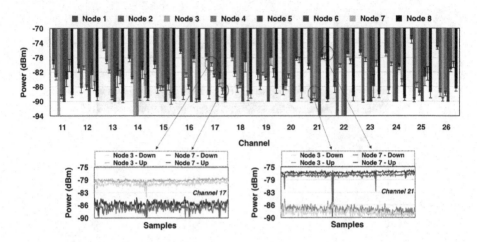

Fig. 6. Spatial variations in the channel quality for different nodes, in the first day of experiment [6].

4   Results

4.1   Environment 1 – Water Treatment and Injection Station

Figure 6 shows the mean received power, and the standard deviation, for each end-node, considering the experiment performed in the first day. The mean received power varies significantly, even for the adjacent channels and for the same end-node. For example, for Node 1, the differences for some channels were higher than 10 dB (e.g. Ch 20 and Ch 25). For Nodes 4 and 5, which were positioned in a place without Line-Of-Sight (LOS) (see Fig. 1(b)), no communication can be set, for example, when using Ch 22, due to a deep fading problem in the channel. All channels shown a low quality for Node 5, but for Node 4 some channels presented high quality, such as the Ch 17. Deep fading problems have also occurred for some other nodes and channels, in which the number of packets received was very low.

From Fig. 6 it is also possible to analyze the spatial variations in the quality of the channels. The values of received power for Nodes 3 and 7 are analyzed in detail for two different channels. These nodes were positioned at nearly the same distance to the coordinator, and with a 1.6 m of difference in the height. The Ch 17 presented a high quality for Node 3, but the quality was significantly lower for the Node 7. On the other hand, the Ch 21 presented a high quality for Node 7, but a low quality for Node 3. The reception power in the two directions of the links are shown. There is a high correlation between the received power in both directions of the links, but with a small difference in the mean values. When the received power is near to the sensitivity threshold of the transceiver, such as is the case of Ch 21 for Node 3, this small difference can provoke an asymmetry in the link quality.

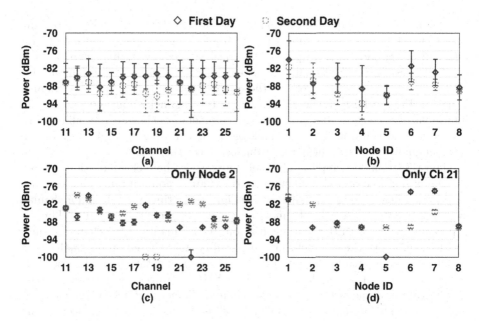

Fig. 7. Comparative results between the two days of experiment [6].

Hence, it is difficult to guarantee a good Quality of Service (QoS) for all nodes when only one channel is used in the whole network, such as in the MAC protocols defined by the IEEE 802.15.4 standard. Even for the new standards defined for IWSN, some problems can arise due to the spatial variations in channel quality. In the LLDN mode, TDMA is used to avoid collisions, with a star topology, to achieve very low latencies [3]. However, only one channel is used for all end-nodes. One possible solution is the use of multiple sink-nodes, using different channels. When the channel being used by an end-node starts to present low quality, that node can switch to another channel and communicate with a different sink. However, some mechanism to estimate the link quality in real-time [7], and a specific synchronization mechanism needs to be developed. The protocol described in [14] uses a tree topology and multi-channel communication for LLDN networks, with adaptive channel selection, but the same channel is allocated to all nodes in the sub-network, and spatial variations in channel quality can also occur inside the same sub-network.

Even for protocols that use channel hopping or channel adaptation, some problems may arise. For example, the TSCH, WirelessHART, and ISA100.11a standards use TDMA and channel hopping. In this approach, all the channels can be used by the end-nodes to perform communication. However, the blacklist needs to be properly managed in order to achieve a good QoS in the network. In [5] it was observed that the larger the size of the blacklist, the better the communication performance. This result corroborates with the results presented in [12]. However, this type of behavior only occurs if an adequate monitoring of the quality of the channels is performed, in order to properly configure the blacklist.

One problem is that, when a channel is blacklisted, all the nodes stop using that channel. In the result shown in Fig. 6, Ch 21 presented a low quality for four end-nodes and could be put on the blacklist. However, this channel is the one that presents the best quality for Node 7, and also presents good quality for Nodes 1 and 6. Thus, the QoS for these nodes can decrease once this channel is put on the blacklist. When the quality of the channel is affected by external interference, as considered in [5], putting a channel in the blacklist for all network can be a good solution, but the challenge is higher when spatial variations in channel quality, due to multipath problems, affect the links.

The DSME mode employs channel hopping or channel adaptation, during the contention free periods. When using the channel adaptation, a pair of nodes can communicate using the same channel for a long time period, and a channel switch only occurs when the channel in use starts to present low quality. Thus, it is possible to deal with the spatial variations in the quality of the channels, since the decision about the channel to be used can be made based on the quality of a specific link between a given pair of nodes. The implementation of this procedure is not defined by the standard [10]. The DSME networks use beacon packets, transmitted in broadcast using a single channel. Sometimes it is difficult to pick one channel that presents good quality for all nodes in the network. Deep fading problems can also occur, and some nodes can remain disconnected for a long time. While the use of channel adaptation can be a good solution for unicast data packets, channel hopping can be a good solution for packets transmitted in broadcast.

Figure 7 shows a comparison between the results obtained in the two days. Figure 7(a) shows the mean received power, and the variance for all channels. The variance was high in all channels, due to the differences in the channel characteristics for the different links. Figure 7(b) shows the mean received power, and the variance, for the eight different links, considering the 16 channels. There is also a significant variance, due to the differences in the characteristics of the different channels in each link. Figure 7(c) shows the results for a specific node (Node 2) and for all channels in both days. It is worthy to notice that while some channels had an increase in quality, the quality of other channels decreased significantly in the second day. For example, the Ch 18 presented a good quality in the first day for Node 2, but presented a deep fading problem during the second day. Figure 7(d) shows the results for a specific channel (Ch 21), and for the eighth different links. It is possible to notice that the characteristics of the channels vary differently for the different nodes. For example, the Ch 21 presented a high quality for the Node 6 in the first day, but a low quality in the second day. On the other hand, it presented a higher quality on the second day for the Node 2.

Some abrupt variations in the reception power for some nodes and channels were also observed during the second day (Fig. 8). This behavior was also observed in [1] for an indoor industrial environment. The quality of the Ch 24 decreased after some time for Node 7, while at the same time the channel showed an increase in its quality for Node 6. Again, a high correlation between the two directions of the links was observed, but with a small difference in the mean value of each direction of the link.

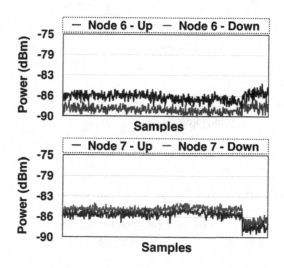

Fig. 8. Abrupt change in channel characteristics [6].

The chart in Fig. 9 shows the path loss $(L(d))$ for a distance (d) between transmitter and receiver. The values obtained for Node 1 were used as reference $(d_0 = 16.5\,\text{m})$. From this experiment, the path loss exponent (n), the shadowing deviation (σ), and $L(d_0)$ were obtained, to be applied in the log-normal shadowing model. Figure 9 shows the curves of the model for three different scenarios: with all nodes, with the LOS nodes (Nodes 3, 6, 7 and 8), and with the NLOS nodes (Nodes 2, 4, and 5). Node 1 was considered in both cases as the reference. Table 1 shows the parameters for the three scenarios. These values can be used to simulate outdoor IWSN.

To allow an accurate simulation, it is important to consider all the aspects and conclusion discussed in this paper, and also nodes with LOS and NLOS, with different parameters for the path loss and shadowing. Also, the level of shadowing in each channel for the different links need to be modified over time. Sometimes abrupt changes can occur in the characteristics of the channel, and the modifications occur differently for the different channels and nodes, and the protocols for IWSN need to be capable to dealing with these modifications to maintain a good QoS over time.

4.2   Environment 2 – Solar Heating System

Figures 10, 11 and 12 show the received power in both directions of the link for the experiments in the positions 1, 2, and 3, respectively. For each position, the received power for two different channels are shown, to compare the behavior

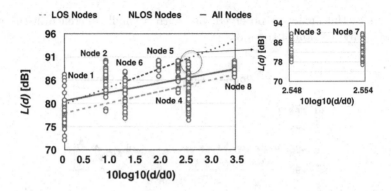

Fig. 9. Relation between the path loss and the distance between transmitter and receiver [6].

Table 1. Parameters for the log-normal shadowing model [6].

	Path loss exponent (n)	Shadowing deviation (σ)	$L(d_0)$
All nodes	2.00	4.53 dB	81.182 dB
LOS nodes	2.43	4.54 dB	78.351 dB
NLOS nodes	4.03	4.98 dB	80.352 dB

of the different channels over time. In the charts it is also possible to see the variation in the angle of the solar parabolic troughs. During the periods without movement of the troughs the channel remains stationary. However, during the periods with movement of the troughs, the channel behavior is very dynamic.

For example, in the Position 1 (Fig. 10) the received power for Ch 11 remains between -70 dBm and -75 dBm for both up and down links during several hours, and during the movement of the troughs the received power was below -80 dBm during some periods. The received power for Ch 15 presented similar behavior, but with different average values for the received power at certain times.

After the period of movement, the received power stabilized in a higher value for Ch 11 in comparison to the values of received power before the beginning of the movement of the troughs. On the other hand, the quality of Ch 15 decreased a little after the end of the movement of the troughs, and its quality become worse than the quality of Ch 11. This probably occurred due to the mechanical imprecision in the movement of the structure. Thus, even with the same inclination degree in the beginning and in the end of the experiment, it is possible that the positions of the troughs in these two periods differ in a few centimeters, which is sufficient to cause a difference in the characteristics of the channels. Despite the temporal variations, in general for the Position 1 all channels presented good quality during all the experiment, since the distance between transmitter and receiver was only 7.8 m, and with line-of-sight.

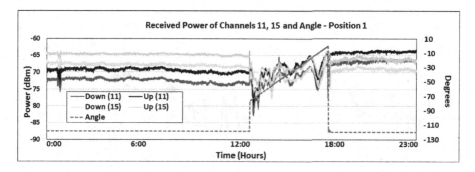

Fig. 10. Received power for channels 11 and 15, and slope angle of the parabolic troughs at Position 1.

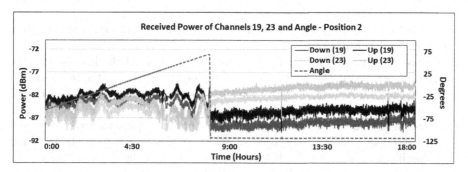

Fig. 11. Received power for channels 19 and 23, and slope angle of parabolic troughs at Position 2.

For the Position 2 (Fig. 11) the received power for channels 19 and 23 are shown. It is possible to notice that during the movement of the troughs the Ch 19 presents a good quality, with received power more than 10 dB above the sensitivity of the transceiver (−94 dBm), despite the variations due to the dynamic behavior of the environment. However, after the end of the movement of the troughs, the average received power dropped to a value close to the transceiver sensitivity. On the other hand, even the quality of the Ch 23 being lower during the movement of the troughs, when compared to Ch 19, its quality increased after the end of the movement, and the Ch 23 become better than the Ch 19 for this particular link.

For the Position 3 (Fig. 12) the overall quality of the channels was worst in comparison to the other two positions, since the end-node was behind a parabolic trough. For this position, it is shown the received power for channels 17 and 19. It is interesting to notice that after the end of the movement of the solar troughs, the quality of the Ch 19 has dropped, and the average received power remained very close to the transceiver sensitivity until the end of the replication. On the other hand, the quality of Ch 17 increased right after the end of the movement

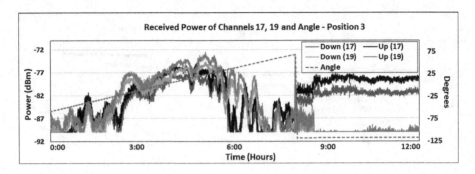

Fig. 12. Received power for channels 17 and 19, and slope angle of parabolic troughs at Position 3.

of the troughs, and the average received power remained more than 10 dB above the transceiver sensitivity for both directions.

Figures 13, 14 and 15 show the channels that presented the highest average received power during the replications, for the positions 1, 2 and 3, respectively. To define the best channel at each moment, the average received power for each interval of one minute was calculated for all channels. These analyses highlight the need of the use of adaptive protocols in order to pick the best channels at each moment, and also the need of selecting the appropriate channels for each specific link, as analyzed in more details through the experiments in the Environment 1. In general, a high correlation between the two directions of the links was observed in all experiments, but with a small difference in the mean value of each direction of the link. Thus, only the up-link was analyzed in the Figs. 13, 14 and 15.

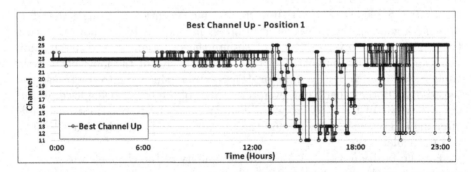

Fig. 13. Channels with the highest received power in each interval of 1 min - Experiment at position 1.

For the Position 1 (Fig. 13), before the beginning of the movement of the troughs the Ch 23 presented the best quality during almost all the time. However, during the movement of the troughs, the best channel varied very much.

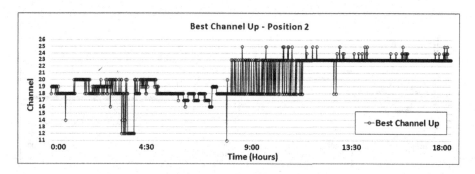

Fig. 14. Channels with the highest received power in each interval of 1 min - Experiment at position 2.

After the end of the movement, the Ch 25 was the best almost all the time, but a higher variation was observed in comparison to the period before the beginning of the movement of the troughs. It is important to notice that due to the small distance between transmitter and receiver in the experiment with the Position 1 all the channels presented good quality.

For the positions 2 and 3, the variation was smaller, even during the movement of the solar troughs (which occurred at the beginning of the experiment for these two positions). This occurred due to the larger distance between transmitter and receiver in comparison to the Position 1, and due to the obstructions. In these scenarios, in a given moment, many channels presented poor quality, and only a small set of channels presented good quality, which diminish the diversity of good channels. For example, for the experiment in the Position 2, during the movement of the troughs, the best channel varied between the channels 19, 18, and 12 during almost all the time. For the experiment in the Position 3, the best channel was the Ch 20 during a long period during the movement of the troughs. These results encourage the development of mechanisms for dynamic management of blacklists in protocols that use channel hopping, such as the TSCH, and the WirelessHART, as proposed in [13,18]. Other possible solution is the use of channel adaptation, in which only one channel is used during a long period of time, and a channel switch only occurs when the channel in use starts to present bad quality, as evaluated in [9] for DSME networks.

Figures 16, 17 and 18 show the received power of the overall best channel during each replication, and the received power considering the best channel for each interval of one minute. It is possible to note that, even using the channel that presents the best overall quality, during certain times the received power for that channel may be low, making the link less robust. By using an appropriate channel diversity mechanism, it may be possible to switch the channel dynamically and try to use a good channel during all the time. For this, mechanisms for link quality estimation, and adaptive channel hopping need to be implemented.

In the experiment at the Position 3 (Fig. 18), in which the end-node was further from the coordinator, when using the overall best channel, during certain

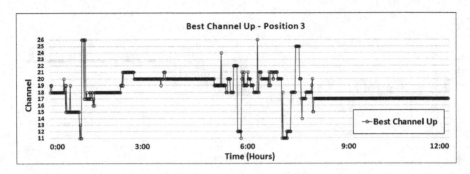

Fig. 15. Channels with the highest received power in each interval of 1 min - Experiment at position 3.

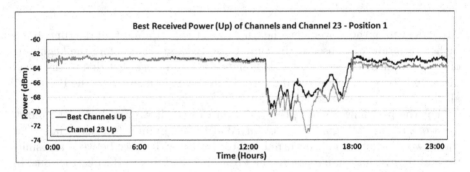

Fig. 16. Comparison between the use of the best overall channel (Ch 23) and the best channels for each interval of 1 min - Experiment at position 1.

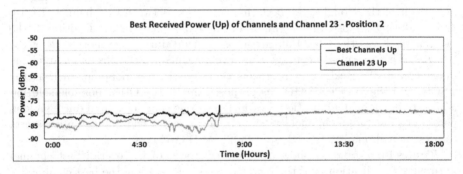

Fig. 17. Comparison between the use of the best overall channel (Ch 23) and the best channels for each interval of 1 min - Experiment at position 2.

periods of time the received power remained very close to the transceiver sensitivity, which makes the link less robust and more susceptible to packet losses due to rapid variations in channel quality or possible external interferences. When using the best possible channel considering each interval of one minute, the received

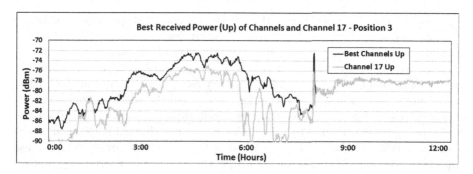

Fig. 18. Comparison between the use of the best overall channel (Ch 17) and the best channels for each interval of 1 min - Experiment at position 3.

power remained above $-88\,$dBm during all the time. Thus, it was shown that by picking appropriate channels for communication in a dynamic way, it is possible to maintain communication with good quality even for end-nodes positioned far from the receiver and close to obstructions that moves over time.

5   Conclusions

This paper describes a set of experiments to evaluate and characterize the performance of multi-channel communications of IWSN in two different outdoor environments. Relevant characteristics of the wireless channel were described, based on the experimental results. Some problems that can occur in the deployment of an IWSN, as well as some possible solutions, are discussed in the paper, considering the characteristics of the wireless channel in the environment under study, and the characteristics of the protocols that are used to implement the IWSN. The parameters of the log-normal shadowing model were also obtained for the first environment. The information contained in this paper can be used to allow the implementation of new techniques and protocols for IWSN, as well as more accurate simulation models.

The first environment is static, and only a few movement of people and equipment occurs over time. However, it is possible to see that adaptive protocols need to be implemented to ensure a good quality of service, due to the spatial variations in the quality of the channels, and due to the slow time variations, as observed in the analysis that compares the characteristics of the channels in two different days.

The second environment is very dynamic, due to the movement of the solar parabolic troughs. In this paper, it was observed the influence of the movement of these metallic structures in the characteristics of the 16 channels defined by the IEEE 802.15.4 standard for different positions of the end-node. The analyses performed for the second environment corroborates the importance of the use of adaptive protocols to pick appropriate channels for each link and to deal with the temporal variations in the characteristics of the channels due to the modifications in the topology of the environment over time.

Based on the characteristics of the wireless channel that were observed in the experiments, some future works can be outlined, such as the design and implementation of mechanisms for dynamic configuration of the blacklist in protocols that use frequency hopping, to deal with the time and spatial variations in the quality of the channels. The use of link quality estimators to monitor the quality of the links continuously can be useful to improve the blacklist management. Other alternative is the use of channel adaptation mechanisms, in which the nodes use only one channel to communicate, but the channel is changed whenever the quality of the channel in use is below a certain threshold. All these aspects will be investigated in future works, as well as new experiments in other types of outdoor industrial environments will be performed.

Acknowledgements. The authors would like to thank the support of the Institute for Advanced Studies in Communications (Iecom), the Brazilian Council for Research and Development (CNPq), the Coordination for the Improvement of Higher Education Personnel (CAPES), and Petrobras.

References

1. Agrawal, P., Ahlén, A., Olofsson, T., Gidlund, M.: Long term channel characterization for energy efficient transmission in industrial environments. IEEE Trans. Commun. **62**(8), 3004–3014 (2014)
2. Amzucu, D.M., Li, H., Fledderus, E.: Indoor radio propagation and interference in 2.4 GHz wireless sensor networks: measurements and analysis. Wirel. Pers. Commun. **76**, 245–269 (2014)
3. Anwar, M., Xia, Y., Zhan, Y.: TDMA-based IEEE 802.15.4 for low-latency deterministic control applications. IEEE Trans. Ind. Inform. **12**(1), 338–347 (2016)
4. Boano, C.A., Tsiftes, N., Voigt, T., Brown, J., Roedig, U.: The impact of temperature on outdoor industrial sensornet applications. IEEE Trans. Ind. Inform. **6**(3), 451–459 (2010)
5. Du, P., Roussos, G.: Spectrum-aware wireless sensor networks. In: 2013 IEEE 24th Annual International Symposium on Personal, Indoor, and Mobile Radio Communications (PIMRC), pp. 2321–2325 (2013)
6. Gomes, R.D., Gomes, E.B., Fonseca, I.E., Alencar, M.S., Benavente-Peces, C.: Evaluation of multi-channel communication for an outdoor industrial wireless sensor network. In: Proceedings of the 7th International Conference on Sensor Networks - Volume 1: SENSORNETS, pp. 60–66. INSTICC, SciTePress (2018)
7. Gomes, R.D., Queiroz, D.V., Filho, A.C.L., Fonseca, I.E., Alencar, M.S.: Real-time link quality estimation for industrial wireless sensor networks using dedicated nodes. Ad Hoc Netw. **59**, 116–133 (2017)
8. Gomes, R.D., Queiroz, D.V., Fonseca, I.E., Alencar, M.S.: A simulation model for industrial multi-channel wireless sensor networks networks using dedicated nodes. J. Commun. Inf. Syst. **32**, 29–40 (2017)
9. Gomes, R.D., Alencar, M.S., Queiroz, D.V., Fonseca, I.E., Benavente-Peces, C.: Comparison between channel hopping and channel adaptation for industrial wireless sensor networks. In: Proceedings of the 6th International Conference on Sensor Networks, pp. 87–98 (2017)

10. Guglielmo, D.D., Brienza, S., Anastasi, G.: IEEE 802.15.4e: a survey. Comput. Commun. **88**, 1–24 (2016)
11. Gungor, V.C., Lu, B., Hancke, G.P.: Opportunities and challenges of wireless sensor networks in smart grid. IEEE Trans. Ind. Electron. **57**, 3557–3564 (2010)
12. Gürsu, M., Vilgelm, M., Zoppi, S., Kellerer, W.: Reliable co-existence of 802.15.4e TSCH-based WSN and Wi-Fi in an aircraft cabin. In: 2016 IEEE International Conference on Communications Workshops (ICC), pp. 663–668 (2016)
13. Kotsiou, V., Papadopoulos, G.Z., Chatzimisios, P., Theoleyre, F.: LABeL: Link-based Adaptive BLacklisting technique for 6TiSCH wireless industrial networks. In: Proceedings of the 20th ACM International Conference on Modelling, Analysis and Simulation of Wireless and Mobile Systems, pp. 25–33 (2017)
14. Patti, G., Bello, L.L.: A priority-aware multichannel adaptive framework for the IEEE 802.15.4e-LLDN. IEEE Trans. Ind. Electron. **63**(10), 6360–6370 (2016)
15. Tanghe, E., et al.: The industrial indoor channel: large-scale and temporal fading at 900, 2400, and 5200 MHz. IEEE Trans. Wirel. Commun. **7**, 2740–2751 (2008)
16. Varga, L.-O., Heusse, M., Guizzetti, R., Duda, A.: Why is frequency channel diversity so beneficial in wireless sensor networks? In: IFIP Wireless Days, Toulouse, France. IFIP (2016)
17. Watteyne, T., Lanzisera, S., Mehta, A., Pister, K.S.J.: Mitigating multipath fading through channel hopping in wireless sensor networks. In: 2010 IEEE International Conference on Communications, pp. 1–5 (2010)
18. Zorbas, D., Kotsiou, V., Théoleyre, F., Papadopoulos, G.Z., Douligeris, C.: LOST: localized blacklisting aware scheduling algorithm for IEEE 802.15.4-TSCH networks In 2018 Wireless Days (WD), pp. 110–115 (2018)

Design of Wireless Sensor Network in the Railway Facilities

Nagateru Iwasawa$^{(\boxtimes)}$, Tomoki Kawamura, Nariya Iwaki,
Satoko Ryuo, and Michiko Nozue

Railway Technical Research Institute,
2-8-38, Hikari-cho, Kokubunji-shi, Tokyo, Japan
iwasawa.nagateru.81@rtri.or.jp

Abstract. In recent years, research and development on the condition monitoring systems using the wireless sensor network in the railway have been proceeded. The railway has a characteristic such as extending linearly, many metal objects becoming obstacles to radio wave propagation. However, there are few cases of the wireless sensor network design based on the features of the railway environment. In this study, we propose the procedure to design the wireless sensor network in the railway. And we introduce the demonstration test and the result in the railway slope based on this procedure.

Keywords: Wireless sensor network · Railway ·
Condition monitoring system · Wi-SUN · 920 MHz · Slopes

1 Introduction

The railway is one of the essential transport infrastructure in many countries. Especially, in Japan, passenger transport in FY2015 stood at 24.3 billion persons, and freight transportation stood at 43.21 million tons [1]. However, most of Japanese railway infrastructures were built before the 1970's, so the average age of many tunnels and bridges is over 60 years. To maintain and manage these aged facilities properly is important for safe and stable operation in railways.

Therefore, regular inspections of these railway constructions are usually conducted once every two years. In addition, depending on the inspections results, the soundness of the structures is evaluated according to the inspection results, and, if necessary, repair and replacement and so on are carried out [2].

In recently, condition monitoring by the WSN (Wireless Sensor Network) has attracted attention, and research on the condition monitoring system utilizing the WSN is under way in the railway as a matter of course. It is expected that we can take necessary measures based on right timing by monitoring the status all the time with the WSN. However, areas with different radio environment such as urban areas and mountainous areas are mixed and there are many metal objects in the railway environment. Therefore, there is concern that the railway environment may not be so created that, in there, we can collect data frequently not enough to monitor the structure states unless network design is properly made.

© Springer Nature Switzerland AG 2019
C. Benavente-Peces et al. (Eds.): SENSORNETS 2017/2018, CCIS 1074, pp. 196–208, 2019.
https://doi.org/10.1007/978-3-030-30110-1_11

Therefore, we propose a procedure for designing a WSN in railway environment considering these problems. Furthermore, based on the proposed WSN design procedure, a WSN using the 920 MHz band wireless communication standard Wi-SUN (Wireless Smart Utility Network) was experimentally introduced to an actual railway slope and a demonstration test was conducted for about 1 year. In this study, we report the outline and results of the verification test.

2   Condition Monitoring Using the WSN in the Railway

2.1   Condition Monitoring

In the condition monitoring system using the WSN that we are working on in this research, data is collected by the WSN installed in the object to be monitored. In addition, the collected data are transmitted to the M2M cloud via the Internet network and accumulated (Fig. 1). These data can be viewed or downloaded via the Internet network as necessary.

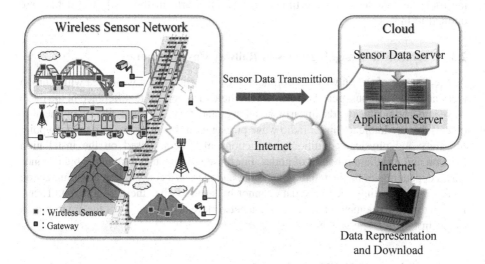

Fig. 1. An example of the condition monitoring system using the WSN [3].

2.2   WSN

The WSN handled in this study consists of a gateway, relays, and wireless sensors. The wireless sensor consists of a sensor for measurement and a wireless terminal, and is attached to the object to be monitored. The data measured by the wireless sensor is wirelessly transmitted to the gateway. If they cannot be directly transmitted from the wireless sensor to the gateway, they are transmitted to the gateway via relay by multi-hop transmission. And the collected data in the gateway is sent to the cloud through a public or private network and accumulated. In this study, the gateways, the relays and the wireless sensors are collectively called nodes.

WSNs have static and dynamic networks [4, 5]. The static network is a network that transmits the data with a preset route. On the other hand, the dynamic network is a network that communicates between nodes and autonomously composes the route.

The static network has the advantage that the power load at each node can be calculated in advance because the route is designed beforehand. For this reason, it is possible to formulate the battery design of each node and an efficient battery replacement plan. However, it is necessary to change the setting for the nodes on the route when a route change occurs due to the addition of a node. Also, sensor data from that node and sensor data passing through that node cannot be obtained until the node is exchanged when a node failure occurs.

On the other hand, since each node autonomously makes a route in the dynamic network, it is not necessary to manually change the route due to the addition of a node. Unlike the static network, it does not always use the same route, so it is not possible to calculate the power load of each node in advance. So, for such a dynamic network, we developed a method of estimating the battery consumptions by stochastically changing the route in time series by the time-series Monte Carlo method [6]. The details are omitted in this study.

2.3   Problems in Designing WSN in Railway Environment

As the features of the railway environment, it can be cited that a wide area which urban areas and mountainous areas between which there may be a large difference in the radio wave environment extends linearly and long, and that there are plenty of metallic objects that are liable to hinder radio wave propagation. In addition, from the viewpoint of safety and physical conditions, restrictions may be imposed on the installation location and installation height of nodes. For these reasons, the communicable distance varies depending on the installation location, and there is a concern that communication quality for collecting necessary data cannot be secured after their installation. Therefore, in this study, a method of designing a network in consideration of the environment of the installation site was examined.

3   Procedure of WSN Design [3]

There is research on the design of WSN, but there seems not to be found the network design considering the railway environment as mentioned above [7–10]. So we propose a design procedure for introducing the WSN in railway environment. It is explained below.

STEP1 Determination of objects and items to be monitored
The railway operator decides the objects and the items to be monitored. And it sets the collection interval and acceptable arrival rate of the data required according to the monitoring item. In the following procedure, the network is designed so as to satisfy the required specifications set here.

STEP2 Determining the location of the wireless sensors and gateway
It selects the location of the wireless sensor according to the monitoring items determined in STEP1. In addition, the location of the gateway is selected the area of public or private network, and a fixed power source is available, if possible.

STEP3 Survey of installation environment
In order to determine the location of the relay, it confirms the location where the relay cannot be installed and check the line of sight and obstruction between the wireless sensor and the gateway. In accordance with the installation environment, we appropriately select the frequency band and the communication standard to be used. In addition, it conducts a radio wave environment survey and so on to derive communicable distance in the installation environment.

STEP4 Derivation of communicable distance in installation environment
From the result of the survey of the radio wave environment at the installation location implemented in STEP3, it derives the communicable distance in this environment. The term "communicable distance" means the distance at which the data arrival rate between the nodes which results in achieving the data arrival rate of STEP1 is secured. Communicable distance in a section excluding the tunnel is calculated considering the influence of weather such as rain and snow [11, 12].

STEP5 Determination of the installation location of relay
If data cannot be transmitted directly from the wireless sensor to the gateway, multi-hop transmission is performed. If the wireless sensor can be transmitted via another wireless sensor between the wireless sensor and the gateway, there is no need to take additional measures. However, if the number is insufficient, dedicated relays should be installed. By setting up this relay, we attain the achievement rate set in STEP1. The details of the method of determining the installation location of the relay apparatus will be described Sect. 4.

STEP6 Power supply design
Since wireless sensors and relays are not necessarily installed in locations where fixed power supply is available, and there is a possibility that many nodes may be installed for one monitoring location, basically, power supply by a battery or an energy harvesting is provided. Therefore, in accordance with the network operation period and so on, the design of battery capacity and energy harvesting generation capacity and so on are properly determined. In order to extend the lifetime of the network, the power saving operation method proposed in Sect. 5 becomes important.

4   The Determination Method of Relay Location [3]

We describe the method of determining the location of the relay in STEP5 of Sect. 3.
In the railway environment, it is necessary to monitor the long distance section along the railway track depending on the monitored object. Therefore, it is important to relay data from each sensor when constructing a WSN in railway environments. In this case, if each sensor data reaches the gateway, it is more economical that the number of relay nodes is as small as possible.

Also, in the railway environment, there are places where installation of nodes is difficult due to physical conditions and the like, so that restriction is imposed on places where the relay nodes can be arranged. In addition, in the railway environment, there are many obstructions that impede radio wave propagation, so it is necessary to decide the placement of relay nodes in consideration of the influence on radio wave propagation by the obstacles.

In this study, we propose a method to decide the effective placement of the relays of WSN, taking into consideration the influence of shielding objects using mathematical optimization, taking account of placement constraints and presence of obstructions. In the proposed method, it is assumed that the positions of the sensors and the gate-way are given as inputs, and it is considered to decide the number and placement of relay nodes in the range from which data can reach from the sensor to the gateway. The objective function of this method can be formulated as the minimization of the number of relays as shown in Eq. (1).

[Objective function]

$$\min(R_{num}) \tag{1}$$

[Constraints]

$$r_{i,gat} = 1 \tag{2}$$

$$P_i(x, y) \neq N_j(x, y) \tag{3}$$

In the above equations, R_{num} is the number of relays, $r_{i,j}$ is the reachability matrix, $r_{i,j} = 1$ if there is a route by which data can reach node j from node i, and ri, j = 0 if there is no reachable route. Also, $P_i(x, y)$ is a position (x coordinate, y coordinate) of the relay device i, and $N_j(x, y)$ is the position (x coordinate, y coordinate) where the relay cannot be installed. Equation (2) represents the constraint relating to the arrival of data from each wireless sensor at the gateway, and $r_{i,gat}$ represents the reachability of the gateway from the wireless sensor i by data. Equation (3) represents the constraint relating to the position of the relay.

Here, the position $N_j(x, y)$ where the relay cannot be installed included in the constraint condition is given as input, and it shall be set according to the conditions of the environment where the WSN is installed. In addition, the conditions such as the position of the gateway, the number and position of the sensors, the communication distance of the wireless devices, the position of the obstructions are given as input. Furthermore, the reachability matrix $r_{i,j}$ is calculated by the following procedure conditions such as the position of the gateway, the number of wireless sensors, the position of each wireless sensor, the communication distance of the wireless devices, and the position of the obstructions.

STEP1 Generation of the adjacency matrix based on the communication distance
STEP2 Updating the adjacency matrix based on internode of line of sight
STEP3 Calculation of the reachability matrix based on the adjacency matrix

Details of the above procedure are shown below.

4.1 Generation of the Adjacency Matrix Based on the Communication Distance

In this study, we consider the reachability matrix showing the reachability of one of the nodes from another by data using the adjacency matrix in the graph theory. The adjacency matrix expresses the presence or absence of the relationship between nodes in the graph, and the adjacency matrix of the graph consisting of n nodes is an n × n square matrix.

Here, if the adjacency matrix is $a_{i,j}$,

> if there is an edge from node i to node j, $a_{i,j} = 1$.
> if there is no edge from node i to node j, $a_{i,j} = 0$.

In this study, the gateway, the wireless sensors, and the relays are assumed to be the nodes in the adjacency matrix, and the availability of communication between each node is expressed as an edge. That is, $a_{i,j} = 1$ when communication from node i to node j is possible, and $a_{i,j} = 0$ when communication from node i to node j is impossible.

Here, the determination of whether or not communication is possible between the nodes is made as follows using the communication distance of the wireless devices of the wireless sensor or relay given as the input condition.

> if $D_{i,j} <= C_i$: Communication is possible $(a_{i,j} = 1)$,
> if $D_{i,j} > C_i$: Communication is impossible $(a_{i,j} = 0)$

Where, $D_{i,j}$ is the distance between nodes, C_i is the communication distance of each wireless device.

By performing the above judgment between any pair of all the nodes, the adjacency matrix is generated here. In this study, we consider the possibility of reaching data from the sensor to the gateway by expressing the possibility of communication between nodes by adjacency matrix as described above.

4.2 Updating the Adjacency Matrix Based on Internode of Line of Sight

Here, the adjacency matrix generated in Eq. (1) is updated based on the presence or absence of the internode of line of sight. The presence or absence of the internode of line of sight is determined based on the position of the obstructions given as input. As shown in Fig. 2, the position of the obstructions is input as the coordinates of the end point of a line segment constituting the area where the obstructions exist like $L_i (x_1, y_1, x_2, y_2)$. In this study, the presence or absence of the internode of line of sight is judged by the possibility of intersection of a line segment constituting a certain area of the obstructions and a line segment connecting the nodes. Here, assuming that the two line segments are $L_1 (x_1, y_1, x_2, y_2)$ and $L_2 (x_3, y_3, x_4, y_4)$, the two line segments intersect when the following Eq. (4) is satisfied.

$$tc \times td < 0 \tag{4}$$

Where,

$$tc = (x_1 - x_2)(y_3 - y_1) + (y_1 - y_2)(x_1 - x_3),$$
$$td = (x_1 - x_2)(y_4 - y_1) + (y_1 - y_2)(x_1 - x_4).$$

Here, the intersection determination is made based on the above Eq. (4), and if any of the line segments intersect each other as a result of the judgment, it is determined that there is non-line of sight and the adjacency matrix is updated as $a_{i,j} = 0$ (communication is impossible).

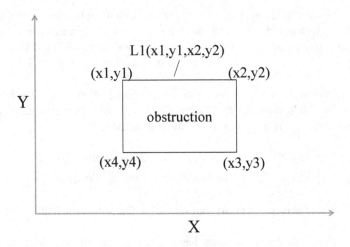

Fig. 2. The coordinates of the line segment.

4.3 Calculation of the Reachability Matrix Based on the Adjacency Matrix

Here, the reachability matrix is calculated based on the adjacency matrix calculated above. The reachability matrix can be calculated by the following procedure.

STEP1 Add unit matrix I to adjacency matrix A

STEP2 Under the Boolean algebra operation, A + I is repeatedly multiplied by r times until the state represented by the following expression Eq. (5) is obtained

$$(A + I)^{r-1} \neq (A + I)^r = (A + I)^{r+1} \tag{5}$$

$(A + I)^{r+1}$ obtained by the above calculation is a reachability matrix. In this way, in the method proposed, the reachability matrix is calculated based on the communication distance of the wireless devices and the line of sight between the nodes.

In this study, we calculate the node placement that minimizes the number of relay nodes considering the presence of obstructions and positions where nodes cannot be placed in the railway environment by performing mathematical optimization shown by Eqs. (1)–(3) on the basis of the reachability matrix calculated above.

5   State Transition Mode Mechanism

We describe one of the methods for saving power in STEP6 of Sect. 3.

In railway facilities such as railway slopes, there are many places where people's access is difficult and fixed power supply cannot be secured. Therefore, development of a battery-driven sensor node is required. However, since the resources of the battery are limited, if they are lost, the data will be lost until the battery is exchanged or charged.

There are restrictions on the length of time the access to the railway field is allowed, and the number of batteries replaced at once is limited. Also, such cost as labor cost for the replacement of batteries is high, so the higher the number of times of replacement, the higher the cost, then, power saving operation is necessary for reducing battery exchange. Therefore, we proposed a mechanism to reduce power consumption by changing the measurement and transmission intervals of data by state transition.

For example, In order to monitor the stationary state of the railway slope, it is sufficient to acquire data about once a day from the inclination wireless sensor. By contrast, if heavy rain causes soil moisture to rise and there is a possibility of slope collapse, it is necessary to acquire data more frequently. However, if you get data frequently, the battery will be lost soon. Therefore, the sensor node switches the measurement and transmission intervals according to its measurement value. Specifically, if the measured value of the sensor node itself does not change greatly, the transmission interval is shortened, and when the measured value greatly changes, the measurement and transmission intervals are lengthened (Fig. 3).

In this demonstration, the case of long interval measurement was set as "normal state" and the case of short interval measurement was set as "alert state". Moreover, the case of the interval between "normal state" and "alert state" was set to "caution state".

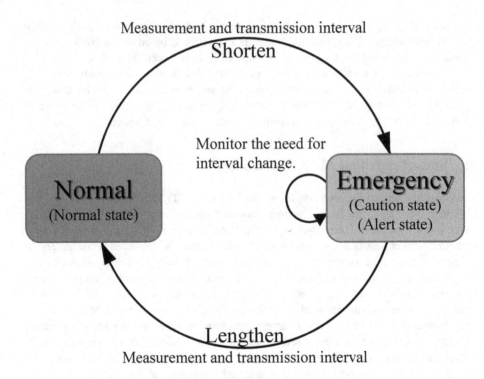

Fig. 3. An example of state transition mechanism.

6   The Demonstration Test on Railway Slope

We conducted a demonstration test on the railway slope, in accordance with the procedure proposed in Sect. 3.

6.1   Wi-SUN

In Japan, the 920 MHz band is allocated as the ISM band in July 2012, and the application of the band to the WSN is progressing. Along with that, the development of the 920 MHz band LPWA (Low Power Wide Area) wireless module is progressing. The LPWA includes the LoRaWAN, SIGFOX, Wi-SUN, and the like. Compared to other LPWAs in the same 920 MHz band, the Wi-SUN has the advantage that, although the communication distance is inferior, the transmission speed is 200 kbps and multi-hop transmission is possible [13]. Therefore, it can be said that it is suitable for a WSN which requires high scalability due to such changes as the addition of wireless sensors, or one to be introduced sequentially. So we decided to design the WSN for monitoring the railway slopes by using Wi-SUN.

6.2 WSN Design on Railway Slope [3]

First, we decided the location of the wireless sensors on the assumption of detecting the sign of land slide and land collapse by measuring the inclination and the soil moisture on the slope. And we decided to install the gateway in the location that can supply fixed power.

Next, we conducted survey of the installation environment, and confirmed the location where the relay can be installed and the shielding object and so on from topographic conditions based on topographic map (Fig. 4). Then, we applied the proposed method in Sect. 4 to determine the setting location of relays for the wireless sensors far from the gateway in Fig. 4. Figure 5 shows the location of the relays by the proposed method. Incidentally, the wireless sensors and relays were powered by solar panels in this demonstration test. Also, Table 1 shows the measurement interval and transmission interval of inclination wireless sensors in each state. For example, when the state is normal, the sensor measures once 1 h, and it transmit 24 pieces of measurement data to the gateway once 1 day as 1 packet. The state was transited the other state according to the change amount of the inclination in this test, which is the difference from the current measurement value and the previous measurement value. However, there are cases where the state is held for a certain period of time, but details are omitted. Also, in order to verify the function, the threshold of state transition is set as follows. When the change amount is less than 0.01, the state become to the normal state. When the change amount is more than 0.01 but less than 0.1, the state become to the caution state. When the change amount is equal to or more than 0.1, the state become to the alert state. These thresholds need to be set appropriately according to the monitoring purpose, the environment and so on. However, these threshold values to set in this study are for testing the function of the state transition mechanism.

			N	N	N	N	O	O	O	O	O	O	O	O	O	O	O	O	O	O	O	O	O	O	O	O	O	O	O	O	O	O	O	O	O	O	O	O	O	O	O
S			N	N	N	N	N	N	N	N	O	O	O	O	O	O	O	O	O	O	O	O	O	O	O	O	O	O	N	N	N									N	N
N	N	N	N	N					N	N	N	N	N	N	N	N	N	N	N	N	N	N	N	N	N	N	N	N	N	N	N	N	N	N	N	N	N	N	N	N	N
	G										N	N	N	N	N	N	N	N	N	N	N	N	N	N	N	N	N	N	N												
									O	O																							O	O	O	O	O	O			S
									O	O																							O	O	O	O	O	O			

1cell = 10m × 10m, N: the relays installation impossible, O: the obstructions,
S: the wireless sensors' location

Fig. 4. The result of survey of the installation environment.

	R		N	N	N	N	O	O	O	O	O	O	O	O	O	O	O	O	O	O	O	O	O	O	O	O	O	O	O	O	O	O	O	O	O	O	O	O	O	O	O
S			N	N	N	N	N	N	N	N	O	O	O	O	O	O	O	O	O	O	O	O	O	O	O	O	O	O	N	N	N	R								N	N
N	N	N	N	N					N	N	N	N	N	N	N	N	N	N	N	N	N	N	N	N	N	N	N	N	N	N	N	N	N	N	N	N	N	N	N	N	N
	G										N	N	N	N	N	N	N	N	N	N	N	N	N	N	N	N	N	N	N												
									O	O																							O	O	O	O	O	O			S
									O	O						R																	O	O	O	O	O	O			

1cell = 10m × 10m, N: the relays installation impossible, O: the obstructions,
S: the wireless sensors' location, R: the relays' location

Fig. 5. The result of the method to determine the location of relays.

Table 1. Measurement and transmission intervals of inclination wireless sensors.

Normal state		Caution state		Caution state	
Measurement interval	Transmission interval	Measurement interval	Transmission interval	Measurement interval	Transmission interval
1 h	1 day[a]	10 min	30 min	5 min	5 min

[a]All Mesasured Data Collectively Sent

6.3   The Result of the Test

We installed 5 inclination wireless sensors, 2 soil moisture wireless sensor and 3 relays. Figure 6 shows the state of installation the nodes on the slope.

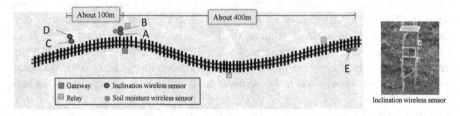

Fig. 6. The state of installation the nodes on the slope [3].

We accumulated the sensor data by the designed network for about 1 year. As a result, except for some sensors, the sensor data arrival rate was more than 99% (Table 2). In addition, we examined the state transition mechanism of the inclination wireless sensors. Figure 7 shows the measured inclination angle and state transition. The horizontal axis represents the date and the vertical axis represents the inclination angle. Moreover, the color of the background represents the normal state (white), the caution state (yellow), and the alert state (red). When the difference between the measurement value and the previous measurement value is large, the state was transited from normal state to caution state or alert state. As a result of the analysis of the acquired data, it was confirmed that transition to arbitrary state was made.

Table 2. Data arrival status of the inclination wireless sensors.

	Number of packets the sensor sent	Number of packets the gateway received	Packet arrival rate
Sensor A	18918	18918	100.00%
Sensor B	39982	39982	100.00%
Sensor C	3277	3277	100.00%
Sensor D	7906	7906	100.00%
Sensor E	5343	5336	99.87%
Total	75426	75419	99.99%

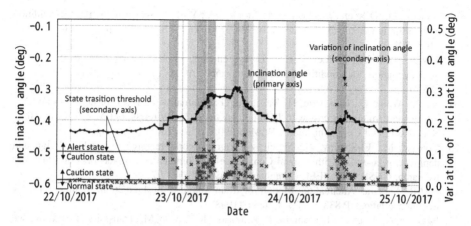

Fig. 7. The measured inclination angle and state transition (3 days). (Color figure online)

7   Conclusions

In this study, we introduced the procedure for designing the WSN in the railway environment. And we reported the demonstration test to the railway slope for 1 year based on the procedure. As a result, we achieved data arrival rate of more than 99% as designed and confirmed that the state transition mode mechanism works correctly. We will plan to improve the proposed method so that we can consider the dynamic environment such as train movement. And we will marshal the idea of threshold at the time of state transition.

References

1. Ministry of Land, Infrastructure, Transport and Tourism: Annual report on railway transportation. MLIT, Tokyo (2016). (in Japanese)
2. Railway Technical Research Institute: Railway structures maintenance standard and commentary [earth structure] (embankment and excavation). Maruzen, Tokyo (2007). (in Japanese)
3. Iwasawa, N., Kawamura, T., Nozue, M., Ryuo, S., Iwaki, N.: Design of wireless sensor network in the railway. In: 7th International Conference on Sensor Networks. INSTICC (2018)
4. Bakaraniya, P., Mehta, S.: Features of WSN and various routing techniques for WSN: a survey. Int. J. Res. Eng. Technol. **1**(3), 348–354 (2012)
5. Potdar, V., Sharif, A., Chang, E.: Wireless sensor networks: a survey. In: 23rd International Conference on Advanced Information Networking and Applications Workshops, AINA 2009. IEEE Computer Society (2009)
6. Kawamura, T., Ryuo, S., Iwasawa, N.: Power consumption prediction method for train-health monitoring wireless sensor networks. In: 23rd J-RAIL 2016. IEEJ (2016). (in Japanese)

7. Hodge, V.J., O'Keefe, S., Weeks, M., Moulds, A.: Wireless sensor networks for condition monitoring in the railway industry: a survey. IEEE Trans. Intell. Transp. Syst. **16**(3), 1088–1106 (2015)
8. Tiwari, A., Ballal, P., Lewis, L.F.: Energy-efficient wireless sensor network design and implementation for condition-based maintenance. ACM Trans. Sens. Netw. **3**(1), 1–23 (2007)
9. Xu, K., Wang, Q., Hassanein, H., Takahara, G.: Optimal wireless sensor networks (WSNs) deployment: minimum cost with lifetime constraint. In: Wireless and Mobile Computing, Networking and Communications, WiMob 2005. IEEE (2005)
10. Youssef, M., El-Sheimy, N.: Wireless sensor network: research vs. reality design and deployment issues. In: 5th Annual Conference on Communication Networks and Services Research, CNSR 2007. IEEE Computer Society (2007)
11. ITU-R: Specific Attenuation Model for Rain for Use in Prediction Methods. ITU-R Recommendations P.838-3, ITU, Geneva (1998)
12. Iwasawa, N., Ryuo, S., Kawamura, T., Kawasaki, K., Nozue, M.: Transmission performance evaluation of wi-sun wireless sensor network during snowing. In: 23rd J-RAIL 2016. IEEJ (2016). (in Japanese)
13. Harada, H., Mizutani, K., Fujiwara, J., Mochizuki, K., Obata, K., Okumura, R.: IEEE 802.15.4 g Based Wi-SUN communication systems. IEICE Trans. Commun. **E100.B**(7), 1032–1043 (2017)

Author Index

Printed in the United States
By Bookmasters